Humanistic Education and Western Civilization

HUMANISTIC EDUCATION AND WESTERN CIVILIZATION

Essays for

Robert M. Hutchins

Mortimer J. Adler
Elisabeth Mann Borgese
Scott Buchanan
William O. Douglas
Philip C. Jessup
Bertrand de Jouvenel
Humayun Kabir
Milton Mayer
Richard P. McKeon
John Courtney Murray, S.J.
David Riesman
Rexford G. Tugwell
F. Champion Ward
O. Meredith Wilson

Edited with an Introduction by
Arthur A. Cohen

Holt, Rinehart and Winston   New York   Chicago   San Francisco

Designer: Ernst Reichl
81496-0114
Printed in the United States of America

Contents

Humanistic Education and Western Civilization

Robert

Maynard

Hutchins:

The Educator

as Moralist

Arthur A. Cohen

At a time when preoccupation with moral principle appears to most men of affairs as an enviable but wasteful luxury; when the formation of habits of virtue is regarded as an almost irresponsible indulgence, it is well to reflect on the career of one who is pre-eminently a moralist, not despite the urgency of events but because of them. It is Robert Maynard Hutchins' understanding of his vocation as an educator that has resulted in his having been outstanding among the nation's moral leaders for so many years—first as Chancellor of the University of Chicago, then as President of the Fund for the Republic, and since 1959 as head of the Center for the Study of Democratic Institutions.

To understand the career of Robert M. Hutchins it is necessary to distinguish between the teacher, the administrator of teachers, and the educator. It is quite possible for a teacher to teach, without manifesting any interest in the quality or substance of his teaching or, for that matter, in the institution in which he teaches. A teacher may teach without becoming either administrator or educator. The administrator, the uni-

3

versity president or dean, may be an efficient and disciplined pragmatist, meeting *ad hoc* challenges from faculty, alumni, or public with *ad hoc* solutions. He is efficient if he balms their querulousness, gives in to their demands, or manages to compromise among the tensions created by opposition of all three; he is inefficient if he allows matters to get out of hand. The administrator may administer without being a teacher or educator. Indeed, if he sets out to be an efficient and famous administrator, the less he knows or cares about either teaching or education, the more efficient and famous he will probably be.

The educator, in contrast to both teacher and administrator, may be a poor teacher and a worse administrator when judged by the efficiency of his performance, but he cannot escape having views about the nature and end of teaching. Moreover, although the educator himself may limit his action to the narrow confines of college or university, his theory of education bears upon the whole life of man and society.

The educator in our times is a theorist whose notions of education are no less comprehensive than were the notions of education developed in the classical cultures of Greece and Palestine, for in that time the education of man was intimately connected to the end of man. A man learned in order that he might live in accordance with a certain view and behave with a certain style and insight; habits of mind and discipline of character were formed that man might order his passions and intellect in the service of his family and friends, his society, and his God. It was not imagined that education might fit a man for commerce or train his vocational aptitudes; it was not imagined that education was but a way station in which to incubate adolescence while it molted painlessly into maturity; it was not imagined that education was a means of adapting the individual to an environment already so fixed and formed as to be impervious to change; finally, it was not imagined that education was an instrumentality of the state, whereby the deficiencies and urgencies of national policy were met by turning the resources of education into its service.[1] None of these were regarded as

[1] The debased doctrines and activities of education, particularly of American education, are examined often in Hutchins' writing. Indeed, there is probably not one essay or lecture which does not turn upon the serious investigation or witty debunking of one of the views stated above. Most noteworthy are the following: "What Is a University?" *No Friendly Voice*, The University of Chicago Press (Chicago: 1936), pp. 5–11; "The Aims of Education," *Education for Freedom*, Louisiana University Press (Baton Rouge: 1943) and Grove Press (New York: 1963), pp. 19–38; *The University of Utopia*, The University of Chicago Press (Chicago: 1953); *The Higher Learning in America*, Yale

proper modes of education, although it cannot be denied that examples of all of them can be found in the history of Western education and all of them are found at present in American education.

The educator of the past—and one may regard most philosophers and religious thinkers as educators by the very nature of their intellectual activity—was concerned with the total formation of man. He was obliged to ask what a man should know and to devise methods of instructing his mind. He was obliged to ask what a man should do and to implement methods of instructing his character. He was obliged to ask: What may man hope for? and to refine principles by which to educate his belief. The process of defining the principles and methods by which man's reason, virtue, and belief were shaped was regarded as education; and only when a student was able to think intelligently about the same questions was he regarded as educated.

Education was a moral enterprise. The morality of man's life consisted less in his attention to the mores and customs of his times than in the training of his mind and habits of action in order that his fellow man and his society might be illumined. The intellectual virtues were practiced in order that the truth might be apprehended and the practical virtues were exhibited in order that the truth might reign in a just society.

Today, most of us would probably regard such a view of education as utopian. The conditions of democratic education are such that they do not conduce to the formation of wise and virtuous men, although some wise and some virtuous men are its fortuitous by-products. The technological revolution of modern times, the endless accumulation of new facts, the divorce of science and the humanities, the complexity of government and communication—these, and more, make the definition of a university along the lines of classical models apparently hopeless, for there is no longer face-to-face communication between the knower (the teacher) and the student who wants to learn; there can no longer be that patient, deliberative, unhurried inquiry into the foundations of a discipline, for not only is the discipline regarded as too complex to be

University Press (New Haven: 1936), pp. 1–58; *Some Observations on American Education,* Cambridge University Press (Cambridge: 1956), pp. 8–45; and finally the quite systematic essay, "The Democratic Dilemma," which was published, with additional lectures, under the title *The Conflict in Education,* Harper & Brothers (New York: 1951) and reprinted, in somewhat altered form, in *Freedom, Education, and the Fund: Essays and Addresses, 1946–1956,* Meridian Books, Inc. (New York: 1956), pp. 101–151.

compassed by any single mind, it is also too dynamic and changing to remain the same discipline long enough to extract from it a definition of its nature. In effect, democracy makes classical education a luxury; and the state of knowledge and civilization makes such classicism romantic, foolish, and irresponsible.

If this résumé of the logic of the argument that Robert M. Hutchins has carried on with American education is accurate, we may regard him as romantic, foolish, and irresponsible. He would undoubtedly admit to each of these charges with more or less of an amused smile, but he would probably remind us that an educator as moralist is a utopian, and utopians—if they are enlightened and moral men—should be somewhat romantic, foolish, and irresponsible. Without a touch of all three —enthusiasm, Erasmian folly, and an indifference to consequence— moral imagination would be hopelessly compromised.

Hutchins, as a utopian, has been the most practical and realistic of men. All utopians are. It is only when utopian thinking slips over into fantasy that utopia ceases to be instructive. When the utopist remains a moralist, employing his mythic kingdom to describe the corruptions and possibilities of our own, he may guide us in the way in which our life and order may be improved. It is appropriate that the educator who has been a teacher and an administrator of teachers should be a utopian moralist.

Characteristic of utopian moralists, whether they be Plato or Campanella or More, Bacon or Swift or implicit utopists such as Moses, the prophets of Israel, Jesus, Buddha or their wise and enlightened followers (who might include St. Augustine, Maimonides, John Henry Newman, and their like) is that the prescription of vision is set forth against the background of a penetrating diagnosis of their own present. It would be foolish to be visionary without clarity about the real world. The vision does not transform an ether or a mist, a chimera or a dream, but a real society with a history and a predicament.

The education for utopia which Hutchins has described numerous times—with seriousness prevailing over wit in his important book, *The University of Utopia,* and wit overwhelming seriousness in his essay "Locksley Hall in 1988–89"[2]—is *educational* because it is devised to resolve the dilemmas of a society which wishes to remain

---

[2] "Locksley Hall in 1988–89," *What Is a College For?*, Public Affairs Press (Washington: 1961), pp. 5–13.

democratic and egalitarian, while training for excellence, and is *utopian* because, however much excellence is desired, the moral predicaments of such a society are not likely to be resolved other than by a transformation of its values.

The transformation of American society is the presupposition for a transformation of American education. "The educational system that any country has," Hutchins notes, "will be the system that country wants."[3] Education does not create nations. Ideals create nations such as the United States and the cultures which nourish and shape those ideals usually train the idealists who realize them. But given the nation and given the realization of its mediate ideals, the task of education is more readily given over to the conservation of ideals than to their refinement; to the assumption of their continued validity regardless of how man and society have altered, rather than to their unceasing examination and reconstruction. Education upholds the past; it rarely reforms the present. If this is the tendency of the education which exists in conservative societies—in monarchies, in oligarchies, in republics founded on wealth and property—how much more devastating is it in a polity whose principle is freedom, whose law is changing and dynamic, and whose rationale is the universality of liberty. For education to be conservative in a democratic society, the education must be bad and the democracy may be threatened.

This is precisely the case with education in the democratic society of the United States. The values of democracy are polarized and in opposition to the education that society appears to endorse. It was assumed by the fathers of American democracy that every citizen would enjoy the right of suffrage. The right to vote was not regarded, as it has lately come to be regarded, as an ineffectual and cynical instrument for influencing the centers of power. It was regarded by such as Washington, Adams, and Jefferson as a primary means of effecting the transformation of private will and judgment into public policy. It was what is sometimes called "direct democracy." At the same time the Founding Fathers instituted universal suffrage they were conservative enough to recognize that such a right was inherently precarious and were aristocratic enough to believe that men less educated than themselves might misuse their right. It was only sensible, therefore, that they should have concerned themselves with the education of the voter. And hence from

[3] *Education for Freedom*, p. 48.

the right to vote arose the right to education and from the notion of equality in the right to vote arose the notion of equality in the right to education. Both concepts were revolutionary. Great Britain, an orderly and principled nation, did not introduce universal suffrage until after the passage of the second Reform Bill and even then universal education was to follow only because, as Lord Sherbrooke said with condescending grace, "we must educate our masters."[4] France, a revolutionary nation, moved in a hurry, but still lagged behind the experiment of the New World.

In effect, political democracy demanded an educated electorate. To this necessity Thomas Jefferson addressed himself, for he was the first American educator, and he addressed himself not to the task of teachers or institutions, but to the purpose of the nation and the people who would advance its cause. At the same time, however, as he raised the task of education to the forefront of the nation's concerns, he defined a doctrine of education which could not help but maintain and insure inequity. Jefferson regarded education as universal, but he did not regard the same education for all as a desideratum, much less a requirement. There are those who must till and harvest, Jefferson seems to have argued, and for these the requirements of vocational training are more pressing than the demands for learning. They must, to be sure, be taught to read, to write, to do sums, to adjudicate between the good and the ill in the practical order, but no effort need be made to define what they should read and what they should write, or what degree of abstraction their mathematics should enjoy. Sufficient that they be sober and sound.

Jefferson has been construed to have said more than this. He is believed to have advocated the higher learning for all. This is not true. The higher learning was for those qualified for the higher learning and the qualified were those already fitted by nurture and disposition to its pursuit. Jefferson was a democrat, but he was also an aristocrat and a practical man.

Hutchins has put his finger on the defect in Jefferson's reasoning.[5] Jefferson was an egalitarian for the mass, but an aristocrat for the gentry. He feared for the intellect and sought to protect it—by disseminating enough knowledge to make men useful but not enough to make

---

[4] *The University of Utopia,* p. 3.

[5] "Thomas Jefferson and the Intellectual Love of God," *No Friendly Voice,* pp. 59–69.

them wise or envious of the knowledge of others. But the dilemma of American life arises from the fact, as Hutchins has made abundantly clear, that the agrarian democracy for which Jefferson planned is not the democracy of our day—the numbers are vaster, the problems more complex, communication more subtle and indirect, and the consequence of excessive practicality offset by insufficient wisdom can prove disastrous. What might have been a neat solution for Jefferson's time—to make the farmer educated enough to elect his betters—can be calamitous in our day, when farmers are often among the betters and the betters are often anti-intellectuals. The higher learning for all is no longer an option; it is a necessity.

What, then, is the higher learning? It consists, as Hutchins has defined it, in the acquisition and application of the intellectual virtues. And what are these? For the moment, let us put aside the definition that Aristotle gives us of the intellectual virtues, and reflect upon the resonance of the words "intellect" and "virtues." It is assumed that if a virtue is intellectual, it is impractical, abstract, and, therefore, not relevant to the immediate goals of life—which might be adaptation, success, wealth. It is also assumed that any virtues that require intellect are artificial, unspontaneous, contrived, and therefore deceptive and untrustworthy. Surely, if both intellect and virtue are not allowed to modify each other, then to insist that their conjunction is the proper discipline for the higher learning might be regarded as gratuitous. We may counter such an assertion by affirming that the intellect is a proper capacity of man and that among its several capabilities is the ability to demonstrate by scientific induction, to deliberate about how things are made or how desirable states (such as health or strength) are achieved, to grasp by intuition the ultimate premises from which science departs, and lastly to speculate concerning the nature of things insofar as that nature may become apparent through employment of the principles of logic, mathematics, or natural science. A program of instruction which might enable a man to civilize his mind to intuit, to deliberate, to demonstrate, and to contemplate would be, Hutchins suggests, an enviable achievement for a democracy. But what has such intellectual achievement to do with virtue and what, it might be asked, has virtue to do with democracy? The utopian presupposition of an education such as Hutchins has defined is not, contrary to what his critics have claimed, dependent upon a closed view of man—an Aristotelian view, an Augustinian view, or a Thomist view. Hutchins has specifically noted that it is not conceivable or desirable to look to theology to define the unity and authority of the higher learning.[6] Similarly metaphysics, which Hutchins properly celebrates as a discipline most appropriate to the inquiry into the highest foundations of the life of nature and the life of man, is wholly absent as a center for the *de facto* ordering of the higher learning.[7] "I am not arguing for any specific theological or metaphysical system," he added to his historical reprise of the waning of theology and metaphysics in *The Higher Learning in America*.[8] However, it is his claim that the fundamental end of metaphysics—the rational inquiry into the ultimate nature of things—is the high end of education. Metaphysics, more than being a discipline with a particular object of inquiry or peculiar type of procedure, is a method appropriate to the learning of any art or science.

"The fundamental problems of metaphysics, the social sciences, and natural sciences are . . . the proper subject matter of the higher learning. These categories are exhaustive. I have used the word 'metaphysics' to include not only the study of first principles, but also all that follows from it, about the principles of change in the physical world, which is the philosophy of nature, and about the analysis of man and his productions in the fine arts, including literature. The social sciences embrace the practical sciences of ethics, politics, and economics, together with such historical and empirical materials as may be needed to supplement them for the guidance of human action. The theoretical principles of ethics, politics, and economics are, of course, principles of speculative philosophy. The principles of ethics, theoretically considered, are to be found in metaphysics. In ethics itself the same knowledge is viewed in the practical order. To speak of ethics, politics, and economics as practical philosophy is to indicate that they are philosophical knowledge organized for the sake of action. In the law we have a practical application of this body of practical principles. By the natural sciences I mean, of course, the study of nature. The natural sciences derive their principles from the philosophy of nature, which depends in turn on metaphysics. In the study of them, such recent observations as serve to illustrate, exemplify, or confirm

[6] *The Higher Learning in America,* p. 97.
[7] *Ibid.,* pp. 98–109.
[8] *Ibid.,* p. 105.

these principles must be included. Medicine and engineering are applications of this whole body of knowledge."[9]

Law without an inquiry into justice,[10] medicine without the metaphysical bent of Galen,[11] the social sciences without an investigation of the nature of politics and society is not education, surely not the higher learning. Such a defective education may well satisfy the penchant of a culture, which concerns itself with supplying skills and vocations to the economy, or with putting into circulation people who will put money into circulation, or with making the dull pliable and content, while permitting the clever to become adept at their particular cleverness; but an education without a vision of first principles does not educate.

It is here, perhaps here alone, that Hutchins is a dogmatist—but since metaphysics is the science of first principles, it is appropriate that Hutchins' only tenaciously held principle should be the pre-eminent importance of metaphysics for education. What relevance does metaphysics have for virtue or democracy? At first blush, it would appear to have none. Metaphysics is abstract, difficult, stratospheric. But let us recall that Aristotle regarded the intellectual virtues as the consequence of the appropriate use of man's reason. If a man reasons patiently, quietly, intelligently, assessing evidence, weighing the interconnection of kinds of knowledge and the bearing of knowledge upon life, it may be expected that such a man may come to lead a wise life. And one believes that the wise man is more likely to be virtuous than is the fool or the illiterate or even the practically educated. The right employment of the natural endowments of men, the turning of these endowments to inquiry into the highest and deepest must help a man to achieve those virtues which we call justice, prudence, courage, magnanimity. Lastly, such a man is prepared to bear other men with affection, helpfulness, and courtesy. He is also likely to assist them along the path toward truth.

The man who has acquired the intellectual virtues is likely to exhibit the virtues compassed by political and personal ethics. Such a man is an aristocrat who desires the aristocracy of all and he is a democrat because he is not prepared, on the basis of IQ tests or psychological sifting, to discount the ability of any but the medically certified as in-

[9] *Ibid.*, pp. 107–108.
[10] "The Autobiography of an Ex-Law Student," *No Friendly Voice*, pp. 41–50.
[11] "Back to Galen," *No Friendly Voice*, pp. 51–58.

capable of asking the most important questions. It is more likely that an education designed in the spirit of an across-the-board egalitarianism is antidemocratic and discriminatory than is the higher learning. The former design calls for a curriculum insistent upon facts and information, standards of accumulation and regurgitation. An education which insists upon pounding the same into all, rather than eliciting the same from all, disqualifies many with a brutality from which they cannot recover.[12] The higher learning, founded upon processes of mind by which facts are defined and incorporated into knowledge, is designed to teach all to think according to their capacity and temperament. It is not that the higher learning seeks to make men metaphysicians—far from it! It does seek to enable men to think critically, judiciously, selectively. Thoughtful men make good citizens—citizens less susceptible than are unreflective men to pressures of opinion or hysteria, less amenable to the attitudes of rashness and haste which lead to repression and injustice.

Robert Hutchins' utopian vision of the higher learning is still unrealized, although happily, during the thirty years that he has spoken on its behalf and in the twenty years that he experimented with its implications at the University of Chicago, some of its emphases and innovations have become ingredients of American education.

The vision nevertheless remains utopian, for, although American universities may be showing responsiveness to the demands of the higher learning, the community which supports these universities remains unpersuaded. This is perhaps because Hutchins decided, after leaving the University of Chicago from whose Chancellorship he resigned in 1951, to become a foundation executive rather than a politician. It cannot be determined whether he would have agitated the conscience of American life more efficaciously from the Senate than he managed to do from the offices of the Fund for the Republic in New York or from the groves of Santa Barbara in which the later incarnation of the Fund, the Center for the Study of Democratic Institutions, is located. In all events, though the scenery and atmosphere have changed, the content of his argument has not. The fusillades which Hutchins and his critics continue to exchange with one another no longer burst over the Midway in Chicago, but across the nation.

[12] See essay, "Innovation and Reaction in Higher Education" by David Riesman, p. 199 for discussion of some aspects of this problem.

The issue is still the higher learning, but the immediacies to which Hutchins addressed his first book, *The Higher Learning in America,* have, in the nearly three decades since its publication, become desperate and urgent.[13] In *The Higher Learning in America* the word "freedom" is hardly used. The more chaste and conservative word "liberty" appears frequently, but it is not a predominating theme. The apocalyptic words of that book, a generation ago, were the call to reason; the goods of the soul; the ordered, just, and wise community. These are no less decisive, but it is the prudent man who puts off the ultimate in order that those for whose sake the ultimate exists may survive to enjoy it.

The issue of the 1950's, as Hutchins described it, became not education for wisdom but education for freedom. The United States were to be preserved as a free society in order that it might endure to become wise. The challenge of leisure and abundance was not present in the thirties; the crises of the Cold War and the threats posed by imperialistic communism were not apparent in the thirties; the automated technology of industry and the lethal technology of atomic and ballistic warfare were not present in the thirties. At that time the task was to make education appropriate to a society given a rude shaking by economic depression. The rethinking of the nation's goals, which commenced then, terminated in the enthusiasm of war and the splenetic peace which followed. It would appear now that American society—rich, powerful, and successful, fulfilled of all the objectives for which the education of that era provided—is floundering in search of new objectives. The institutions of freedom persevere; undoubtedly they will survive, but they have not gone unchallenged.[14]

[13] Referring in the preface to the paper-bound edition of *The Higher Learning in America,* Yale University Press (New Haven: 1962), p. ix, Hutchins observed: "This book was written twenty-five years ago, during the Great Depression, when Russia was a backward nation, when colonialism was in flower, and when people in the advanced industrial countries still believed that technology could menace neither their livelihood nor their lives.

"This was before television, before World War II, before the United Nations, before the Cold War, before the Affluent Society, before the forty-hour week, and before the rise and fall of the labor unions. It was before oligopolistic arrangements among giant corporations superseded competition as the distinguishing characteristic of our economic system, and before American culture became bureaucratic. It was another world."

[14] "The Bill of Rights: Yesterday, Today and Tomorrow," *Freedom, Education, and the Fund,* pp. 30–34.

It is characteristic of the anxiety of a people to foreshorten or constrict the breadth and amplitude of principles of freedom on the mistaken assumption that, since the majority is not directly threatened, the dissenting and precarious minority can be limited without danger to the whole. The fact is that it is not the majority as majority which made the American Constitution or the Bill of Rights, which guarantees its provisions and spirit. It is rather the responsible freedom of individuals who, confident of their own intelligence and with respect for the intelligence of others, determined to guarantee an optimistic environment for the expression of freedom. "The leading principle of democracy," Hutchins has affirmed, "is that we are to think for ourselves. The ideal American is the perpendicular man."[15] It is, however, when the part is substituted for the whole, when the legitimate concern that the nation not be subverted by violence becomes the excuse for curtailing freedoms of speech; when procedures of investigation, confrontation of witnesses, scrutiny of evidence are modified to permit the often slipshod conviction of the guilty and the irreparable damaging of the innocent; when, in effect, the encouragement to individual thought and judgment is replaced by mass persuasion and propaganda—that the nation is not protected, but endangered.

The conjunction of Hutchins' preoccupation with education and his concern for freedom during recent years, have their common foundation in his ongoing interest in the principles of justice and the instrumentalities of the law. It was as a teacher of law and as Dean of the Yale Law School (1927–1929) that he first became aware of the precarious assumptions of contemporary legal education and of education in general. It was his recognition that the law pursued justice, that justice was indispensable to a free society, and that such a society could remain free to pursue justice only if its citizenry was properly educated that served to integrate his interest in law, education, and morality.

It is as lawyer, become educator and moralist, that we may understand Hutchins' willingness, earlier in his career, to direct the Commission on Freedom of the Press (1942–1946)[16] and to initiate and

[15] *Ibid.*, p. 31.

[16] *A Free and Responsible Press* by the Commission on Freedom of the Press, The University of Chicago Press (Chicago: 1947). Also see the excellent and witty essays, "Freedom and Responsibility of the Press: 1948," and "Freedom and Responsibility of the Press: 1955," *Freedom, Education, and the Fund*, pp. 46–56, 57–67.

become President of the Committee to Frame a World Constitution
(1947). In both cases the motivation was the same: the press had to
rethink its proper objectives in relation to the free society and to discipline itself to insure the instruction of public opinion rather than
to continue to serve the narrower interests of profit or prejudice; similarly, the nations of the world, if they wished the human community
to survive, had to seek brotherhood "under law."[17] Law—whether
construed as the bringing of discipline to the passions and self-seeking
of the private man, or as the seeking of the common foundations by
which the nations might discipline their public passions and self-seeking for the benefit of all mankind—is related to the pursuit of justice
and the preservation of freedom.

The interrelation of Hutchins' concerns with education, freedom,
and the law moved him later, through the Fund for the Republic
to press, among other projects, research and inquiry into the nation's
loyalty-security program under the auspices of the Association of the
Bar of the City of New York; to assist the League of Women Voters
to examine the condition of civil liberties; to support the efforts of the
National Citizen's Commission on the Public Schools in promoting
debate about the state of public education, particularly as it relates
to academic freedom and racial discrimination; to commission Clinton
Rossiter and a considerable staff to write the history of the Communist
party in the United States; and to enable John Cogley, former executive editor of *The Commonweal,* to investigate techniques of political blacklisting in the entertainment industry.[18]

The work of the Fund for the Republic—diffused and far-ranging
as it was—and the subsequent work of the Center for the Study of
Democratic Institutions—more precisely targeted and defined as it is—
is the relation of freedom to education and the bearing which education
may have upon freedom. Freedom must be preserved within the civil
order, for freedom is the natural condition of a society which still
seeks to grow and mature. (It is implicit in Hutchins' analysis that the
only societies which submit to the elimination of freedom are those
which have never known it or those which have become fearful of it.)
Freedom is not, nor has Hutchins understood it to be, an unqualified

[17] "1950," an editorial by Hutchins in *Common Cause,* the monthly report of the
Committee to Frame a World Constitution, July, 1947, Vol. I, p. 1.

[18] "The Fund, Foundations, and the Reece Committee," "Some Truths about the
Fund for the Republic," "The Fund and Freedom," *Freedom, Education, and the Fund,*
pp. 201–212; pp. 213–220; pp. 221–232.

good.[19] Freedom is a potency, a condition for the achievement of ends which, without freedom, cannot be achieved. No man wishes to be free simply for the sake of being free. He wishes to be free to pursue the goods of his life—to be with his family; to go boating; to meditate in the Lotus position; or to secure peace, order, and justice. Freedom is the precondition of securing what men believe to be good—good for themselves, good for others, good for mankind. The achievement of the goods of life is no less qualified than is the good of freedom, for some goods are more desirable than others. This may not be self-evident to many for whom all goods are equally valuable, but presumably justice is preferable to boating and peace is the end of Yoga meditation. In all events, without argument on the substance of the principle, most men (unless they are tenaciously solipsistic or tediously selfish) will grant that the goods which enable them to realize more fully the ends of a just, peaceful, and noble life are to be preferred to uncomplicated hedonism.

The life of freedom is thus related to ends which organize the energies of freedom. Without moral, intellectual, spiritual purpose freedom can become either anarchy or tyranny. To know the goods of the moral, intellectual, and spiritual life is the aim of education. Education is then indispensable to a free society, for without an appropriate education, the mind of man is deprived of the talent and discipline to search properly and intelligently for the goods of life. Hutchins concludes several analyses of this question by referring with frank admiration to the observation of John Dewey (with whom he appears often to be placed in disagreement)[20] that "the discipline that is identical with trained power is also identical with freedom." Freedom was never, for John Dewey, license or uninstructed desire; for Dewey as for Hutchins freedom was the acquisition of a disciplined mind. When the mind is trained by education to inquiry and investigation, it is prepared to become free.

"The mind cannot be free if it is a slave to what is bad. It is free if it is enslaved to what is good. To determine the good and the order of goods is the prime object of all moral and political educa-

[19] *Education for Freedom*, p. 88 *et seq.*
[20] *Education for Freedom*, p. 91; John Dewey, *Experience and Education*, Collier Books (New York: 1963), pp. 61–65.

tion. We cannot hope that one who has never confronted these issues can be either a good citizen or a good man."[21]

The educator as moralist, the moralist as educator—for they are interchangeable persons—is visionary without being apocalyptic, hopeful without being optimistic, anxious without being despairing, ironic without being cynical, open without being undiscriminating, principled without being fanatic, free without being disorderly. The educator as moralist is a utopian. Robert Maynard Hutchins, has exemplified these—educator, moralist, utopian.

[21] *Education for Freedom*, p. 91.

Part One

Democratic

Values and

Western

Civilization

1

International

Democracy

Philip C. Jessup

The democratic values of Western civilization must exclude parochialism, must include a readiness, not so much to proselytize as to share. The wide extent to which the term "democracy" or "democratic" has been adopted, in the evident belief that it is a label which attracts, should be gratifying. Without condoning false use of labels, Western democracy should welcome developments which progressively make its geographical adjective unnecessary except in examination of historical perspectives. The contributions of what we loosely call "the West" need not be either exaggerated or ignored. Today one hears—in rather tautological terms—of "peoples' democracies," and of "basic democracy," of "panchayat democracy." It is not my purpose to argue how these or other types of democracies resemble or differ from democracy as understood in the United States. These pages are concerned with "international democracy."

A paragraph of explanation may be worth a volume of definitions. This paragraph is one of explanation in which I wish to make clear that in speaking of "international democracy," I am not referring to a possible (or actual) global or even widespread repetition of the pattern of Periclean, or town-meeting, or American, or any other type of democracy which may exist within the borders of a single state. I am referring to a democratic system in which the "individuals" or units, instead of being natural persons, are, or would be, collectivities, usually states themselves.

Since the theory has actually already been conceived, one is bound to admit that an "international democracy," in the sense that all of the billions of the world's population would participate as individuals, is theoretically possible. The period of gestation which must elapse before this theory is born into reality is sufficiently long to make it permissible at this moment not to analyze the designs of the political forms in which the child will eventually be swaddled. I would not deprecate the use of the wide learning and imaginative ingenuity which others have made to this end, but I am considering a different question which, in the sequence of historic time, may come to have priority. Nevertheless, something new and vital is already emerging. The Court of Justice of the European Communities has held that the Community constitutes "a new juridicial order in international law, for the advantage of which States have limited—so far as certain restricted fields are concerned—their sovereign rights, and of which the subjects are not only the Member States but equally their nationals."[1] Here, then, in a regional context, human beings and states are being democratically associated with a measure of equality.

To a degree, the United States (by comparison with my "international democracy") is an interstatal democracy in which the *demos* is composed of fifty individual states or statal individuals. The United Nations is an international grouping of some one hundred and eleven individual states; the question remains whether the United Nations is or can be an international democracy: I shall answer this question in the affirmative. A like question could be posed about the older (and more loosely constructed) Organization of American States or the newer (but tighter) European Communities.

Democracy is a philosophy and it is also a societal arrangement. It is often analyzed in terms of the relationship between the individual and the state or the governing power in the state. But since, fundamentally, it is the *demos* which is the governing power, the individual

[1] *N. V. Van Gend and Loos v. Tariefcommissie*, Feb. 5, 1963, IX *Recueil de la Jurisprudence de la Court de Justice des Communautés Européenes.*

is himself a part of the governing power and the essential relationship is that of one individual to the others in the society. The lack of a super-state or supreme international authority does not therefore preclude a consideration of international democracy as a relationship between the individual states which compose the international society.

"Law," if I may borrow Majid Khadduri's phrasing,[2] "is a system of social control established for the purpose of maintaining an ordered society among men." Mark that it is not a system merely for maintaining order, but for maintaining "an ordered society."

The law for maintaining an ordered society among states, that is, the law of international democracy, is, or would be, international law. It would not necessarily be identical with the law of nations recognized, *eo nomine,* by the drafters of the American Constitution in defining the powers of the Congress, nor with the international law invoked in the Charter of the United Nations for application by the International Court of Justice. International law, like the law of all modern societies, has changed, is changing, and will change. Maurice Bourquin could say, in 1931, *"C'est devenue une banalité de dire que le droit international est en pleine transformation."*[3] It is only the law of the Medes and the Persians "which altereth not," and where now is the empire of Darius? The spate of books and articles dealing with the current changing phase of international law may not as yet have crested and it is much more desirable that this should be so than that we should be slaves to—in Loren Eiseley's phrase—"the fossil ape encrusted in our hearts." Much of the writing has to do with the impact on international law of the emergence of many states which had heretofore, by their colonial status, been foreclosed from participation in an international democracy. Another large segment is concerned with the status of international law in a world divided in what is commonly called its postwar bipolarity.

The rate of change will, of course, be aggravatingly slow to those who are most impatient with old norms, the application of which seems detrimental to their interests or at least to their desires. This is a common phenomenon not peculiar to the international scene, but perhaps more keenly felt at that level because the machinery for peaceful change in international affairs is so painfully inadequate; consider, for instance, the *relative* facility of amending the Constitution of the

[2] *Islamic Jurisprudence: Shafi'i's Risala* (Baltimore: 1961), p. 3.
[3] Hague Academy of International Law, 35 *Recueil des Cours* (Paris: 1932), p. 5.

United States as contrasted with the almost insuperable difficulties of amending the Charter of the United Nations. Difficult, but yet not really insuperable, because in due time, as Bynkershoek wrote over two hundred years ago: "as customs change, so the law of nations changes." When Margaret Mead says "Nations are, and should be, different from one another," one may well add Felix Frankfurter's dictum: "Anybody who is any good is different from anybody else. That is the point about being good—you're different." And one also recalls that a great North American international lawyer, John Bassett Moore, decried the "passion for uniformity."

It is a commonplace that international law has developed, *i.e.,* changed, to meet new conditions created by advances in the physical sciences. Thus with progress in aviation, the law of the air developed. As it became feasible to extract oil from the continental shelves, international law evolved changes in the historic law on freedom of the seas and on territorial waters. The use of atomic power for peaceful purposes is pointing toward new rules of liability comparable to those evolved long since in private law. So with man's entry into outer space. Physical scientists have been apt to demand that to meet the changes in political conditions like changes in the law of nations should emerge. But just as lawyers were of no use in splitting the atom, so the scientists are apt to be wide of the mark in trying to cut the political knots which still tie the society of nations to old rubrics of sovereignty, even as so experienced a person as Lord Franks denounces such "sentimental romanticism which has no place in the world today."[4]

Charles Morgan in his "Reflections in a Mirror" suggests views which Metternich might express if he were available to discuss today's dilemma. "A peace that ends a great war," he imagines Metternich saying, "should be regarded neither as a sleeping draught nor as a stimulant. Peace is like a pair of stockings. My life consisted in darning Europe's stockings. But you are too lazy. Remember what Goethe said to Eckerman: 'Man is not born to solve the problems of the Universe but to find out where the problem lies and then to keep within the limits of what he can comprehend.' I would urge you, if you are in pursuit of an ideal, to take with you a map and a darning needle."

[4] Lord Franks, "Cooperation Is Not Enough," 41 *Foreign Affairs* (New York: 1962), pp. 24, 33.

How many fragments of international democracy have already been stitched together?

Recalling that the units of the international democracy are themselves collectivities, the question poses itself whether the internal structure of these units, of these statal individuals, must itself be democratic. The answer is "no," just as one does not demand a probe into the mind, heart, and conscience of the individual in a national democracy when it is a question of his exercise of his democratic rights. (I shall not attempt here to enter into the field where the courts have drawn distinctions between permissible and unlawful individual activities, for one reason, because I am treading dangerously close to the perilous brink of excessive reasoning by analogy in applying to the international community the norms which are applicable to some national communities.) The task of constituting or maintaining, an international democracy may therefore involve the co-operation of states with widely differing ideological, social, economic, and political systems. (Some fifteen years ago one could speak of "coexistence" in this context, but the word has now acquired such a psychic fringe that its use leads to misunderstanding.)

I have already suggested that the United States may be considered an "interstatal democracy," just as I maintain that the United Nations is an "international democracy"—one always encounters the semantic difficulty caused by the uses of the term "state" to mean the units in our federation and to mean the national units—including the United States itself—in the world society. The form of association and of participation in governing power in our federal system is a democratic form; in essentials, a comparable democratic form characterizes our international organization.

How democratic are the existing international organizations? They are organizations within an international society which is itself passionately democratic. In the United Nations there is equality of voice and vote except for the special status of the five permanent members of the Security Council. This specialty is perhaps no more undemocratic than the constitutional right of one-third plus one of the Senators of the United States to veto the ratification of a treaty. The Charter says the organization is based on the sovereign equality of all its members. It might as well have said that it was based on the equality of its sovereign members. Aside from those security issues, in most situations the rule is by majority and the vote of the least (in size, population, wealth, or other magnitude) equals that of the greatest. The fact that the organization does not have general legislative power is evidence of impotence, but not of autocracy. I shall not argue whether there is a necessary connection between the party system and the democratic form of government within a national state,[5] and it really matters little whether one seeks to assimilate the blocs in the United Nations to parties in a national state. If there be democratic criticisms of a one-party system, such criticisms cannot be leveled at the United Nations.

Qualifications for membership in the United Nations, as administered in practice, are not exacting; requirements for citizenship, *i.e.,* individual membership, have been more rigorous in many modern states considered to be democracies. That certain potential members have failed to command in the Security Council and in the General Assembly the vote which is needed for admission is merely evidence of the play of political forces such as those which separated the proslavery and antislavery forces when Kansas sought admission to the Union in the 1850's.

Those who bemoan the instances of undemocratic solutions of international problems today, or who are distressed by the troubles which beset the UN in the Congo, may recall, perhaps with a feeling of hope, that the United States has left far behind and, indeed, has largely forgotten the unhappy story of "bleeding Kansas," when Free Staters sought to settle the territory of Kansas, and five thousand armed Missourians crossed the border, controlled the polls, and elected proslavery delegates to the legislature. President Pierce failed to support the Governor of Kansas who had expected him to nullify the election. The proslavery legislature made it a penitentiary offense to deny orally, or in writing, or in print, the right to hold slaves in the territory; no man was eligible to serve on a jury if he was conscientiously opposed to holding slaves. The antislavery men held their own convention at Topeka and adopted a constitution under which they elected a new governor and the two rival governments began to arm and drill their adherents. President Pierce denounced the Topeka free-soil group as "revolutionaries." With federal support, the pro-slavery government proceeded to arrest their opponents. The free-state stronghold town of Lawrence was attacked. The sheriff destroyed the printing press,

---

[5] See Mboya, "The Party System and Democracy in Africa," 41 *Foreign Affairs,* 650 (1963).

turned his guns on the new hotel which was the town's pride, and then burned it to the ground while a drunken mob pillaged the town. For three months there was war in Kansas; two hundred were killed and property damage was estimated at two million dollars. Federal troops restored order at last and the proslavery group drew up a new constitution at Lecompton. The referendum on the constitution wholly lacked the element of democratic freedom, but President Buchanan submitted it to Congress with the recommendation that Kansas be admitted under it as a slave state. Congress required a new popular vote, which resulted in the rejection by a large majority of the proslavery Lecompton Constitution. But when Kansas was admitted as a state of the Union it was legally "equal in power, dignity and authority" to all other states of the Union.[6]

New states have been admitted to the United Nations after comparably bloody conflicts and also, as has been true in the history of our Union, in peace and harmony. There is no need to despair of international democracy because, before man makes internationally a more perfect union, some madman may "Cry havoc, and unleash the dogs of war."

The Charter of the United Nations recognizes that the principle of equality applies to nonmembers as well as to members: Article 35 of the Statute of the International Court of Justice, which "forms an integral part" of the Charter, requires that the conditions under which the Court shall be open to other States shall not "place the parties in a position of inequality before the Court."

Indeed, the principle of the equality of States is among the oldest in international law. "No principle of general law is more universally acknowledged," said Chief Justice Marshall in 1825, "than the perfect equality of nations. Russia and Geneva have equal rights."[7] Without continuing with Marshall's interesting choice of symbols, one must at once admit that in much of history, small states have been denied the equal protection of the laws as have individuals within national democracies. On the international plane, self-determination and numerous slogans of the new nationalistic aspirations, have been promoting the

[6] One borrows the words used by the Supreme Court later in regard to Oklahoma: *Coyle v. Oklahoma* (1911) 221 U.S. 559, 566. The account of "bleeding Kansas" is adapted from the author's *The International Problem of Governing Mankind* (Claremont: 1947), by kind permission of The Claremont Colleges.

[7] *The Antelope,* 10 Wheaton 66, 102.

establishment, on a footing of equality, of many new states which now find the door to the United Nations wide open to them; the rostrum freely available to their orators; their words, or a summary record thereof, enshrined in at least two and, according to the pertinent regulations, often in all five official languages. Although the Councils and the Court have limited numbers of members, the members are, in the majority, freely elected by the total membership. In the General Assembly, all seven committees are committees of the whole on which every member is entitled to be represented; chairmanships, by tradition, are open to representatives of any Member except the five permanent members of the Security Council. The Secretary-General serves by virtue of a vote of the General Assembly and a qualified individual from the smallest state has on the whole a better chance of appointment to the Secretariat than one with the nationality of say, the United States. In this event, the larger powers cannot complain of disparity of representation.

In May, 1963, states of the African continent and the Malagasy Republic adopted the Charter of Addis Ababa to establish The Organization of African Unity. The governments of the participating states are various, but the Charter is a democratic constitution. It includes the principle of equality of states both great and small (as well as among individual persons) which had been stressed at the Conference by the representative of the largest of the new African States, Sir Abubakar Tafawa Balewa, Premier of Nigeria.

The United Nations, to a degree, deserves Senator Vandenberg's characterization of "the Town Meeting of the World," but as Eugene Rostow says, "Neither the town meeting nor the Swiss referendum is an indispensable feature of democratic decision making,"[8] and "Representative government is, after all, a legitimate form of democracy." The labels multiply: Section 4 of Article IV of the Constitution of the United States says that the United States shall guarantee to every state in the Union a *Republican* form of Government. In the arguments pro and con the acceptance of the Constitution in Massachusetts, James Sullivan said, "At the perusal of this clause, anti-federalism must blush. . . . The inhabitants of America are surely acquainted with the principles of republicanism, and will certainly demand the establishment of them. . . ." But James Winthrop *contra,* insisted that "Republicks

[8] Eugene V. Rostow, "The Supreme Court and the People's Will," 33 *Notre Dame Lawyer* 573, 577 (1958).

are divided into democraticks and aristocraticks."[9] The Britannica (eleventh edition) assures us that the term "republic" is now "universally understood to mean a state, or polity, in which the head of the government is elective, and in which those things which are the interest of all are decided upon by all." The United Nations is not a "state" and has no "government," but one may call it "a polity" and the power of decisions therein fits the prescription, at least in a formal sense. Of course, in the best of democratic republics, one knows that many important things "which are the interest of all" are not decided by *governmental* processes at all.

The world "polity" has been through phases of tyranny and has at times also been directed by those states which considered themselves the "aristocrats." Now is the era of international democracy, and "Western civilization" could not wish it to be otherwise.

[9] *The Federalist and Other Constitutional Papers,* E. H. Scott ed. (Chicago: 1894), pp. 502, 546.

2

The

Future of

Democracy:

A Swan Song

Mortimer J. Adler

The last great book in political theory—a work that stands in the line of Plato, Aristotle, Aquinas, Marsilius, Hobbes, Spinoza, Montesquieu, Locke, Rousseau, Kant, and Hegel—was published in 1861, a little more than a hundred years ago. John Stuart Mill's *Representative Government* has, in addition to its intrinsic greatness, the distinction of being the first major work in political philosophy which, addressing itself, as is appropriate to a treatise in political philosophy, to the question of the ideally best form of government, answers that question by a fully reasoned and critically cautious defense of the proposition that democracy is, of all forms of government, the only one that is perfectly just—the ideal polity.

At the time that Mill wrote *Representative Government,* democracy in his sense of the term—constitutional government with universal suffrage operating through elected representatives—did not exist anywhere in the world. Republics there were and constitutional monarchies, but all of them were oligarchies of one type or another: the ruling class—the enfranchised citizenry in the republics or the citizenry and the nobility in the constitutional monarchies—comprised only a small fraction of the population. The rest were disfranchised subjects or slaves.

Nor had democracy, in Mill's sense, ever existed in the whole of the historic past. From the beginnings of constitutional government in the city-states of Greece right down to Mill's day and beyond that into the twentieth century, the republics which went furthest in the direction of popular government were all oligarchies, in which "the people"— the constituents of the government, the enfranchised citizens—formed a privileged ruling class, rising above the subjects and slaves who formed the rest, usually the majority, of the population. In the Athens of Pericles, where what Aristotle would have regarded as an extreme form of democracy prevailed for a short time, the citizens numbered 30,000 or less in a population of 120,000.

We should certainly not allow ourselves to be distracted or confused by the fact that the Greeks invented the name "democracy" and used it, either invidiously for mob rule as Plato did or descriptively as Aristotle did for a form of government which, as contrasted with oligarchy, set a much lower property qualification for citizenship and public office. The democracies of the ancient world differed from the oligarchies only in the degree to which participation in government was restricted by property qualifications for citizenship and public office—which could result, as it did in the case of Athens, in the difference between a democracy of 30,000 and an oligarchy of 500. However significant that difference must have seemed to the 30,000, it could hardly have had any meaning for the 90,000 disfranchised human beings who, in Aristotle's terms, were useful parts of the political community, but not members of it.

We have no reason to complain about how the Greeks used the word "democracy," but it is disingenuous, to say the least, for contemporary writers to use it as a synonym for "popular government," and then make that term applicable to any form of government in which some portion of the population—the few, the many, or even all except infants, idiots, and criminals—participate somehow in the political life of the community. By that use of the term, anything other than an absolute monarchy is a democracy in some degree, more or less, according to the proportion of the population that forms "the people"—the ruling class. According to such usage, "democracy" in Mill's sense of the term is merely the limiting case in the spectrum of popular governments, the case in which the people is co-extensive with the population, excepting only those who, as Mill says, are disqualified by their own default. We are then compelled to say that the Greek oligarchies were simply "less democratic" than the Greek democracies; and that modern democracies became more and more democratic as the working classes and finally women were granted suffrage. It would take the semantic sophistication of a six-year-old to recognize that this is a use of words calculated to obscure problems and issues rather than to clarify them.

It can be said, of course, as it has been, that democracy in Mill's sense represents an ideal which, through the course of history, diverse forms of constitutional government have been approaching in various degrees; and hence, to whatever extent they are popular—to whatever extent "the people" is an appreciable fraction of the population—they are entitled to be called "democratic" by virtue of their tending to approximate the ideal. But to say this is worse than confusing. While it may be poetically true to describe the course of history as tending toward democracy as the political ideal, it is simply and factually false to attribute that tendency to our ancestors as if it were the manifestation of a conscious intention on their part. Democracy, in Mill's sense, was not the ideal to which the past aspired and toward which it strove by political revolutions or reforms. With the possible and qualified exception of Kant, no political philosopher before Mill ever argued for the inherent or natural and equal right of every human being to be a citizen actively participating in the government of his or her community; none regarded it as an ideal; none, in fact, even contemplated the possibility of a genuinely universal suffrage.

In the sphere of political action, as distinct from that of political thought, Mill did have some predecessors, such as Colonel Rainborough and Sir John Wildman among the Levellers in Cromwell's army; Mr. Sandford and Mr. Ross in the New York Constitutional Convention of 1821; Robert Owen in the formation of the community at New Lanark and similar communities elsewhere. But even in the sphere of practical politics, Mill is the first to advocate the enfranchisement of women and hence the first to conceive universal suffrage as including the other half of the population.

The prior uses of the term "democracy," both descriptive and denigrative, should not prevent us from perceiving what is genuinely novel in the political conception for which Mill appropriated that term. (1) It involves an adequate appreciation of the full extent to which universal suffrage should be carried on the grounds of a right to participate in government, a right inherent in every human being. Hence, (2) it regards constitutional government with truly universal suffrage as the only completely just form of government—the ideal polity.

In what follows, I shall be exclusively concerned with this new conception which, under any other name, would be exactly the same. Since no other name, nearly as appropriate, is available, I shall use "democracy" in Mill's sense of the term, hoping that the reader will remember why, *when the term is used in that sense,* nothing prior in theory or practice can be called "democracy" or "democratic." Anyone, of course, is privileged to use words as he pleases, but that privilege does not justify obfuscation or confusion in their use.

My main purpose in this paper is to consider the question: Under current and future conditions, is democracy *possible?* Is government by the people *practicable* in the world as it is today and as it is likely to become? Or to state this still another way: *Can* the people participate through suffrage in the government of a modern state?

There is, of course, a prior question: *Should* they? *Should* all human beings, as a matter of right and duty, actively participate in the political affairs of their community? If political democracy is not, as a matter of right and justice, the ideal polity, then why waste time concerning ourselves about its practical feasibility?

One might also ask, Do the people—or most people—really *want* to participate in government, or would they, as a matter of fact, rather concern themselves exclusively with their private affairs while someone else takes care of the business of government? This question is, in a sense, a subordinate part of the question about whether democracy is practically feasible; for certainly one major obstacle to its being effectively practiced would be a general indifference to political affairs on the part of most people. That indifference, if it exists, would have to be overcome by education or other means if democracy is to become effectively operative.

Let us return to the primary question: Is democracy the ideal polity —the most just, the only completely just, form of government? I share Mill's affirmative answer to this question. My explication of the answer, which I cannot attribute wholly to Mill, can be briefly stated as follow:

There are three principles or elements of political justice. (1) Government is just if it acts to serve the common good or general welfare of the community and not the private or special interests of those who happen to wield political power. By this principle, tyrannical government, exploiting the ruled in the interests of the rulers, is unjust; and, by this same principle, a benevolent despotism can be to some extent just.

(2) Government is just if it is duly constituted; that is, if it derives its powers from the consent of the governed. The powers of government are then *de jure* powers, and not simply *de facto:* we have a government of laws instead of a government of men. By this principle, constitutional governments of all types have an element of justice lacked by all absolute governments; by this criterion, an absolute monarchy, however benevolent the despotism, is unjust.

(3) Government is just if it secures the rights inherent in the governed, *i.e.,* the natural, and hence the equal, rights which belong to men as men. Among these rights is the right to liberty, and of the several freedoms to which every man has a natural right, one is political liberty—the freedom possessed by those who have some voice in the making of the laws under which they live. When political liberty is thus understood, only men who are citizens with suffrage enjoy political liberty. The unenfranchised are subjects who may be ruled paternalistically or benevolently for their own good, but who are also unjustly treated in so far as they are deprived of a natural human right. By this principle, every constitutional oligarchy is unjust, and only a constitutional democracy is just.

The last of these three principles is the critical one, the one that is essential to democracy. With the exception of tyranny, other forms of government may have certain aspects of justice, but only democracy, in addition to being constitutional government and government for the common good, has the justice which derives from granting every man the right to participate in his own government. This right needs a word or two more of explanation.

Like every natural right, this one is rooted in the nature of man. Its authenticity rests on the truth of the proposition that man is by nature a political animal. To affirm this proposition is to say that *all* men, not just some men, should be *constituents* of the government under which they live and so should be governed only with their own *consent,* and that in addition, they should be citizens with *suffrage* and be thus empowered to *participate* in their own government. (I have italicized all the crucial words in the statement of the proposition's meaning.)

It was Aristotle, of course, who said that man is by nature a political animal, but he himself denied one of the crucial elements in the proposition's meaning when he also said that some men are by nature slaves; for to assert that some men have natures which fit them only for slavery (*i.e.,* naturally incapable of participating in government) directly contradicts the proposition that all men are by nature political (*i.e.,* fit to participate in government).

To accommodate modern ears, let me translate Aristotle's remarks about natural slavery into the proposition that some men are intended by nature (*i.e.,* by their endowments at birth) to be governed for their own good and for their own good should be deprived of any voice in their own government. If this proposition is true, then political democracy could hardly claim to be the ideal polity. It has no special justice in excess of that possessed by a constitutional oligarchy, administered for the benefit of those subject to its rule. In fact, it might even be said to involve a certain injustice, in so far as it gives political power to those who *should not* have it—all those who are not by nature fit for suffrage. In short, *only if all men are by nature political animals*—only if all are naturally endowed to live as free or self-governing men—do all have the right to be enfranchised citizens and the duty to participate in government. Only then is democracy, of all forms of government, supremely just.

This is not the place to argue the truth of the central proposition or of its contradictory. But we ought to spend a moment considering what the best form of government would be *if only some men are by nature political animals.* Would the "some" be a small or a large proportion of the population? Would they be the few or the many? Undoubtedly, the few. These, then, should comprise a political elite, a corps of officials, a professional bureaucracy that should govern the people at large for their own good. So far we have a benevolent despotism; but if we now add (1) that the government should be duly constituted (*i.e.,* should be constitutional or limited rather than absolute—a government of laws) and, (2) that, except for the political distinction between the official ruling class and the rest of the people, an equality of social and economic conditions should prevail (*i.e.*, all men should equally share in the general welfare that the government aims to promote), and (3) that the government should safeguard, equally, the private rights and liberties of each individual or family, then what we come out with is the kind of government recommended by certain commentators on the present political scene; *e.g.*, Bertrand de Jouvenel, with a fondness for Gaullism, or Walter Lippmann, with nostalgia for Platonism.

Such a form of government can appropriate to itself the name "democracy" by appealing to Tocqueville's sociological rather than political conception of democracy as a society in which a general equality of conditions prevails. Equality of conditions can, as Tocqueville recognized, tend toward completely centralized totalitarian government, more oppressive than any ancient despotism; but if a community retains the limitations and checks of constitutional government, and if the general welfare that is promoted by the government includes the protection of the private rights and liberties of the people, then, perhaps, it does deserve to be called, as De Jouvenel calls it, a "social democracy." But it is not a political democracy; for while the community enjoys government *of* and *for* the people, government *by* the people has been replaced by the rule of a professional bureaucracy (which, it is hoped, comprise the few who are by nature competent to govern).

A "social democracy," thus conceived, might very well be the best— the most just—form of government *if it were true that only some men are by nature political animals.* But if the contradictory proposition is true—*if all are*—then it involves the same essential injustice that is to be found in any benevolent despotism. As Mill helps us to see, what is pernicious about the idea of the good and wise despot—in all the forms that it has taken from Plato to De Gaulle—is not the myth that any one man or any few actually have the superior qualities that merit putting the government entirely in their hands; the point is rather that, granted such men can be found, letting them rule, with wisdom and benevolence, reduces the rest of the population to a perpetual childhood, their political natures stunted rather than developed. By the standards of wisdom, efficiency, or competence in government, political democracy may not compare with the excellence in government that can be achieved by a specially qualified bureaucracy; but if all men deserve political liberty because they have a right to a voice in their own government, then government by the people must be preserved against all the tendencies now at work in the opposite direction—and for one reason and one alone, its superior justice.

The question remains: Can it be preserved?

In the hundred years since Mill wrote *Representative Government*, a small number of political democracies have come into existence for the first time in history, most of them since the turn of the century and most of them in Europe or North America. This is not to say that the ideal polity has been actually and fully realized on earth in our time. Far from it! What came into existence in our time were the legal enactments—the constitutional provisions or amendments—which established the form of democratic government in a small number of political communities. But in most cases—most notably, perhaps, in the United States—the discrepancy between democracy on paper and democracy in practice was vast at the beginning and has nowhere yet become negligible.

If significant inequality of conditions, if educational deficiencies, if the obstinate persistence of privileged minorities, on the one hand, and the failure to eradicate underprivileged minorities, on the other, prevent the effective operation of democratic institutions, then the full realization of democracy still belongs to the future, even in the politically most advanced countries. Nevertheless, one might have been cautiously optimistic twenty years ago, as I was, in thinking that the future belonged to democracy, that the general direction of change in the conditions of human life promised not only the legal institution of democracy where it did not yet exist, but also a slow and steady progress toward its fuller realization in practice wherever it did exist. It looked as if Tocqueville were right in thinking that "an aristocracy cannot again be founded in the world" and that "the nations of our time cannot prevent the conditions of men from becoming equal"; and therefore right in predicting that "the gradual development of equality of conditions" is inevitable.

It looked, in other words, as if all of Mill's fears about "the infirmities and dangers to which representative government is liable" would gradually be made groundless by the social and economic changes that have been taking place since his day. While advocating the extension of the suffrage to the laboring classes (because it was clearly unjust "to withhold from anyone, unless for the prevention of greater evils, the ordinary privilege of having his voice reckoned in the disposal of affairs in which he has the same interest as other people"), he feared that the enfranchised masses would exercise their new-found power in their own factional interests and tyrannically subjugate the upper class minorities to their will. He also feared that the judgment of the uneducated would prevail, by sheer weight of numbers, over the judgment of their betters to the detriment of the community as a whole.

The marked inequality of conditions which, in Mill's day, separated the working masses from the upper classes and brought them into a sharp conflict of factional interests led Mill, the proponent of democracy, to have the same fears about it that led others to oppose it. And, let it be said in passing, that the remedies—proportional representation and plural voting—which Mill proposed as ways of safeguarding democracy from its own deficiencies would as effectively have nullified democracy in practice, if they had been carried out, as the devices proposed by James Madison or John Calhoun to prevent the will of the numerical majority from prevailing. To be in favor of universal suffrage (which makes the ruling class co-extensive with the population) while at the same time wishing somehow to undercut the rule of the majority, is as self-contradictory as being for and against democracy at the same time.

This is not to say that the problems which concerned Mill were not genuine in his time. These problems—especially the problem of factions (the age-old conflict between the haves and the have-nots) and the problem of an educated electorate—can be solved, not in the way that Mill, or Madison, or Calhoun, proposed, but only through the development of a general equality of conditions, which, by gradually substituting a classless society of haves for a class-divided one, tends to reduce and ultimately to eliminate the conflict of economic factions; and which also, by gradually giving all equal access to schooling and enough free time for leisure and learning in adult life, enables every educable human being (i.e., all except the incurable feeble-minded or insane) to become educated to the point where he can be as good a citizen—as sensible in the exercise of his suffrage—as anyone else.

All men are not equally intelligent at birth; nor will all ever become equally wise or virtuous through the development of their minds and characters; but these ineradicable inequalities in human beings do not in themselves undermine the democratic proposition that all normal men are educable enough to become good citizens. To think otherwise is to revert to the aristocratic proposition that some men are so superior to others in natural endowment that they alone are educable to the extent required for participation in government. I am not saying that the problem of producing a sufficiently educated electorate (when it is co-extensive with the population of the community) has yet been solved. It certainly has not been, and we are still a long way from solving it. I am only saying that the changes which have taken place since Mill's day—especially the technological advances which have brought affluence and ample opportunity for learning and leisure in their wake—give us more hope that it can be solved than he could possibly have summoned to support his wavering democratic convictions.

Herein lies one of the paradoxes of the present situation. The same technological advances which have created relatively affluent societies for the first time in history, and without which it would have been impossible to effect all the social and economic reforms that have tended to create a greater equality of conditions, are now made the basis for despair about the feasibility of democratic government. Again and again, in discussions conducted by the Center for the Study of Democratic Institutions, for instance, it has been said that government by the people is no longer possible, because, in our technologically advanced societies, the problems of government have become so complex that neither the people themselves nor their elected representatives in congress or parliament can contribute to their intelligent solution. It has been suggested that, if not now, then certainly in the foreseeable future, decision-making will have to be taken over by computers and by the experts who know how to program them.

Government by the people may have been a feasible polity in ancient Athens when the *few* who constituted the citizenry met in the agora and debated questions of policy which they could understand and think about in terms of the relatively simple state of facts with which they were generally acquainted. It may even have made some sense in certain countries during the eighteenth and nineteenth centuries, when the significant citizenry were still a very small portion of the population and when their elected representatives in congress or parliament could still have understood the questions they debated and have had some command over the facts relevant to reaching decisions. But now that the citizenry is, in effect, the whole population—now that, at last, we have constitutional democracy with universal suffrage—most of the basic questions which confront a twentieth-century government can no longer be intelligently debated, much less decided, by the public at large or even by representative assemblies.

There are other sources for the current despair about the feasibility of democratic government—if that is really taken to mean participation in government by the whole population through voting and through other ways of expressing their views on public policy, either directly or by pressure on their representatives. One is the ever-increasing size of the population and the intricately complicated and ever-changing conditions under which the enlarged population now lives and struggles to form a community. Another is a series of studies of the voting process, made in recent years by social scientists, which tends to confirm the worst suspicions of antidemocrats concerning the folly of supposing that the voters pay any attention whatsoever to the real public issues involved in an election when, in fact, they merely express their emotions or their prejudices at the polls. Still another is a mathematical analysis of voting which leads to the conclusion that the principle of majority rule does not work when the voters are presented with more than two alternatives.

One could go on, either to spell out in detail the sources of despair about democracy or to add many others of similar vein, but that is not necessary in order for us to face the fact that today the prevailing opinion among the learned—the professional students of sociology and politics—is that a realistic approach to the processes of government leads to the conclusion that the ideal of democracy, as Mill envisioned it, is simply a misleading myth. Even if democracy were ideal in terms of the principles of justice (a matter which most of the learned no longer deign to discuss, or else dismiss as the kind of loose talk in which only philosophers indulge), it does not now have and probably never can have any reality in the world of things as they are.

Since I am only a philosopher—and also a relatively ignorant man with regard to the current state of learning in the behavioral and social sciences—I cannot assess the validity of the conclusion just stated in terms of the evidence or considerations on which it is based. Such questions as: *Does democracy now actually exist to any degree?* or *Under present and future conditions, is the realization of democracy highly improbable?* are questions of fact. I do not know the answers to these questions; and, being a philosopher, I suspect that no one else does either. I also doubt, as any philosopher would, that such questions can be answered demonstratively. The answers to them always remain in the sphere of opinion and are always likely to be subject to reasonable differences of opinion in the light of all the evidence that can be gathered.

Confronted with the opinion about democracy that is now prevalent among the learned, at least among those of realistic persuasion, a phi-losopher is impelled to ask questions.

Let me begin by assuming the truth of the realistic denial in its most extreme form; *i.e.,* let us assume the *impossibility* of government by the people in any sense which tends to realize, in some degree, the ideal of democracy. What then?

First, must we not conclude that the ideal is a purely visionary uto-pian one, not based on men or conditions as they are? For if it were a practicable ideal, based on things as they are, then how could it be im-possible of realization—in the strict sense of impossible? Those who thus eliminate democracy as a practicable ideal must therefore be asked whether they have any genuinely practicable (*i.e.,* actually realizable) political ideal to substitute for it. If they say no, they must be further asked whether the reason is that they reject normative political think-ing entirely and so refuse to take the question seriously. In that case I, as a philosopher, have no interest in questioning them any further. But if they concede the possibility of sensible and reasonable talk about good and bad forms of government, and hence are seriously concerned with thinking about the best of all possible (*i.e.,* realizable) forms, then they should either have some alternative to democracy as the ideal polity or be in search of one. In either case, they must be asked to state the stand-ard, principle, or norm in terms of which they would propose a partic-ular form of government as best, or better than some other. Justice? Wisdom? Efficiency? Strength? If they appeal to any standard other than justice, or do not include justice among the principles to which they appeal, I must remind them that democracy is said to be the best form of government only in terms of justice, not in terms of wisdom, efficiency, strength or any other criterion; and so they have failed to find a substitute for democracy. If they then reply that justice is totally irrelevant to the goodness of government, I either have no more ques-tions to ask them or too many to set forth here.

Let me turn next to a milder form of the current despair about de-mocracy—to the view that the difficulties in the way of realizing it are now very great and, the way things are going, are likely to become even greater in the future. Let us assume that this is true. However great they are or are likely to become, they cannot be regarded as insurmount-able; for that would throw us back to the extreme position that govern-ment by the people is impossible. Here we have only two main questions to ask.

The first is addressed to those who are so deeply impressed—and claim to be so sorely distressed—by all the difficulties which now loom up and stand in the way of making democracy work, especially the difficulty that arises from the complexity of the problems which governments now face, a complexity that seems to place them beyond the competence so far manifested by the electorate or by representative assemblies, or any degree of competence that might reasonably be expected of them in the near future. I must, in passing, warn our friends not to overstate this difficulty lest it become insurmountable and we be once more thrown back to the extreme view that democracy is impossible. If they heed this warning and continue to concede that democracy is practicable, however difficult putting it into practice may be, then I would like to ask them whether they also concede that it is the ideal polity. My question, I must remind them, is not about democracy in *any* sense of that term, but about democracy as defined: constitutional government with genuinely universal suffrage, operating through elections and elected representatives, with majority rule, and under conditions of social and economic as well as political equality. Do they regard democracy thus defined as the ideal polity, and if they do, do they hold it up as the ideal by reference to principles of justice?

If they answer this compound question with a double affirmative, then there is only one further question to ask. Let me assume that they take the view that the difficulties confronting democracy—if not now then certainly in the future—are likely to be so great that, even if they are not, absolutely speaking, insurmountable, we may nevertheless be unable to overcome them in any really satisfactory manner. Hence, they may say, we should prepare ourselves for this eventuality by thinking of a second-best form of government, one which, while less just, would be more workable because it would get around the difficulties now besetting democracy. What shape would that take?

I do not know whether there is more than one possible answer to this question; but I do know, and have already mentioned (see page 36), one alternative to democracy that is espoused by those who wish to discard government by the people while retaining government of and for the people. I am even willing to concede that if political democracy should prove to be impossible, then so-called social democracy may very well be a second-best. But I am not yet willing to yield—and I see nothing in the contemporary discussion of the difficulties of democracy which requires me to yield—on the proposition that all men are by nature political. I must, therefore, repeat what I said earlier; namely, that, men being what they are, "social democracy" is a poor second-best, for it imposes upon the many who are disfranchised the essential injustice which characterizes any benevolent despotism. Hence, until—as nearly as possible demonstrably—insurmountable difficulties force us to surrender all hope in democracy and for its future, we should be loath to settle for anything less than the best form of government that befits the nature of man.

Until then, the only course for us to follow—with courage and intelligence—is the one outlined by Robert M. Hutchins in a recently published conversation in which he engaged with Joseph P. Lyford on the subject of man the political animal.

Summing up, Mr. Hutchins said, "The Center [The Center for the Study of Democratic Institutions] is committed to constitutional democracy. Its reasons lie in the nature of man. Man is a political animal. It is unjust to deprive him of his political life." He then went on to say in conclusion:

> The task of those who are committed to political democracy is to discover how democracy can work in a technical, bureaucratic society in which all problems appear to be beyond the reach, to say nothing of the grasp, of the citizen. The task calls for more than haphazard thoughts and random discussions and the dusting off of ancient but irrelevant slogans. It requires a prodigious effort of the best minds everywhere to restore the dialogue that is the basis of the political community. Above all, the effort calls for faith that, whatever the defects of our society, self-government can and must endure because it is the only form of rule consistent with the nature of man.

3

The

Society

of the

Dialogue

William O. Douglas

Robert M. Hutchins, testifying in 1952 before the House Select Committee to Investigate Tax-Exempt Foundations and Comparable Organizations, made a classic statement concerning the Society of the Dialogue:

> . . . a university is a place that is established and will function for the benefit of society, provided it is a center of independent thought. It is a center of independent thought and criticism that is created in the interest of the progress of society, and the one reason that we know that every totalitarian government must fail is that no totalitarian government is prepared to face the consequences of creating free universities.
>
> It is important for this purpose to attract into the institution men of the greatest capacity, and to encourage them to exercise their independent judgment.
>
> Education is a kind of continuing dialogue, and a dialogue assumes, in the nature of the case, different points of view.

The civilization for which I work and toward which I am sure every American is working, could be called a civilization of the dialogue, where instead of shooting one another when you differ, you reason things out together.

In this dialogue then, you cannot assume that you are going to have everybody thinking the same way or feeling the same way. It would be unprogressive if that happened. The hope of eventual development would be gone. More than that, of course, it would be very boring.

A university, then, is a kind of continuing Socratic conversation on the highest level for the very best people you can think of, you can bring together, about the most important questions, and the thing that you must do to the uttermost possible limits is to guarantee those men the freedom to think and to express themselves.

Now, the limits on this freedom cannot be merely prejudice, because although our prejudices might be perfectly satisfactory, the prejudices of our successors or of those who are in a position to bring pressure to bear on the institution, might be subversive in the real sense, subverting the American doctrine of free thought and free speech.

The principal guide in this matter is due process of law. *The limits that are set, then, on this dialogue* on the conversation, on the independent thought and criticism, *are the limits set by the law.* (Italics added)

The law in this context can mean either legislative enactments punishing certain kinds of speech or constitutional limitations on the power of government to restrain or punish utterances. The two are not necessarily synonymous; and it seems obvious that Dr. Hutchins used *the law* in the latter sense.

The law in the legislative sense has had a narrow or broad spectrum depending on the predilections of the ruling group. A religious group possessing secular power has usually used it to promote the "true" faith and to inhibit or destroy heretical ones. A religious group, though not exercising secular power as such, may be so powerful that it can obtain monopolies or concessions from the ruler, as have Catholics in Spain; or, as in Ireland, where religious authority is so influential that it is able to fasten on the state the literary standards of the *Index Librorum Prohibitorum*. Nations dominated by one religious sect have not, however, always tried to cast *the law* into one religious mold. Modern Nigeria—predominantly Moslem—has not undertaken to revise Nigerian law to conform to the Koran. Pakistan, on the other hand, in a devout effort to establish its mark as a Moslem regime has energetically tried to do so.

Theologians usually have been as fearful of heresy as kings have been of treason. One of the charges against Socrates was "impiety"—that is to say, he denied the existence of the gods that had been recognized by the state. Every religion at some time and place has been denounced as heresy; and those in power have tried to put it down. Sects within Christianity have shown the same intolerance. The Reformation is associated with Martin Luther; however, prior to Luther, reformist movements appeared many times only to be crushed. When in time the Protestants gained control, they tried to repress Catholics; and wherever Catholics regained or maintained the upper hand, they ferreted out the Protestants. Many devices of turning up and repressing heresy were used. Heretical books were destroyed; heretics tortured, burned or banished. Among devices of repression, particularly noteworthy is that those charged with the crime of printing books without a license and those charged with heresy were both required to take the oath *ex officio.*

The oath *ex officio* made unnecessary an indictment, trial by jury, and confrontation of accusing witnesses. The judge *ex officio, i.e.,* by virtue of his office as judge, summoned the party to court on suspicion, on probable cause, or on whim or caprice, and instituted action against him. This practice of requiring the accused to testify or to go to jail for contempt was ended in England by Act of Parliament in 1368. After that a presentment or indictment, returned by a man's peers, was necessary to require him to answer. But that obtained only in the King's Courts. The ecclesiastical courts and the notorious Star Chamber continued to use the oath *ex officio.* The Puritans learned that this was the most awesome power the government had over them. It was used to make them conform to objectionable religious ceremonies, to punish them for speech and thought, and to seek out the nonconformists who surreptitiously published "dangerous" tracts. The European experience of political and religious repression transmitted to the shores of the New World a bitterness against all devices by which men convicted themselves against conscience and dignity. The oath *ex officio* was used against John Udall in 1589 and against John Lilburn in 1647 in trials touching freedom of the press that were burned into the memories of the American colonists.

Religious groups whose economic interests have been in the *status quo* have often conditioned politics, philosophy, and law to protect not only their dogma and creed but their wealth as well. In spite of its stout advocacy of the principle of equality in the United States, the Catholic Church has been closely linked with feudalism in Latin America. With only intermittent (but happily increasing) exceptions, its voice there has been on the side of the *status quo* and against reform.

At times the religious influence in secular affairs has appeared most subtly. Prior to the dominance of Puritanism, the Western world did not concern itself with obscene literature. Pornography marched down through history, gaining few recruits, though not punishable as an offense nor subject to the censor's pencil. The Puritan influence changed all that, beginning in the seventeenth century. Poetry, novels, the stage, became punishable if they "corrupted the morals." Prison sentences and fines were imposed. The *Index* was added as a sanction on some nations, the censor reigning supreme. Censorship became fastened on parts of the press in this nation and in England; and neither has been completely removed.

There have also been other watchdogs of ideology. These guardians of the "public good" were once members of the royal class and the vested interests they represented. In early American history workers were disenfranchised, only property owners qualifying for suffrage. Aristotle discussed the danger of turning the power over to the masses —"for their folly will lead them into error, and their dishonesty into crime"; and the danger of not doing so—"for a state in which many poor men are excluded from office will necessarily be full of enemies." Centuries later, in 1821, Chancellor Kent spoke much more dogmatically when he expressed the classic position against universal suffrage— the danger of giving the vote to "men of no property" and to "the crowds of dependents connected with great manufacturing and commercial establishments and the motley and undefinable population of crowded ports" and to "every man that works a day on the road or serves an idle hour in the militia." Even today many states have property qualifications for voters. Five states still have poll taxes, an institution against which the proposed Twenty-third Amendment is aimed. Nine states in America bar paupers from voting.

Property—free enterprise, private farming, private housing—is an ideology and it has conditioned American politics. The dominance of the proletariat is the communist ideology and it has dominated the politics of China, Russia, and Eastern Europe. Subversion in a communist regime is advocacy of the creed we espouse. Constitutional limitations apart, subversion here is advocacy of communism. Subversion in either place includes, of course, action as well as speech. But the fact that on each side of the curtain subversion is understood to include speech marks a sharp limitation to the modern Dialogue.

The legal conception of punishment for words spoken has a long history. The matter of belief has created some of the bloodiest chapters of history. Kings, sitting on uneasy thrones, always sought out the "subversives" among their people. Those who schemed and plotted against the king, collecting arms, making plans for riots, assassinations, and seizure of government arsenals, were, of course, punished for their overt acts. But what of those sullen, silent people who wished the king were dead, but never put their wishes into action? What greater uneasiness is there than that created by a host of enemies who have not moved into action but may do so? The law—which was usually the instrument of the ruler—designed a method of reaching this "subversive" group.

British law made it a treasonable crime to "compass or imagine the death of the King," the crime known as constructive treason. This crime was borrowed from Dionysius (430–367 B.C.) who executed a subject for dreaming that he had killed him. That was sufficient proof, Dionysius said, that the subject had thought about killing him when he was awake. Jefferson said that this crime of constructive treason "had drawn the blood of the best and honestest men in the Kingdom." Men were, indeed, executed merely for uttering treasonable words. In 1351 the British Parliament, while retaining as one definition of treason the compassing and imagining the death of the King, ameliorated the plight of the suspects by requiring that there be an overt act. In other words, wishing that the King were dead was not enough; doing something about it was necessary. The deed, rather than the thought alone, became a necessary ingredient of the crime of treason. But reducing treasonable words to writing was considered an overt act.

Dangerous talk has been the bane of the theologians and of uneasy rulers. Dangerous talk has been the excuse for oppression from our colonial days down to the present—an excuse that has had many distinguished proponents. One was Samuel Johnson, who thought that "no member of a society has a right to *teach* any doctrine contrary to what the society holds to be true." He said:

> . . . every society has a right to preserve public peace and order, and therefore has a good right to prohibit the propagation of opinions which have a dangerous tendency. . . . He may be morally or theologically wrong in restraining the propagation of opinions which he thinks dangerous; but he is politically right.

This view obtains in most nations, for in most of them the legislative branch is supreme. In highly disciplined England, the House of Commons is a conscientious guardian of freedom of expression. Many nations, however, took steps to preserve the Dialogue through written constitutional limitations. Examples of this kind are conspicuous in the constitutions of Latin American countries and of nations newly emerged since World War II. But more often than not those constitutional limitations are window dressing only. In practice the iron hand of a military clique or a dictator bears down heavily on the nonconformist. Some nations, notably India, have provided in the Constitution considerable leeway for legislative action. While freedom of expression is guaranteed, the legislature may make "reasonable" regulations of it. In the United States we built the fences higher both as respects treason and free speech. The ease with which the concept of an overt act establishing treason was expanded resulted in a narrow American definition: "Treason against the United States, shall consist only in levying War against them, or in adhering to their Enemies, giving them Aid and Comfort." Since, moreover, the treasonable act might be only a drummed-up charge, the Framers of our Constitution provided that in order for a charge of treason to be proved, it was necessary to have two witnesses to each overt act: "No Person shall be convicted of Treason unless on the Testimony of two Witnesses to the same overt Act, or on Confession in open Court."

More relevant to the creation of a Society of the Dialogue is the First Amendment which reads:

> Congress shall make no law respecting an establishment of religion, or prohibiting the free exercise thereof; or abridging the freedom of speech, or of the press; or the right of the people peaceably to assemble, and to petition the Government for a redress of grievances.

This prohibition has by judicial construction been extended to the States as a result of the Fourteenth Amendment, adopted after the Civil War, which provides, *inter alia:* ". . . nor shall any State deprive any person of life, liberty, or property without due process of law." Denial of "freedom of speech or of the press," or of "the right . . . peaceably to assemble, and to petition the Government for a redress of grievances" violates the "due process" clause of the Fourteenth Amendment since they have been construed to be included in the term "liberty." (See *Stromberg* v. *California*, 283 U.S. 359; *DeJonge* v. *Oregon*, 299 U.S. 353.) And, the cases hold, the same is true when a state violates the "establishment of religion" clause of the First Amendment or prohibits "the free exercise" of religion. (See *Engle* v. *Vitale*, 370 U.S. 421; *Abington Township* v. *Schempp*, 374 U.S. 203; *Murray* v. *Curlett*, 374 U.S. 203.)

The beginning of our experience under the First Amendment was not auspicious. In 1798 the Congress, in fear of the French and their agencies of espionage, enacted the Alien and Sedition Laws making it a crime, among other things, to publish any "false, scandalous and malicious writing" against the government, the Congress, or the President with intent to defame them or bring them into "contempt or disrepute" or "to stir up sedition." This was a short-lived law, lasting by its terms only until 1801 and never extended. It brought, however, a reign of terror to the nation. Matthew Lyon of Vermont was fined and imprisoned for criticizing President Adams and condemning his policy toward France. Thomas Cooper was fined and imprisoned for criticizing Adams for delivering an American citizen to the British Navy for court-martial. Anthony Raswell of Vermont was fined and imprisoned for denouncing the political persecution of Matthew Lyon. James T. Callender of Virginia was fined and imprisoned for criticizing Adams and accusing him of attempting to embroil this country with France. He wrote, "Take your choice, then, between Adams, war and beggary, and Jefferson, peace and competency." David Brown was fined and imprisoned for proclaiming against those laws and saying, "Downfall to the tyrants of America; peace and retirement to the President; long live the Vice President and the minority." Luther Baldwin was fined for a comment he made when a cannon was fired in Adams' honor. Baldwin was heard to say that he hoped the wadding behind the powder would hit Adams in the seat of his pants.

During the trials under the Alien and Sedition Laws, counsel for the defendants got nowhere with their objections to the validity of these Acts. The power of the federal judiciary to declare Acts of Congress unconstitutional was not announced until 1803 when *Marbury* v. *Madison* (1 Cranch 137) was decided. The federal courts undertook only to enforce the Alien and Sedition Laws, not to pass on their validity. Those laws would not, of course, pass judicial scrutiny today, as Justice Holmes indicated in his dissent in *Abrams* v. *United States* (250 U.S. 616, 630), since they would strike at the very heart of free political comment.

We atoned as a nation for the injustices perpetrated under the Alien and Sedition Laws. When Jefferson was elected in the 1800 campaign, he promptly pardoned those who had been convicted for seditious utterance; and for the next fifty years Congress passed laws remitting the fines of those who had been convicted.

While any *federal* law forbidding criticism of the government is at war with the First Amendment, by judicial construction the States have greater leeway. Libel or slander of an individual *under state law* are not outlawed. But the desirability of having full discussion and debate of public issues has resulted in the rule of "fair comment" which means that, though one on the hustings speaks falsely, he is immune from suit if he acts not maliciously but reasonably in light of the facts as he understands them.

Puritanism was bent on censorship of the press to protect the morals of the public. The Anthony Comstocks brought many sanctions to bear, including restrictive state laws. Sex became taboo. But *the law—constitutional law*—inched slowly forward. It is not isolated parts of a book by which a work is to be judged, but its effect as a whole; it is not what a prude or a psychopath would call "filth" but what "the community" would condemn; it is not the mere presence of sex which casts a book into outer darkness. Free speech and free press protect dissemination of ideas on sex except for material which treats sex "in a manner appealing to the prurient interest" (*Roth* v. *United States,* 354 U.S. 476, 488). Even so, there is no room for the unilateral action of the censor. If a book is to be condemned, there must be a criminal trial with all protective safeguards. Movies, however, may within limits still be censored, for they are thought by judges to be a more dangerous medium of expression.

At the political level the American Dialogue has suffered greatly because of a loose construction of the First Amendment. The First

Amendment is not a command, said Learned Hand, but only counsels "moderation." "It does not mean what it literally says," ruled the judges. "Otherwise speech might be the undoing of a nation"—as if a nation could be saved if it was already so weak as to be undermined by speech!

The "clear and present danger" test was formulated by Holmes, the libertarian (*Schenck* v. *United States*, 249 U.S. 47). That test was made meaningless by *Dennis* v. *United States* (341 U.S. 494) where "clear and present danger" was defined to mean that the danger need be neither "clear" nor "present" but realizable only "as speedily as circumstances would permit" (*Id*. at 499). A conspiracy to teach communist doctrine (accompanied by no overt act except the teaching) became, thereby, a crime, even though the Communist Party was too weak to carry any precinct. Moreover, "advocacy" of communism was established as a constitutionally permissible crime in *Barenblatt* v. *United States* (360 U.S. 109).

Advocacy means more than an intensity in tone of voice; it assumes an intent to promote an idea as speedily as circumstances permit. Making advocacy a crime expresses fear of the incitement of the idea. All talk, all writing, all methods of expression are incitement. Where the legislature is supreme, the toleration point is reached not with pleasant ideas but with ideas despised or feared. Where there are no constitutional limitations, the essential difference, so far as the Dialogue is concerned, between a totalitarian regime on the one hand and the Free Society on the other is the point where that intolerance is reached. When there are limitations on governmental control of speech as severe as the ones in the First and Fourteenth Amendments, one would expect that the Dialogue would be much freer. But, as noted, even constitutional limitations are eroded by construction.

Another serious invasion upon the Dialogue was made by legislative committees as a consequence of the "clear and present danger" test. Since Congress or the States could, in spite of the command of the First Amendment, restrict speech if a "clear and present danger" existed, they could investigate to determine whether that danger existed, the authority to investigate being an aid to the exercise of legislative power. Investigation of speech meant investigation into "What did you mean?", "What did you believe?", "What did you advocate?" It also meant investigation into all the associational rights implicit in the First Amendment: "What party did you join?", "What magazines did you read?",

"What club did you join and who were its members?" Thus many of the fences of privacy, protected by the Constitution, were broken down and roving commissions hunted the new heretics of a new age.

The law has always set the boundaries of the Dialogue—narrowly, when a church, a clique, a class, a party held all power; broadly, when a society became more mature and more responsive to multi-racial, multi-religious, multi-ideological needs and adopted by tradition unwritten constitutional limitations as in England or written ones as in the United States. But the rulings on constitutional law have not always been the true measure of tolerance. Community attitudes, legislative committees, vigilantes of one sort or another have often had repressive effects. While constitutional law condemns only advocacy, bigotry condemns *per se* the unorthodox view. The ideas placed by bigots beyond the pale may be as personal as birth control or as impersonal as foreign policy. He who becomes identified with an unpopular view may jeopardize his job. The modern inquiry into an employee's security or loyalty covers a wide range and dredges deeply his or her past. The number of employees affected is almost without limit, for local, state, and federal bureaus grow annually; and those who contract or subcontract with government under the Pentagon's vast procurement program employ the great majority of industrial workers. It is safe only to conform; it is hazardous to embrace ideas that are unpopular. Government preoccupation, first with the punishment of "anarchists," I.W.W.s or "wobblies," "socialists," and later with punishment of "communists" led officials, who were in search of *overt* acts to settle for mere utterances deemed un-American. And *the law* in its application (though not always in its formulation) usually accommodated the prosecutor. Those retreats, tragic as they were, were not the true measure of the decline of the Dialogue. The level of the editorial page and of television was lowered; the pulpit became complacent; the school boards followed the masses. Thus it was that belief in an unorthodox view, let alone advocacy of it, was avoided. Public opinion moved more to the center and to the right; and public affairs lost much of the ferment of the Dialogue. Freedom of expression and belief suffered from regimes of intolerance that had extralegal sanctions. A nation, great in tradition, became petty when it came to ideas. Intolerance drained much of our strength.

The result is the same, whether *the law* or a popular mood restricts talk and debate. For when traffic in ideas is slowed, a nation is changed.

New and different ideas may then even seem dangerous; inventive genius is thwarted and some of the dynamism of the Society of the Dialogue is lost.

If the Dialogue is to flourish, the First Amendment must be accepted in full vigor, as distinguished from a rule fashioned from day to day to fit the mood of the dominant group. Ideas make men free; the real un-American is he who suppresses them. Yet whatever the Constitution says, whatever the judges rule are not important if our communities do not honor free expression. If that is to come to pass, we must accept moderation in debate and discussion, the role of an opposition, the right to dissent. If the Society of the Dialogue is to flourish, our people must reflect a spirit of respect for the First Amendment, a tolerance even of ideas that they despise and of their advocates. If that kind of regime is to be established, we must accept a moral responsibility to make the First Amendment work for all groups, not just for one faith, one race, or one ideology. That means a vision broad enough to permit discourse on a universal plane; only then will we be able to communicate with a multi-ideological world. Community attitudes as well as *the law* must be shaped so that they become instruments which encourage, not the suppression, but the release of talents and energies in the Dialogue.

4

Toward a

Political

Theory of

Education

Bertrand de Jouvenel

The Fundamental Purpose of Society Is to Rear the Young

It is a tautology that the perpetuation of any living species depends upon the successful rearing of its young. It is an empirical finding that such rearing poses to parents a problem of increasing difficulty as we ascend the ladder from the simplest to the most complex organisms. When we are dealing with the lower forms of life, the adults' perpetuating function is completed in the very moment of germ discharge. Of such germs of life, produced in sufficient quantity, and abandoned to water or air, enough enter a favorable environment in which to develop autonomously. Such autonomy of development is denied to superior animals, which require, for survival and growth, the nurture and care of the mother. The greater the perfection to which they are called, the more pronounced their initial helplessness, the more delayed their ability to fend for themselves. These features so culminate in the case of man that I find it impossible to picture a being deserving the name of man developing without the benefit of already elaborate arrangements for his protection. It seems reasonable to regard the mother's need for help in the nurture and protection of the young as having provided the nexus of society, which sufficiently explains the many matrilineal traits of primitive societies.[1]

We must picture, therefore, some social coalition built around the mother as the necessary precondition for the emergence of man. Some species offer instances of such coalitions which, however, dissolve when the young all reach adulthood at the same time. It could not be so in the case of man or his forerunners, since the period of maturation was much longer than the interval between births: the coalition therefore had to be permanent, a requisite condition for the devolopment of language.

We do not have to explain how the forerunners of man came to form permanent associations, but we can safely assert that the biological character of the species made its survival impossible but for such groupings; and that, indeed, only within such groupings could man acquire characteristics such as significant speech, which we regard as defining him. Man was born in and of society.

Have I any justification for so farfetched a beginning? I think so, because it emphasizes that the care of the young is the sufficient reason and fundamental purpose of society.

The Main Social Task Is the Education of the Young

It would be futile to bring the young to physical adulthood without endowing them with competence. It seems true of all creatures that they break away from their protectors as soon as they feel apt to cater for themselves: if that occurs after only one season, the time during which they can learn from their seniors is short. It is a boon to us that our period of inevitable dependence is so long: while this has, on one hand, made society necessary, as a corollary it gives us much time to be taught.

What are children taught everywhere, even in the most primitive groups? Skills, manners, and judgment. I put skills first because the teaching of skills can be observed already in the behavior of animals: we can easily watch birds being taught to fly, kittens being taught to hunt. Manners are these modes of conduct which contribute materially

---

[1] Note that the rearing of Romulus and Remus by an isolated fostermother (called tellingly a she-wolf) is meant to excite wonder.

and morally to group co-operation. Judgment is the capacity to make the best decisions for oneself and for the group.

Anthropologists have stressed that, in a primitive group, any child gets attention from his seniors: as his seniors pet him in his infancy, so does every senior chide him for bad manners when the occasion arises. Training in skills is given by all, but it is mainly under the tutelage of the best performers that the child learns to fish or hunt. As those who have lived longest in a dangerous world are deemed by their success (longevity) to have given positive evidence of their prudence, it falls to them to teach judgment: which these elders do by telling tales which imply a moral, and become "lessons of history." It does seem that more of adult activity is addressed to education in primitive conditions than in our advanced societies. It is understandable: survival is doubtful enough to make it essential that the coming generation should be as well or better endowed than their contemporaries in skills, manners, and judgment.

Education Is the Mirror of Society

The behavior of adults is dependent upon, though not uniquely determined by, the education received. But also the education given reflects the values of society.

However much one would like to think of war as a decreasing function of civilization, the evidence is to the contrary. The primitives seem to have less thought of conflict than societies with an already higher organization. Lacedaemon is the classic example of a society where the training of the young tended to make them battle-worthy. It is only fair to point out that the purpose seemed to be defense rather than conquest,[2] and also that their training did more than prepare warriors: it overcame laziness, clumsiness, and selfishness. The founder of anthropology, Father Lafitau, stressed the similarities between the institutions and education of Sparta and those of the Iroquois Indians.[3]

It is trite to contrast the Athenian education with the Spartan. In

[2] Because military capacity was so much in the minds of the Spartans and so colored their institutions, one should not jump to the conclusion that theirs was an aggressive city. Thucydides shows that its leaders tried to avoid or terminate war. It may be, however, that the small numbers of Spartans compared to the large number of their subjects was a motive for military vigilance.

[3] See *Moeurs des Sauvages Américuains comparées aux Moeurs des Premiers Temps,* par le Père Lafitau de la Compagnie de Jésus, 2 vols. (Paris: 1724).

Athens we find a "liberal education." In social terms, this means nothing but an education for free men. But I think it may also be taken to mean an education for those who may look forward to a life free from pressing cares. Productive skills have no part in this education because production is entrusted to slaves. War skills have but a subsidiary part because the City glories in a safe hegemony.

"Music" becomes essential in such an education: it includes literature in its many developing forms, and thus corresponds to what will come to be known as attendance upon the Muses. Philosophy is introduced at a later stage of history, and also for students more advanced in years. Thus liberal education takes shape as a quickening of the esthetic and intellectual faculties, as a formation of taste and thought, promising a fruitful use of gentlemanly leisure.

Such education can properly be called "culture" because it causes what Alfieri called the *pianta uomo* to flourish: it was, however, only for a minority. Surprisingly enough, it is Friedrich Engels who argues vigorously that slavery and other forms of subjection of the greater number have been historically necessary to allow minorities the leisure necessary for the development of culture.[4]

It is easy enough to recognize that the great cultures of the past, marked on the one hand by a liberal education for a minority,[5] were marked on the other hand by the subjection of the multitude. Nor does it seem true that, as Engels implied, the favored minority, by its very existence, stimulated the development of productive forces. Its members owed it to their position to turn their backs on sordid pursuits. As

[4] See Friedrich Engels: *Anti-Dühring*, Second Part, Chapter 4. "Without slavery, no Greek City, no Greek art or science; without slavery, no Roman Empire. And without this basis of hellenism and Roman empire, no modern Europe. We should never forget that our whole development, economic, politic and intellectual had as its prior condition, a state of affairs in which slavery was quite as necessary as generally acknowledged. Thus, we have reason to say: without ancient slavery, no modern socialism."

[5] For a minority, does not mean for privileged classes alone. It is well known that the Church seeded medieval Europe with so many schools that, as an historian puts it: "Except in thinly populated districts, there were few parts of Western Europe in which a boy needed to go far from home to attend a regular grammar school, where in addition to instruction in reading, writing and religion, he could acquire Latin both as a spoken and as a written language, and perhaps even rhetoric and logic, which were still regarded as 'trivial' subjects, to be learnt at school." William Boyd, *The History of Western Education* (London: 1921 and 1947). It is equally known that promising subjects could hope to rise to the highest Church dignities, and indeed to the Holy See. The same seems to have been the case in China.

Seneca remarks of such devices as central heating or stenography: "These are nothing but the devices of our vilest slaves: wisdom sits higher, and does not educate hands but souls."[6] If, due to the practice and example of the Church, the upper classes of Western Europe were open at all times to those rising from below, such ease of access, however laudable in itself, worked rather against the improvement of the common lot than on its behalf. And this, for a simple reason, which Bonald expounds[7]: as soon as a businessman had done well enough, he hastened to become a nobleman, and this implied "living nobly," that is renouncing all interest in materially productive processes. Thereby the chief talents of the productive multitude were skimmed off, removed by their own choice, from further contribution to the material progress.

The Coming of "Productivity"

Swift, in his *A Voyage to Laputa,* rails against the "projectors" who propose new ways of performing material tasks, "whereby, as they undertake, one man shall do the work of ten."[8] His mockery proves that the state of mind to which we owe so much was then already in vigorous ascent. No political or social reformer could possibly have transformed the condition of the multitude as it has been transformed by the ceaseless introduction of new technological processes. Our age is properly "the Age of Productive Capital," meaning that installations and equipment afford to labor a productivity previously inconceivable. And nowhere is this better recognized than in the Communist countries, which concentrate on capital building.

We can deem ourselves fortunate to live in times when the material condition of the common man is continuously improving, when he obtains an ever-increasing flow of goods and services in exchange for work of shorter duration, exacting far less physical effort. Those who turn up their noses at this technological civilization should see in what misery, and at what cost of labor the masses of the people live in the countries where this great advance has not yet occurred. They would then speak just like that Jesuit missionary to China whose initial admi-

---

[6] Seneca, Epistle 90.

[7] See Louis Bonald's *Observations sur l'ouvrage ayant pour titre Considérations sur les principaux évènements de la révolution française par Mme la baronne de Staël* (Paris: 1818).

[8] *A Voyage to Laputa,* Chapter 4 (first published in 1724).

ration for the refined culture of the mandarins turned to angry sorrow when he saw the life of the peasant, toiling throughout the day in water to his knees and fed in the evening on a bowl of rice.[9]

Whatever the indubitable welfare-consciousness of seventeenth-century China, it could not remedy its lack of productivity. This lack is surprising in a country which made major inventions many centuries before they reached Europe or were rediscovered there.[10] Political good will of itself cannot cure economic ills, nor can inventions of themselves procure economic goods: there must be an attitude of mind which turns them to productive purposes. A productivity-conscious society such as ours is without precedent in human history.

Before our times, there have been so-called rich civilizations. In fact, however, the eye was drawn to islands of wealth amid a sea of poverty. Now, for the first time, wealth is general—nothing proves this better than the denunciation of "patches of poverty" which now seem to us to be anomalies.

What does this imply for education?

Quantitative Progress in Education

Education is "a good thing," and there should be more of it. On this statement, couched in naïve terms, there is pretty unanimous agreement.[11] The rough and common meaning of "more education" is "more years spent at school." This, indeed, is the criterion of "educational attainment" used by the U.S. Bureau of the Census, whose reports rank the adult population according to the number of years of schooling completed. Its reports inform us, for instance, that the median education in 1940 for workers in the age group from 18 to 64 consisted of 9.3 years

[9] Lettre du Père de Premare, Missionnaire de la Compagnie de Jésus, au Père Le Gobien, de la même Compagnie, November 1, 1700, in Lettres Edifiantes et Curieuses (1781 ed.), Vol. XVI, pp. 394 seq.

[10] See in Joseph Needham's admirable Science and Civilization in China (Cambridge: 1956), pp. 154 ff. the table displaying the lags between China and the West in mechanical and technical inventions: the median lag of the West is ten centuries!

[11] I find the data collected by Eva Mueller very impressive, if one remembers firstly that American opinion is averse to public spending, and most averse to the raising of taxes, and secondly that American usage offers alternative financing of education. No less than 60 per cent of people consulted agreed that Government should spend more on education, and as many as 41 per cent persisted in this assertion even if such spending had to be financed by the raising of new taxes. No other item of public expenditure obtained so high a score when the condition of increasing taxes was included in the query. Eva Mueller: "Public Attitudes towards Fiscal Programs," Quarterly Journal of Economics, May, 1963.

of schooling, while by 1957 this median had risen to 11.8 years.[12] We are also told that, at a given moment, say 1957, the age group 25 to 34 had a higher "educational attainment" than the 45 to 64 age group, the median of school years completed being 12.1 for the first against 9.5 for those older. The "educational attainment" of the whole adult population is, of course, affected by the continuous addition of generations with a higher educational attainment.

If we turn to what is presently being done for education, still employing a quantitative concept, the best presentation consists in ranking the young population by age, taking the ratio of school attenders for every age class, plotting such ratios on a chart and drawing a curve through these points. The curve stays in the neighborhood of a 100 per cent straight line for a period of years, and then falls off. Curves of this kind can be compared for the same country at different times or for different countries. Obviously such a curve begins to fall off later when legal age for leaving school is raised, also its shape beyond that age depends upon the opportunities given and taken for further study.

The surface defined by this curve can be called "the tuition area": it is remarkably large in the United States by comparison with other countries.

The Economist's Plea for More Education

Quite recently, there has been a considerable expression of interest among the economists, for increase in education. It is not suggested that their concern for it, as individuals, is novel! What is new is that their plea for more education should be made in their capacity as economists and be based upon economic considerations. It is supported by three important positive findings.

1. The study of economic growth has gone far beyond any explanation based upon the cumulative increase of fixed capital alone. It is now stressed that such growth also depends upon the development of "the economic capacities" of individuals, capacities which are enhanced by education. Education therefore is "investment in man," deemed no less necessary for growth than investment in capital equipment. Theodore W. Schulz, a pioneer in this area of study, asks us to imagine some low-income country acquiring overnight the set of natural resources and means of production possessed by an advanced country. Would not its output fall very far short of that of the advanced country to which it is

[12] Bureau of the Census. *Current Population Reports*, "Labor Force," November, 1957, Series P-50, No. 78.

now materially comparable, for want of comparable skills? Conversely, Schulz feels, that the remarkable rates of growth achieved by some European countries after World War II may be due to their having been "long on human capital relative to their stock of reproducible non-human capital," so that successive increases in the latter paid off startlingly well in terms of output—this, because they remedied an imbalance, because there was an excess of skills available to put the new tools to work.[13]

2. The comparison of individual incomes has brought out that personal income is an increasing function of the number of years of schooling completed.[14]

3. The analysis of the unemployed population has shown a clear correlation between unemployment and inadequate schooling.[15]

Of these findings, the second is, by far, the least novel: parents have always assumed that they improved their child's chances of social advancement by affording him more education. The third is quite alarming: technological progress seems to increase the risk of superfluity for the ill-qualified. It is worth noting how far this new fear belies the old fear, so frequently expressed in the past, that the development of "machinism" would grind down the great majority of workers to the performance of witless tasks! On the contrary, it is now felt that economic development as it were makes more room at the top while leaving less at the bottom of the job structure, tends to manifest itself by excess demand for highly qualified personnel, simultaneous with excess demand for jobs by the least qualified. In other words, the labor market tends to divide itself into "floors" with a possibility of inverse situations at different "floors." Whatever the immediate implications of such a situation—and they are of very great importance, but not our present concern—the long-term implications are clear enough: the structure of qualifications should keep pace with the changing structure of jobs.

At the same time that parents may regard the future benefits accru-

---

[13] The most convenient presentation of the whole subject is offered in the October, 1962, supplement to *The Journal of Political Economy,* a supplement entitled *Investment in Human Beings,* and organized by Theodore W. Schulz. Therein can be found references to the many relevant papers published elsewhere.

[14] For a crisp, clear statement of the findings and a critical appraisal, see H. S. Houttaker "Education and Income," *The Review of Economics & Statistics,* February, 1959.

[15] See the reports of the U.S. Commissioner for Labor Statistics, especially the results of the April, 1962 survey of persons unemployed five weeks or more in 1961.

ing to their children from more advanced education, their fear of unemployment for lack of sufficient education is an additional negative incentive. For society as a whole, the progress of education seems a condition not only of over-all growth, but of preventing that great evil, unemployment.

Some Implications of More Education

Still thinking in quantitative terms, the progress of education means: (a) that the period of mandatory education is lengthened; or (b) that the ratio of those studying beyond the mandatory period is raised; or —and more probably—(c) that both of these phenomena occur, in whatever mixture. In any case, it means that, besides the general increase which the school population must undergo in coming years for merely demographic reasons, a specific increase (corresponding to the idea of "more education") must considerably swell the school population above the age of seventeen.[16]

Stressing that the problem to be dealt with essentially concerns the population above seventeen immediately implies that the attendant increase in teaching personnel requires people capable of giving junior college, or college, or university tuition. In short the teaching population, which must increase in numbers throughout all grades, must be expanded to a much greater degree at its more advanced levels. This requires that capable people should be tempted away from the competing attractions of the professions, business, public administration, advertising, and, to some degree, of research itself. This should accelerate the process, already visible, of heightening the material and moral status of professors. Incidentally it will make the teaching profession a far more influential and powerful group in society.

Securing teachers in adequate quantity and of sufficient quality is no mean task. It is, however, in my view, the only economic problem which results from the lengthening of the educational process.

I have found that the foregoing statement often arouses surprise and incredulity. It can be easily justified. Everybody takes it for granted that continued gains in productivity will permit a progressive shortening of the work-week. A general shortening of the work-week by one hour deprives the economy of as much labor as the delay by one hour of the

---

[16] I choose the dividing line of seventeen because, from the American statistics available to me, this seems the age beneath which the very great majority already attend school under present conditions.

commencement of work by all the youth of the nation.[17] Thus if the economy can afford the shortening of the work-week, it can just as well afford an *alternative* deprivation of labor by lengthening the required time for study. It must, however, be clearly put to public opinion that these are *alternative* benefits accruing from gains in productivity. The shortening of the work-week is assuredly the self-regarding alternative.

It is not, however, the economic but the psychological problem which concerns me. It seems the natural bent of physically mature human beings to embark upon the active life—the urge is very strong in the late teens; it is quite easily overcome in the case of those who truly delight in study. But they are a minority. For the majority there is a painful tension—often manifested in disorderly conduct—which makes the task of teachers more difficult. The phenomenon is well known, but it is often said that this phase passes away. True enough, but quite frequently such passing away leaves a certain limpness in the individual. As he has not started "doing" when he first felt impelled to the active life, he may subsequently find himself more phlegmatic and less energetic. Moreover, the life and environment of the student are abnormal, especially in the residential universities of the United States. It is worth remembering in this context that such a life was devised long ago in England for men promised to Holy Orders, and that those destined to an active life came to Cambridge or Oxford much earlier and left much earlier than is the case in the American universities.

Undoubtedly this is a real problem, one, however, which I do not feel experienced enough to discuss further. It does inject a doubt into my mind about the desirability of lengthening progressively the duration of formal education for all, regardless of individual propensities.

In any case, at some point, it becomes absurd to think in terms of adding "more years" and we shall have to think of more fruitful years. This again is a problem for thoughtful educators, of which I am not one. I shall leave it for the moment.

Education for Production and Education for Leisure

It is time, indeed, that I should come to consider the purpose and nature of education. I have stressed that continued gains in produc-

---

[17] Skeptics can be convinced by this rough calculation. Take 60 million fully employed as the equivalent of the occupied labor force, strike off 50 hours per year and per person: that is a loss of 3 billion hours of work. Assuming that 1.5 million youths are kept at school instead of doing 2,000 hours of work a year per head: that is also equivalent to 3 billion hours.

tivity constitute the characteristic feature of our modern civilization: tellingly enough, it is the only one which nations formed by a different civilization than our own are eager to take over from us.

I have noted, as well, that economists champion more education because it serves to increase productivity. Productivity benefits the worker in two ways: (1) by an increase in the flow of goods he gets and (2) by a decrease in the amount of work which he must do. When we think of less work or more free time, we are all too prone to consider it only in terms of a shorter work-week. Considerations of increased holidays or increased longevity beyond the age of retirement are but different forms of one and the same phenomenon. It is the most telling index of our technological civilization that life expectation has so increased: workers no longer work until they drop, because on the average they live longer than they used to and because individual or (increasingly) social provision can be made for old age.

If one reflects on the career of a hypothetical young man who goes to work at the early age of seventeen, he has a long career of work stretching before him. We may make some revealing calculations. He can look forward to fifty-three years of life, of which he can expect to spend ten after retirement. The very most he can expect to spend at work each year, assuming forty-three years of work is approximately 1900 hours per year. Taking these figures, which surely do not err on the side of optimism, the most our young man can expect to spend at work is less than 18 per cent of the time of life he has before him. If he assumes that during the coming forty-three years, the average time worked will be forty-eight weeks and thirty-five hours per week (1680 hours per year), then the share of the time at work during his lifetime falls to 15.7 per cent. I think it is permissible to state that work-time will absorb one sixth of the time he has before him.

Assuming that sleep will absorb one-third of the remaining time, our young man has one-half of his prospective life unconsumed by work or sleep. In more striking terms, a man's waking hours (two-thirds of his whole mature life) will be divided one-quarter for work and three-quarters for free time. I find it surprising that people seldom make such simple arithmetical calculations—calculations, moreover, which are likely to shed light on pressing problems.

Let us by all means so educate our young man so that his hours of work will be more productive. Of course, if we delay his entry into work by one year, it will mean so many hours less (possibly as much as 1900 hours) available to him in his lifetime. At the same time it may well be that the loss of one year of work consumed by education might add to his economic capability in such a way that the life-product for the total hours remaining will be increased, not diminished—and, indeed, so increased that the shortening of the normal work year to come may ensue. All this is quite right.

But what seems very wrong is to educate our hypothetical young worker for one-quarter of his waking hours to come, and not for the other three-quarters! I am quite willing to recognize that not all of the three-quarters is, in fact, available time: much of it is taken up by travel to and from work—but even during this trip the fruits of education may appear. Using public means of conveyance, one may as well read Pascal as look at comic strips. In short, all the waking hours ahead of us—those hours not consumed by work—depend for their use upon the education we receive.

Let me put it another way—and for this purpose I shall provisionally adopt the vocabulary of aristocratic civilizations which contrast the laborer bent upon his task, and the gentleman of leisure who bears his head high, *os sublime*. In our day the man who is all the time a "gentleman of leisure" has utterly disappeared. But the laborer who was nothing but laborer, a mere "hand," has also disappeared. The man of our day is part laborer, part gentleman of leisure. If we want to call work "slavery," then the contemporary is a good deal less than "half-slave" and a good deal more than "half-free": look to the foregoing figures.

The case for developing the average man's skill as a laborer is unanswerable, since among the benefits procured, despite the loss of work-time, is the progressive enlargement of that share of time during which he is a freeman, a "gentleman." But the greater the share thus liberated, the more pressing it becomes to educate man for the fruitful use of this free time. Sebastian de Grazia puts things very nicely when he used the term "free time" negatively, to signify that part of time which is "saved from the job," while reserving the term "leisure" to signify something positive," a state of being in which activity is performed for its own sake or as its own end." And he says: "To save time through machines is not easy. To transform free time into leisure is not to be easy either."[18]

While the contrast here drawn between "free time" and "leisure"

18 Sebastian de Grazia *Of Time, Work and Leisure,* The Twentieth Century Fund, (New York: 1962).

may well be deemed excessive, it does point to a major problem of our
times which is well expressed in the popular expression: "How shall I
spend my time?", or even better the childish question: "What shall I do
with myself?" According to the way we spend our time, we improve or
harm ourselves—and it is truly a question of *ourselves* and not of such
externals as our job or status.

No term is clearer than that of "culture": it means something
done to us for our improvement, and something we do to ourselves
for improvement. There is a wealth of examples to show that a man
who has not been cultivated can, later in life, cultivate himself. But it
would be optimistic to believe that more than a small minority are
capable of this—most of us depend for our cultivation upon the good
start given us by our teachers.

In short, future generations, which can look forward to an increasingly lighter burden of work, and to an increasing share of free time,
require a liberal education.

And those so aristocratically minded as to think that the delights
of art and thought can be enjoyed but by the "happy few" play a fool's
game. We live in majority societies where beautiful things will be
wiped out unless the majority appreciates them. The selfish sage
(were these terms not contradictory) who wants the harmony and
silence of Nature only for himself will find the silence destroyed by
noisy hordes and the landscape ruined by bulldozers unless he can convert the majority. "Convert or perish" must be the motto of the self-
regarding man of taste. Surely it is better, as indeed it is more natural, to undertake such conversion for the good of one's fellow men and
especially of coming generations.

A Trivium

Education then has a dual purpose: to make man's labor more
productive, and his leisure more fruitful. And the greater the gains
in one direction, the more necessary is progress in the other. But here
a great difficulty arises. I have expressed doubts about the feasibility
and advisability of successively lengthening the term of formal education. If it must be lengthened in order to accommodate increased
productivity, how much more must we lengthen it in order to make
room also for a liberal education? If that is the problem, we are, indeed, in trouble. But I think, or hope, that the formulation above is
erroneous. It contains two assumptions, both of which I reject: the

first is that education for efficiency and education for improvement are radically distinct, and that to give both is twice as much trouble and takes twice as much time; the other is that the time presently spent in education is well employed.

Would anyone doubt that the art of correct expression (literature) and the art of rigorous reasoning (mathematics) are basic both to business and to culture? I would contend that the acquisition of these two skills is far the most important part of education.

I would draw the sharpest contrast between mental skills (such as I have just mentioned) and factual knowledge. We are lazy, and most of us have to be driven very hard to progress in lucid exposition and correct inference. However, such progress as we do make becomes part of our personality. It is otherwise with factual knowledge: we receive it from outside, store it, and it wastes away in storage. Factual knowledge does not become part of us—no more, be it noted, than what is in the "memory" of a computing machine is an integral part of it: you can change the content of its memory; it still is the same machine. Personal experience has made me most strongly aware that we forget factual knowledge.[19] Therefore I ask: How much of the history, geography, physics, chemistry, biology, or geology taught at school do we remember? And since these things are going to be forgotten anyhow, instead of wasting upon them efforts better applied to the gaining of durable skills, one may as well present them in the form of educational films, which will at least associate vividly in a child's mind with a given historical event. I regard it as very important that a child should realize ecological relationship, the dependence of human life upon its natural environment, and while it can be expected that he will remember how the rains come and the simple circuit of water, it is idle to hope that he will memorize the pathways of biosynthesis and photosynthesis. Nor is it good to grade on the basis of how much is remembered:[20] proper grading should be on the degree

---

[19] A quarter of a century ago I spent two years steeped in the French administrative correspondence of the Revolution and Empire relating to the "Continental blockade." As the author of a book on this subject, I was asked last spring to say a few words about it in a broadcast discussion. I found that I had to turn back to my book, which I studied almost as if it had been written by another man—the main difference being that some pages acutely brought back to me the excitement felt when I discovered this or that enlightening report.

[20] No quiz is a measure of educational attainment.

of achievement in the use of mental skills. These are what truly survive the end of the formal educational process. To the two named already, I would add a third, as soon as gifted expositors[21] have found means of making it readily accessible to the young: this I would call the art of checking factual statements; of measuring whether the evidence in favor of a given statement is sufficient to carry conviction; of asking the right questions, the answer to which would clinch a case.[22]

This art, along with literature and mathematics, would constitute my *trivium*.

Of course the art of correct expression is considerably enhanced if a great deal of translating is required—and, without hesitation, I would suggest Latin as the other language from which and into which translations should be made, for its prosaic neatness offers such a useful contrast with the colorful vagueness of English.[23]

But as I have no qualifications as an educator, it is most foolhardy to venture so far.

Disciplina Facit Mores

My excuse for venturing as far as I have arises from my insistence upon the acquisition of skills as revelatory of the nature of Education. "Getting education" is not like being given a car; it is more like becoming capable of swift and prolonged swimming. What one really learns is to use one's powers. Brain specialists now tell us that we intellectuals use but a small fraction of the resources of our brain. I feel sure that they are right, and our descendants should be stimulated to do better. This is, to a considerable degree, a moral problem. Lack of attention, the great original fault of the mind, is properly a lack of courage—" 'tis good enough" is a lack of honesty. Everything which Xenophon says in his *Cyropedia* regarding the necessity of a hard training for the body is valid for the mind. It seems to me a shocking paradox that one praises the exacting trainer who forms athletes, and that the same hard-driving spirit is not demanded of or approved in trainers of the mind.

---

[21] I have in mind such admirable examples of pedagogic exposition as G. L. S. Shackle's *Mathematics by the Fireside* for younger children, or G. Polya's *Mathematics and Plausible Reasoning* for older students.

[22] The development of decision theory and information theory should, in time, give rise to an elementary course in the art of evidence.

[23] If not Latin, then French, but let it be pre-Romantic French.

Factual knowledge we acquire throughout our life according to opportunity and need, and we lose it through disuse. But it seems clear that the capacity to use the mind is acquired in youth only: and it is therefore a betrayal of youth, and of mankind, not to challenge this capacity so as to give it the fullest development. It takes moral virtue to respond, and response develops moral virtue.

The Ancients used to say, *Disciplina facit mores.*[24] It is true, indeed, that the way of life depends upon education. It seems that this venerable truth is best understood in our day by the commercial community, whose advertisements are increasingly aimed at the receptive mind of the child, to educate him for conspicuous consumption. Strangely enough intellectuals seem to make little of this truth.

We are all anxiously asking ourselves what is the future of individual liberty. The answer lies in our hands. Our power to preserve or procure it cannot be efficiently exercised by the means which seemed decisive to late eighteenth-century and early nineteenth-century minds. Experience has made us fully aware that the establishment of institutional devices offers no durable and solid guarantee of freedom. We have seen the collapse of too many constitutions and the abuse of others. We realize that whatever the influence we expect from political institutions upon mores, mores have a far stronger influence upon institutions, which stand or fall, work well or ill, according to the mores of the people. But *disciplina facit mores.* The tone and style of the society depend upon education. Of this the ancients were so convinced that Xenophon's *Republic of the Lacedaemonians* deals mainly with the educational system. The persistence and right use of the political institutions depend upon the will of the adult, whose character and judgment have been formed in the educational institutions.

But let us look closer. It is at least a twenty-five-hundred-year-old debate whether "right conduct" should be taught by the pedagogue, or by parents. In Rome there was no question but that such instruction fell to parents: the family was called the "seminar of the Republic." In the Middle Ages, when the teaching establishments were run by the clergy, it was only natural that they should impart religious principles. The day-school system, prevalent in France, naturally leaves moral education to parents; the boarding-school system prevalent in England seems to turn it over to teachers. Presently most of

---

[24] *Disciplina facit mores* is, indeed, the appropriate theme of an essay contributed to honor my eminent friend, Robert M. Hutchins.

our contemporaries are convinced that right conduct is not efficiently taught by "laying down the law," by way of *Diktat,* but by responding to the child's anxieties. As a Catholic, I must and do believe that man has a natural appetite for the good, which only needs to be encouraged and enlightened. So here again it is not a question of imprinting upon the mind a code coming from outside, but of fostering a faculty of the individual.

How school can contribute to this process is quite a problem. Only two positive ways occur to me. First, in literature, a choice of authors with strong ethical content, and these, indeed, seem to be preferred by children (the preference of French children for Corneille, as an example). Second and mainly, the ceaseless practice of virtue in study. *Laborare est orare:* learning to do an honest piece of work is apprenticeship in virtue. A slovenly performance is a spurning of God's gifts and should never be tolerated. And here again, direct familiarity with great authors, as championed by Robert M. Hutchins, is inspiring.

Incidentally, Americans can never cherish enough the independence of educational establishments which exists in their country, not in mine, and which makes it possible to develop experiments, such as the teaching from "great books" practiced at St. John's College in Annapolis.

Education and Equality

We must not only teach intellectual honesty, but also practice it. Liberal thinkers of the past held that progress in education would promote equality. This now seems, to say the least, very doubtful. What is in doubt is not that equal opportunity for education should be afforded to all children. What is in doubt is that, on the basis of equal opportunity, a society of equals will result. Of course we have been and are moving toward equality of opportunity in schooling,[25] an evolution wherein the European countries lag behind the United States.[26] We all favor this equalization of opportunity, but we no longer trust that this equal nurture of children will result in the equal

[25] I say "equality of opportunity in schooling" rather than in education because that part of education which is received at home, of course, depends upon the knowledge and solicitude of parents. And you could not abolish this advantage for some without a general loss to society.

[26] I understand that Japan is here also ahead of European countries.

development of adults. This was believed by some eighteenth-century liberals on philosophic grounds: men, born equal, and receiving equal treatment, should develop equally.

Modern educators, who do not rely upon metaphysical assumptions but speak from experience, tell us that children and youths are quite unequally receptive to education. The longer and more elaborate the curriculum, the more pronounced the disparity becomes. I have been told by American high-school teachers that they felt an obligation to help along the stragglers, but, in so doing, failed to provoke and stimulate the gifted; contrariwise the French *lycée* professor addresses himself to the elite of the class.

It would be a crime against our descendants if education were slowed down to the pace of the least apt, and limited to their ingestive capacity. Education must perforce have for its maxim: "To each according to his capacity." From very different performances by students, there naturally arises a hierarchy within the generation reaching manhood. This hierarchic ordering sits well with an increasingly integrated society. I find it hard to understand how "progressives" can at the same time cherish centralization and champion equality. Integration means nothing other than bringing a great number of individuals into one organization, which naturally assumes a pyramidal shape, and has more grades and rungs the larger it is. A society of large organizations (never mind whether they are called public or private) is a society of many grades; this corresponds very well to the great hierarchy of grades which arises out of education. Michael Young has called the resulting social system "Meritocracy."[27]

This seems to be the modern pattern. Great anxiety has been expressed as to its implications for individual freedom; however, much depends upon what one means by freedom. If one thinks of freedom as enlarged in proportion to means and narrowed in proportion to constraints, one will find it hard to deny that the common man's freedom on balance has increased, and is continuing to increase. The model is not incompatible with freedom in private life but with equality.[28] It is a natural law of organizations—quite flagrant in organisms—that the more elaborate the organization, the more differentiated and hierarchically structured the roles. Increasingly, incompati-

[27] Michael Young: *The Rise of Meritocracy 1870–2033* (London: 1958).
[28] The French have a telling term for this—*"la liberté du particulier."*

bility will be found between the equality proclaimed and its practice. What allows us to believe that we are moving toward greater equality is that there is still a great deal of pre-technological inequality to be liquidated. It is an ironical thought that the more long-drawn-out the process of liquidating antiquated and now dysfunctional inequalities, the more it will help to mask the emergence of a new strongly inequalitarian system. While people are still discussing the abolition of Lords by birth, they are but faintly aware of the new lordships.

However the inequalitarian system we are moving into has much to offer the "inferiors." Not only will they have little to envy their "superiors" as to the material conveniences of life, but the "inferiors" will do less work and will be subject to far less strain than the "superiors." We are witnessing a great upward shift of responsibility and a great downward diffusion of leisure. The advantages of a lower position may, indeed, become such as to tempt even some of the highly qualified.

Aurea Mediocritas

The expression of *aurea mediocritas* may, indeed, become a true description of the common man's condition in a technological civilization. Freed from want and worry, leaving it to a responsible elite to dispose of his work and to insure his welfare, our man can spend a great deal of time according to his taste. He can paint or drink, raise flowers or make the air ugly with the sound of his outboard. The aspect of our civilization already depends and will increasingly depend upon his taste. In this sense (though not in its management) our society promises to be increasingly democratic. In every past culture, religious rites and public edifices have been taste-forming. During the Middle Ages and, indeed, up to recent times all the tunes of popular songs were drawn from Church music composed for the glory of God; Athenian citizens discussing on the Pnyx, faced the beauty of the Parthenon. In our day, a managerial elite, obsessed with the progress of efficiency, has little time or thought to spare for the formation of taste. That is a glaring deficiency which the teaching community must seek to repair.

Just as it is important to express oneself lucidly, so it is important to speak in a voice which does not grate upon the ear: and, for everyday life, the latter is the more important. It is a very good thing that modern transportation makes it easy to visit "beauty spots," but their beauty can easily be destroyed by the behavior of visitors. As men are more closely packed, manners are more indispensable to their enduring each other's company. We are not merely, or even mainly, a thinking machine. We are a sensitive organism. The joys of the mind are experienced by only a few. Is that a good reason to regard them as superior? I think not. I think the more important experiences are those of our affective nature, and that its right cultivation will come to be recognized as the most important part of education. How is this to be achieved? This is beyond my ken.

But I would stress that our Christian faith, perpetually presenting to our minds the passion of Jesus, thereby stresses that the Incarnation was the assumption of our sensitive nature, and so dignifies it. This had been the basis of a policy directed toward the lessening of what human sensitivity has to endure; it can also justify a policy directed toward enriching this sensitivity. And the body of teachers, promised as they are a major influence in society, will therefore find itself stressing the development of our capacities in that direction.

5

The

Universalization

of Western

Civilization

Elisabeth Mann Borgese

Most people take for granted today that sooner or later the world will be governed democratically. As civilizations "grow up" they will not let themselves be ruled in any other way. That "democracy" and "democratic values" will be profoundly transformed by this process may be equally taken for granted.

Space and time have shrunk under the impact of Western civilization. This, too, is a fact no longer open to discussion. The entire world is smaller now in terms of distance-in-time than any of the principal nation states were only a century ago. Men all over the globe have begun to resemble one another more than they ever did before, and a single "world culture" or "world civilization" is beginning to take shape. There can be no question about this. What will be the ultimate contribution of Western civilization to this world culture is another problem. Undoubtedly Western civilization itself will be transformed as it is being universalized.

If we want to understand these impending changes in the nature of democratic values and of Western civilization, we must inquire into this process of universalization.

The term "Western civilization" does not need any definition. We all know what we mean by it. For our purpose it may be useful, however, to point out the factor that distinguishes it from all other civilizations we know. Western civilization, it seems to me, contained from the beginning the seed of its own disintegration. This, one might say, was intrinsic in the unstable amalgam of its heterogenous origins. Other cultures grow, mature, age, and ossify as more or less self-contained organisms. By fusing Greek, Roman, Hebrew cultures, however, and by grafting them on the wild but vital Germanic trunk, Western civilization became a superorganism which was potentially both self-disruptive and all-encompassing. Where other civilizations strove for permanence, Western civilization remained a permanent striving. Others crystallized in being; Western civilization alone was ceaseless becoming. Other civilizations were like wall-enclosed gardens nourishing delicate plants in the midst of the wilderness. Their "cultural evolution"—or, as Thomas Huxley called it, their "ethical evolution"—ran in a sense counter to "natural evolution"—Huxley's "cosmic process"—which was wild, chaotic, based on struggle, a white whale lurking constantly within men and around them. Eventually, the cosmic process resumed its course, back toward the state of nature, and the fine garden inevitably decayed.

In Western civilization alone "cultural" evolution is no longer opposed to "natural" evolution, but has become its continuation and spearhead. This, one might say, is the real meaning of Western history from the Renaissance to the twentieth century: the emergence of modern man, a *mutant* from the species *homo sapiens,* who, with humanism and the New Learning, set out to discover the individual and the universe, not only in order to explore nature but to control it and to take evolution in his own hand.

When evolution—non-directed "un-rolling" (*e-volvere*)—becomes intentional, directed, "led" (*e-ducere*) by man, *evolution* becomes *education*. For if evolution now aims, as Julian Huxley believes, at the ever greater perfection of an ever greater number of individuals, what else, indeed, is it but education?

But since this mutation, giving rise to modern man, was not genetically but culturally produced, the physical dominance of Western man, as manifested by imperialism, could be only a passing phase:

a contact—as much as sufficed to create systems of transmission. A dominant type of ant extirpates rival species. A dominant type of man—like the ant—assimilates rival cultures to his own. That is the difference: which is merely a consequence of the method of transmission of the species' hereditary matter, or its "values."

Still, in our day one often reads that the people who are now in process of development need to "hurry up"; "to catch up" with Western man; to traverse in a few decades the phases of cultural, social, and economic development it took him centuries to pass; to "recapitulate" his history; and then one pauses and wonders at seeing that things turn out so differently in the "new countries." Westernization is there; but of "recapitulation" one sees no trace. What is being adopted from the West, moreover, is the worst. Ancient cultures and customs are being undermined without replacement by new values. And then we in the West beat our breasts, crying that we are no good and that our culture is both ruined and ruinous.

All this seems to me to be rooted in a misunderstanding of the nature of the transmission of "values" in cultural evolution.

This transmission follows its own rules: quite different—almost diametrically opposite—from those governing the transmission of genetically conditioned mutations.

Culture is transmitted *on contact: by communication.* Hence it is absurd to assume that the transmission of culture should begin from the center of values; or from the past (which is the same, because the older a cultural substance, the more interiorized it is). Transmission begins peripherally. Impressionistically. Behavioristically. Externals, the accessories, are transmitted first. Thus bushwomen take to high heels and tight skirts. Cigarettes and alcohol make their triumphal entry.

The missionary's work obviously can have no deep influence on the "primitives'" life at this stage. At best he may slip in a few miracle tales—which are promptly misunderstood and put through a Procrustean process of "adaptation"—provided he makes himself acceptable otherwise by catering to the desire for the accessories of life. To consider the missionary as an avant-courier of Western culture is to misunderstand the nature of its transmission.

What comes next, after the "accessories" and proceeding from the external toward the essential, is technology. Television aerials will spring up from slums and rock caves; the "primitive" will be able to tune in London or Paris long before he knows anything about decent housing. The motor scooter will be sheltered affectionately along with the goat and the ten-head family in their one-room dwelling, long before anything is known about adequate sanitation. And we must not blame ourselves too much for dumping that useless or even damaging stuff on them. We couldn't sell it if they did not want to buy it. But they do want to buy it: because the transmission of the culture of *homo mutans* proceeds from outside to inside, from effect to cause, from the contemporary back to history, from the collective to the personal.

This is why Marxism does not make sense for this stage of development in the "new countries." The epigonal theories of its Western apologists simply don't apply. For the industrial revolution here is not a consequence of capitalism, of the grievances of a class structure. Again, the process is reversed. In Western civilization industrialization led to mass production; in the new countries the mass products arrive first and industrialization follows in the wake of the technological produce.

At this particular point in the universalization of Western civilization, however, a phase sets in, during which Marxism seems to become most actual and convincing: much more so than for us Westerners. For if we look back into our own history, we must recognize —unless we are uncritical and orthodox—that economic rights were created *after* political rights. The philosophical revolution preceded the political revolution which preceded the economic revolution which gave way to industrialization and mass production.

In the new countries democratic rights are born out of economic rights. Democracy, in the new countries, would be unthinkable except in the wake of an industrialization which, by dissolving the tribal order with its values and taboos and by concentrating and equalizing populations in cities, creates the human basis for democracy. Can we blame our African friends for becoming economic determinists?

Thus parliamentarianism is not rooted, as in the West, in the noble aspirations of the few. It lacks a previously reasoned basis. It lacks also the impetus of a start in a phase of historical greatness. It starts, in fact, where ours is leaving off: with a phase of malfunction and decay. The complexities of international life, the exigencies of economic planning, the threats of massification and totalitarianism, all the dangers besetting our parliamentary system at the end of its glorious history—here they are at the beginning. Cause and effect are reversed, and as the universalization of Western culture proceeds, from exterior to interior, the future, as it were, acts on the past, and the essence of Western civilization is profoundly modified.

The universalization of Western culture is proceeding in two directions simultaneously: horizontally, as it were, across the globe, and vertically, *i.e.,* downward toward the disinherited and the poor from an elite which through centuries had been its legitimate repository— just as elites had been the legitimate repositories of all other cultures. The vertically directed process is the same as the horizontally directed. This becomes palpable in border cases like, let us say, the lower classes in southern Italy, which could be considered both vertical and horizontal extensions of Western civilization. The symptoms are the same: slums spiked with TV aerials and the motor scooters. Fixtures come before houses. (A dramatic case in point is a certain housing project in Puglia: blocks of beautiful modern buildings, which cost the state a fortune and took some years to build, and which were to house a population still vegetating in moist rock caves. The renting of caves to cavemen, incidentally, is still a lucrative business in some parts of southern Italy. Thus the great day came, and the cave dwellers moved into their new homes. But who could have imagined what happened next! They broke into wild weeping. The light was too strong, the air was too dry. The furniture was like what one saw on TV, but not to live with. Their grandmothers would turn over in their graves if they saw it: the place was inhuman. They would not stay. At night they unscrewed all the shining fixtures, which were theirs, after all; they drove their goats into the inhuman building, and took the fixtures back to their caves, where they lived happily ever after.) In short, the process is the same: from the externals and accessories of civilization through technology: products first, and then production. From industrialization and the maturation of economic rights to democracy and the re-evaluation of democratic values; and only at this stage do people begin to suspect the fact that these democratic values, although dependent upon the future, had better sink their roots into the past, or else they will not be viable; that democracy calls for the universalization of education; and that leisure, a universalized product of Western civilization, must in turn produce a universalized Western culture if the whole process is to be kept from going haywire. In other words, in the transmission of the culture of modern man—Western man, the dominant mutant—which is a transmission proceeding from outside to inside, there comes a moment when the essential inner values of civilization begin to be reached.

To look at cultural evolution and its transmission in its wider, biological context affords various advantages. First of all, it gives a re-assuring, more optimistic view. Where the old perspective seemed to reveal a culture in the process of disintegration, externalizing and flattening in a most disheartening way its ever-thinning nucleus of untenable values, the wider, new perspective shows us the very op-posite process: a process integrating and internalizing a culture which has become "dominant" in the biological sense. The older perspective shows the sad end of a process. The new perspective reveals a promis-ing beginning, pointing to a future no less marvelous than the past which we nostalgically covet when we look through the old perspec-tive.

Second, by projecting this line of transmission somewhat further into the future, we are in a better position to understand ourselves and reinterpret our values. For the big wind does not halt at our own doorsteps. The process of interiorizing, of reducing matters to their innermost essence, is in course within ourselves as well.

It is, indeed, unlikely that Episcopalianism, Jugend-style and nine-teenth-century symphonic music will be universalized. The fads and frills of yesterday will be shorn off, and universal assimilation will seize upon the deepest, universally human layers of our culture. This implies a re-evaluation of all our arts, of all our thought. Only those works capable of universalization will withstand judgment.

Such re-evaluation, in the perspective of universalization, is, indeed, already in the making.

A typical example is the evolution of the Christian religion in the context of the Ecumenical movement. The universalizing force of this movement, acting not only on those who are Christian today but even on those who may become Christian tomorrow, tends to shear off all that is sectarian, accidental and divisive, and to emphasize a return to the origin, the nucleus: the *individual* that precedes any schisms: the essence capable of universalization. This process is most dramatic in the case of the Catholic Church, where the accidental superstructure —identifiable with a most powerful stratum of Western civilization— had been most imposing, so imposing indeed as to be easily mistaken for the essence itself of this religion. Catholic theologians, encouraged by the greatest of all modern Popes, John XXIII, have been busy tearing down this superstructure: the pomp and the glory, power and politics, tradition, scholasticism—all that was accidentally Occidental; and they are bringing to light the indivisible and universalizable essence of essentially "catholic" Christianity. Let Christianity be Occidental in the West; but let it be Buddhist in India, Confucian in China: "delatinized." "It is undoubtedly true that the Indian Church, or the Chinese Church, must graft Revelation to the trunk of the natural beliefs of their people, 'using' Buddha and Confucius for a new theological and spiritual synthesis, just as the Latin Church 'used' Plato and Aristotle to the same end," writes an Italian Catholic scholar, Mario Gozzini, one of the official commentators of the Vatican II Council. All that remains is the dogma, the sacraments, and the indivisibility of the Ecclesia under the guidance of the Pope and his Bishops. The Pope, however, need not even be Latin and might even cut loose from Rome. All this implies a return to origins, to the early Fathers of the Church who, according to Jean Daniélou, "offer nourishment more suitable for the needs of modern man: for we find in them a number of those categories which are characteristic of modern thought, but which scholastic theology had lost sight of."

Current attempts—from Teilhard de Chardin and Daniélou to Weizsäcker—to find a common denominator for faith and knowledge, on which to reconcile religion, science, and technology, are, in a way, another symptom of the movement back to origins: back, that is, to a state of mind preceding any specialization: a state of mind of the essential, in function of its universalization.

One of the high dignitaries of the Church, Cardinal Frings of Cologne, has compared technology, which today is conquering and unifying the world, to the koine, the language universally understood during the earliest days of Christianity. "The Church today finds herself face to face with a new kind of koine, that is, a universal way of thinking and speaking. This koine is the product of the progress of technology, which is valid across all frontiers and iron curtains." And Jean Daniélou says, "Nothing is more *biblical* than technology."

But even within the sciences themselves there is an unmistakable tendency toward new-old syntheses, a drawing back from specialization, a search for essential unity, within which each science will have its place: the whole body of physical and biological phenomena. Says Louis de Broglie: "If human thought, which by that time may have had its powers extended by some biological mutation, can one day rise to those heights, it will then perceive in its true perspective something of which, no doubt, we have no idea at present, namely the unity of the phenomena which we distinguish with the help of adjectives such as 'physico-chemical,' 'biological' or even 'psychic.'"

This indeed means to go back: to the deepest layers of our collective subconscious, to the beginnings in time. For the "primitive," though he undoubtedly did not "perceive" this state "in its true perspective," nevertheless *lived* it.

Other aspects—numerous and most striking—common to the most advanced modern science and the most ancient wisdom are elucidated in a brilliant book entitled, tellingly enough, *The Dawn of Magic,* by Louis Pauwels and Jacques Bergier. What comes to light here is not only the similarity between modern science and ancient lore, but the fact that the character, the function of the *scientist* are changing. He is growing into situations analogous to those of ancient times, and his problems are much like those of that older transmuter of matter, releaser of energy, the alchemist. The promise, today again, is the same, and so is the danger. The same secrecy surrounds him today, the same air of initiation and conspiracy. Gone is the time when the scientist could afford to be "detached," "objective," "amoral." Today, as in the beginning, physics is inseparable from metaphysics, and scientific work is charged, as never before in modern history, with moral responsibility. Western science, universalized, turns back to the essential, to the deepest layers of the remote past. A Soviet writer, Vladimir Orlov, is quoted by Pauwels and Bergier as having written, in Paris in 1957, as follows: "The 'alchemists' of today would do well to remember the statutes of their predecessors in the Middle Ages, now preserved in a Parisian Museum, in which it is laid down that no man shall devote himself to alchemy who is not 'pure in heart and inspired by the loftiest intentions.'" Also Weizsäcker discusses the advisability of introducing a sort of Hippocratic oath for natural scientists and technicians. "It will not be easy to formulate such an oath in sufficiently concrete terms. Yet it may prove necessary. I believe, for that matter, that an obligation of this kind should at first not be imposed from on high, but that a beginning should be made by the voluntary decision of a few."

Thus the beginning resembles the end, and though nothing that has been achieved in the intervening centuries need be sacrificed, today's science and today's scientists hark back to the beginnings, where science, religion, ethics, and magic were all one.

Art also, of course, was close to magic, and was the handmaiden of religion. It was *engagé*. And thus undoubtedly it is today, too. The universalization of Western art—its contacts with African and other savage sculpture, music, poetry—forced it back to the essential: away from techniques, toward the elementary. Or maybe it was this trend—well on its way in the nineteenth century—that threw our art open to primitive influences of all sorts. The two movements, universalization and a return to the essential, innermost in the work of art and the mind of its creator, pristine in time—the two movements are strictly connected. Contemporary painters, sculptors, poets, composers are re-discovering the primitive state of mind that made magic work. The new forms and symbols, which so strikingly resemble the most archaic ones, thus are, more often than not, re-creations of an inner condition, not external imitations. When the artist, who usually is not an archae-ologist, discovers the old forms, he discovers himself.

This, incidentally, is one of the strangest features of the human mind, that it is able to discover outside itself only what it already con-tains within. And this applies not only to art. It applies to science as well. Man needed to invent the computer before he began to understand an important aspect of the living brain. He used radar and sonar before discovering how bats or dolphins communicate among them-selves; and as long as he tried to imitate the flight of birds, his flying machines were sad failures. Only having invented planes and rockets is he now able to learn more about flying things in nature. Technology is not an imitation of nature. It is an extension of nature in both di-rections, back and forth. The surprises, the today unimaginable new vistas that nature has in store for us, are as unlimited as the unlimited potentialities of technological evolution. The further we advance, the further we are able to go back.

If modern science, in its search for the essential, tends to create new syntheses among its various specialized branches, the same is true to-day of the arts. This is obvious for architecture, painting, and sculp-ture. But even music seems about to lose its abstractness and self-sufficiency. This is what is behind the pretentions of the lunatic fringes of "Fluxus": A Beethoven sonata, these people claim, is in itself ab-stract and therefore bad. To re-connect it with the concrete, action is needed. Therefore, they conclude, the performing pianist must go through an act of strip tease between one note and another, culminating, with the closing chord, in the emptying of a ketchup bottle over his stripped torso. All of this, of course, is absurd; but the idea of reintegrating music with the other arts and with life—to let it act on us—is definitely in the air. In the air in a horrible, literal sense, in the halls, offices, and even elevators of our modern apartment buildings, persecuting us with sweetish poisonous little melodies that pour incessantly from hidden loudspeakers. But then there are more promising experiments in reintegrating music—electronic or conventional—with color, with motion, with action. The Italian composer Luciano Berio has recently set to music a number of poems—in English—by W. B. Yeats. The fact itself is interesting and indicative of the universalization of Western culture. The soprano voice, chanting the text, is accompanied by a splendid harp, symbolizing, as it were, Western tradition, surrounded by a stunning battery of the most exotic percussion instruments, drums, and gongs, beautiful to behold. There is the world. There is no trace of tonality or dodecaphony. The superstructure is razed to the ground. The piece is universal and essential. And the speaking or singing or chanting is integrated with action. The singer walks, gesticulates, takes part in the drumming.

> "All men are dancers and their tread
>   Goes to the barbarous clangour of a gong."

It is difficult to imagine anything more unharmoniously harmonious, more wildly beautiful, than this work of Berio's which I think is among the most significant things contemporary Western art has produced: essential because universal, universal because essential, primitive because post-individual.

Granted, ours is an art of transition. But transition precisely does not mean stagnation or disintegration. There are new great things beyond, and our relentless concentration on the barest innermost is like the step back and the crouching before the great leap.

Politics is the most conservative of all arts and sciences. Bergier and Pauwels say, in the *Dawn of Magic,* that there has not been an original political thinker since Lenin. And, I would add, as a political *thinker* he was not very original either. Neither the revolution in the arts and sciences nor the evolution of new forms of collectives nor the uni-

versalization of Western culture—which are three of the main characteristics of our age—has penetrated official political thinking or the
practice of government: which, obviously, accounts for the fact that
official political thinking is becoming more and more schizophrenic,
and the practice of government is impractical. There have been times
—in the seventeenth or eighteenth century—when political theory was
in the vanguard. Those were the times in which political revolutions
were maturing. Ours is not a time of political revolutions. Politics, today, is a contingent science, a secondary art: an accompaniment.

Yet the trend is unmistakable. The universalization of democracy
makes inevitable a return to origins, to essence. The whole accidental
Occidental superstructure—including even parliaments as we know
them and the division of powers upon which our constitutions are
based—may disappear: which probably accounts for the fact that
Westerners—especially Europeans—often take such a skeptical view
of the future of democracy.

The essence of democracy, in the biological sense, is that men (and
women) govern themselves: control their own destiny. This is the evo-
lutionary significance of democracy. This is what makes it "dominant," that is, in the long run, universal. The mechanisms by which
it is achieved are accidental. Ours, which, indeed, worked splendidly,
are not likely to work on a totally different level, that is, a worldwide
and classless society: both qualities are intrinsic in this basic concept
of democracy. For how can I control my own destiny if an extraneous
nation, controlled by others, is dangling atom bombs over my head?
How am I to control my own destiny if I belong to a "lower class"
which is constitutionally controlled by others?

To go back to the essential, it seems to me, means to re-create the
pristine equilibrium between man and community: both by articu-
lating communities in human dimensions, and by raising the stature
of man. The human figure must be reintegrated. This is true of politics
no less than of art. Political man, with his political rights, is a phantom unless he coincides with economic man, with his economic rights,
which include the right to physical and spiritual health and self-ex-
pression. In our own post-individual phase of cultural evolution, the
emphasis, during the coming decades, will probably be just on this:
the reintegration of the human figure, its educational-evolutionary ele-
vation to a higher rung from which it can increase its share of control
over human destiny. This, I think, applies particularly to the Soviet

Union and the United States. In other parts of the world, lagging at this time in more or less pre-individual phases, communal institutions will probably need to evolve further before the individual person can pass to a more advanced level; and this becomes more plausible if one remembers that it is the peculiarity of the transmission of cultural values to pass from the accessory to the essential, from outside to inside, from the collective to the individual. In northern Europe and Great Britain it would seem that the relationship between man and community has been least upset, relatively speaking, and that institutions and individuals will probably continue to evolve together.

Western civilization could conceivably have run its course without universalization; but only Western civilization could have evolved democracy and become universalized. There is nothing proud in this statement. Universalization and pride, indeed, are irreconcilable. The prize of universalization is, not self-negation, but sublimation of self. Only he who throws away his life, will find it. This, after all, is the basic tenet of Christianity, this un-Western rock of our no-longer-Western civilization.

6

The Conjugation
of a Greek Verb:
Persuasion and
the Life of Politics

Scott Buchanan

Almost two generations ago a revered teacher persuaded me to study Greek. In what for me at that time was a very dark saying, he told me that it might be the most important choice of my life. He apparently knew how often I would gratefully come upon an insight because the Greeks had a word for it. I here would like to report one instance.

Back in those early days of the century we began the study of Greek by memorizing bits of vocabulary, identifying the parts of speech, declining nouns and adjectives, and conjugating verbs. We also studied Latin in the same way, *amo, amas, amat.* But very early in Greek, in spite of the dry forms, the words began talking to us through the paradigms. The word *polis* with all its political derivatives is a case in point. But the word, *peithein,* to persuade, is the word I want to discuss as a paradigm, a *paradeigma,* for all politics. Its conjugation provides the anatomy and physiology for political science and political philosophy today as it did in Athens twenty-four hundred years ago.

Consider the citizen talking to a fellow citizen in the present indicative, "I persuade, you persuade"; as they both listen to a candidate for office, they admit "he persuades." Or sitting at the collective bargaining table, the union business agent says to his colleagues "we persuade," to the management "you persuade," and then in chorus they all say "they persuade" meaning respectively the union members and the stockholders. The present indicative dialogue could take place in many political situations. Its recall could often serve a salutary purpose as a reminder of the primitive political facts which lie at the base of high and complicated affairs.

It may be unfortunate for English-speaking communities, as it is for my own discussion here, that the English translation of the Greek word, *peithein,* is derived from Roman Latin. The Romans apparently thought that persuasion was suave, even sweetly seductive, in its main effect. There is a touch of sneakiness and genteel whitewash in the word and in the deed, and our English still carries the warning to be on guard when it is used. The Greeks would have recognized this side effect, but it apparently did not deter them from the full use of the idea and the practice.

The Greeks would have enjoyed the American cowboy's wit in calling a gun a "persuader of men," also the spurs on his boots "persuaders of horses," even green money the "persuader of sheriffs." They had a word for such coercion and duress, *peithanangke,* persuasion by necessity. But this portmanteau word did not collapse in their minds either into the behavior of stimulus and response nor evaporate into mere sweet reason. In the process of persuasion force is intelligible and has intelligence, and reason intends operation and operates through means. The holdup man or the cop is presumably a rational animal. When he draws his gun, he is presumably trying to influence truly human behavior. His purpose is intelligible to his victim, and he is hoping that it will be reasonably accepted. He therefore allows time for the victim to argue with and persuade himself. He has a hard respect for human freedom. He hopes for willing obedience. In case the persuasion fails, his willingness to shoot marks the collapse of his purpose along with his rhetoric. The Thucydidean account of the dialogue between the Athenian envoys and the Melian city council spells out in exhaustive detail the ratio of force and reason in such encounters, and provides the paradigm for all the situations where power makes right. This is one extreme of the persuasive art. No one will deny that it makes politics.

The grammatical paradigm provides the political model. The verb *persuade* in Greek, has three voices: the active voice means to *persuade;* the middle voice means to *believe,* to persuade oneself; the passive voice means to *obey,* to be persuaded. All three voices are implicated in any act of common deliberation, which is the basic elementary unit of any political transaction, no matter how high or low it is. The agent proposes, the intended victim opposes, and the ensuing deliberation disposes. In the course of the deliberation persuasion becomes mutual, the agent and the victim exchange roles, and the transaction closes, if it is successful, with a common obedience, both parties being persuaded.

But the paradigm is embedded in a wider grammatical construction. The verb "persuade" in all three voices is a very transitive verb; it takes objects, both direct and indirect. We persuade or are persuaded to do or not to do something; we persuade or are persuaded that something is or is not the case; we persuade ourselves to or of something. In the deliberative process we become of a persuasion or of many different persuasions. In all the elaborations that these constructions suggest it should not be forgotten that the primary or proximate objects of the verb are men, characters, persons, citizens with all their idiosyncrasies, prejudices, social places, and momentums. The persuasive process is variable, expansive, and dynamic, but we should also perhaps remember a Greek pun: the verbal noun meaning persuasion, as in the phrase, to be of a persuasion, also means a ship's cable. Ships of state sail many seas, but they also come to port and tie up at wharves. They rest in their constitutional persuasions.

But if we look at the many objects, direct, and indirect, of the verb, they seem to fall into two great categories, one reasonable, theoretic and speculative, the other active, forceful, powerful, pragmatic, and programmatic. The results of persuasion are beliefs, and they run through all the dimensions of culture, opinions, sciences, metaphysics, and theology. But they also guide all the practices, arts, organizations, programs, and policies, and reach all the virtues and vices, both intellectual and moral. When persuasion fails, the two great categories become confused in movements and ideologies.

The naked force of the frontier gunman, or of the old-fashioned striking workman, or of the perhaps equally old-fashioned rebel who became a founding father by his generative acts in a revolution; or, on the other hand, the naked reason of a Socrates on trial, an Antigone before Creon, Jesus under Pilate, or a fasting Gandhi; these two extremes of force and reason set the boundaries of the body politic, the circulation of whose lifeblood is persuasion. Below the holdup man is the beast. Above the martyr are the gods. The city exists between them, but it can tolerate neither. Within the city the political animal wields power and gives reasons in the home, in the marketplace, in the legislative assembly, in the executive offices of corporation and government, in courts of law. These institutions can be distinguished by the kinds of rhetoric they cultivate. In fact they have been made by, and in turn maintain, the kinds of persuasion that are practiced in them.

The family, if it can be called a polity, is the institution that generates and maintains the greatest variety, the most faithful practice, and the highest intensity of persuasion. Hopes, fears, passions, imaginations, reasons, follies, and wisdoms are all grist for the mills of mutual persuasion. The Greek verb, or the words of any other language, do not have enough inflections to discern and trace the manifold range of domestic persuasion, from the family quarrel to the many ecstasies. Every other institution seems to be a partial cut or a violent break from this familiar archetype. This is the place to note that many persuasive processes become habitual, are frozen in custom, and have been inherited from generation to generation, so that any individual family has only to learn to use them. Perhaps the deepest and most comprehensive of these common habits is the habit of persuading itself.

The mutual persuasion of the marketplace is of two kinds, which, no matter how sharply distinguished, are prone to mixture. One of these is commercial in origin, concerned with the exchange of goods; the other is political. They are said to have taken place at opposite ends of the agora in the ancient city state.

In the commercial transaction, two parties, in effect, offer parcels of force and power in the shape of exchangeable goods. Each wishes to acquire the goods of the other, and each withholds his goods as inducement or persuasion of the other to part with his. A special kind of argument—bargaining—ensues, in which relative measurement of value and trial equations of price successively imply the conditions under which exchange will become free consent. As in the simple case of persuasion, one persuader and one assenter, each makes a shrewd estimate of the power and the intention of the other. If the conditions do not make an equation, and there is no meeting of minds, no exchange or contract is made. Each may test his persuasive powers on other parties in pursuit of his individual ends. If there is a meeting of minds, each purpose is served, there is mutual benefit. It is just here in the mutual benefit that there occurs the deceitful appearance of a common purpose and many a political scientist has gone astray in accepting the apparent common good of the contract as the basis for the common good of politics. Actually there is no common purpose. The lines of persuasion have crossed at a moment and at a point, as it were, but each continues on its separate course.

The body politic contains within it many such transactions, and Adam Smith thought he saw a pattern in the cross-purposes that integrated the wealth of the nation. By now we seem to have learned that the arithmetic sum of the sales and the consequent wealth of the individual parties, the so-called Gross National Product, does not constitute a common wealth; nor do the many points of intersection of private purposes determine the locus of general welfare. Adam Smith was a professor of rhetoric, and he was pointing out to the members of Parliament the mutually persuasive processes that, left to themselves, would result in the wealth of the nation. We have been so blinded by this vision that we fail to note that bargaining is a form of persuasion in which the ratio of reason to force is very low. It is a refinement of mutual threat and calling of bluffs, not good training for the political forum at the other end of the agora.

A witty American judge confused the two kinds of persuasion in his famous statement that the truth of a political idea consists in its ability to make its way in the marketplace. This has encouraged politicians, both great and small, to indulge their freedom of speech in threat and bluff, and to settle their bouts of persuasion in deals, fixes, and compromises. In the early days of the American republic Tocqueville described this low working of political persuasion in a bitterly ironic phrase. He said that generating a majority consisted in getting "self-interest rightly understood." He was describing the initial habits that have later developed into that confusion of salesmanship and politics that we recognize in Madison Avenue with its blatant and hidden persuaders. The phrase now fits the political platform that conceals the deals and fixes that it summarizes, a Gross National Product of individual cross-purposes.

But the body politic is not completely sold out. In any bargain or contract there sits a third party, the reasonable community, approving, disapproving, and persuading. The public rhetoric contains reason as well as power and force, and reason, while sweetening and facilitating persuasion, aims at the truth, or that measure of truth that human minds can claim. When this is formalized and generalized, it becomes contract law under which the freedom of the parties is measured, the legitimacy of the persuasion is tested, and the fulfillment of the promises insured, if necessary by enforcement. Not many contracts, whether petty deals or heavy and complicated commitments, would be made if the public persuasion were absent.

The confusion of the styles of persuasion in the marketplace has for a long time been institutionalized. If the business under a contract is heavy and complicated enough, there is a need and a wish to invoke stronger persuasions and to formulate the conditions that will make the contract permanent and institutional. The parties in effect will invite the public to grant them a charter in which the organized persuasion of the community will be permanently present and in which they pledge their consent to recognize the public interest. The charter originally represented a determination to maintain an equilibrium of persuasion and consent. It implies the pledge to operate under rules that limit as well as enable and protect the corporate activities. The notorious fact of grumbling and evasion on the part of corporations is a kind of inverted respect that private interests pay to the common good.

If we consider the business corporation as the typical creature of the chartered contract, its structure and functions, its physiology, as it were, can be seen as a model for all sorts of independent associations. The corporate managers see their organization as an organism in an environment. Some of the environment is favorable, some of it threatens. Adaptation to these conditions is necessary. The corporation therefore sets up organs of adaptation: a research department to imitate and compete with the personnel and apparatus of the university laboratories, a labor department to deal with the unions, a corporation counsel to find a way around government regulations or to build corporation law into internal policy, a sales force to deal with customers, public relations experts to improve the climate for business, buyers to deal with the suppliers of materials and tools, a finance department to deal with banks and shareholders, a procurement department to get government contracts. These organs of adaptation constitute the organizational structure of the corporation. A similar table of organization could be drawn up for the organizations of all kinds that imitate the management of the business corporation. Management, of which these devices are details, has one over-all function, which is called "satisficing." This barbarous word "satisficing" is a rather crude attempt to extend the biological analogy to cover the confused internal struggles of corporate organisms to survive in what is imagined to be a competitive and hostile environment.

We can recover from the biological reduction if we remember that the corporation is an association of men, rational animals who operate through force and reason; it is a system of mutual persuasion. It lives within an institutional shell, and the legal form allows it to add management and planning to the free play of competitive purposes. Its parts are members of the whole and they can act externally as its agents on occasion. If, as some say, the corporation has taken the place of the economic man in the economic system, it is more rational than any man. Strange as it may seem, the corporation has increased the ratio of reason to force in the marketplace. The corporation has discovered after a long period of forgetfulness that it is a body politic.

The Greek middle and passive meanings of the verb, *persuade,* are *believe* and *obey,* but these meanings become clearer if they are understood in the context of the perfect tense of the verb. I believe when I *have* persuaded myself, and I obey when I *have been* persuaded. The Greeks made on this basis a whole family of verbal nouns and adjectives, the chief of which is the word *pistis,* the word which even in the New Testament is translated *faith.* The other words in the family extend from faith through confidence, trust, consent, and loyalty to obedience, even to affection. They tend to become political words and finally seem to precipitate concrete words, such as certified copy, safe conduct, delegated authority, trusted representative, and the association of meanings seems to indicate that the Greek mind was seeing the political things ordered by these words as instruments and results of persuasion, completed acts of persuasions that aid further persuasions.

I would be surprised at this point if the reader were not a bit annoyed at this indulgence in etymology. But I want to beg his indulgence for one further step to which I am persuaded by my reading of Plato's *Laws.* I was first struck by this family of words a long time ago in my first reading of the *Laws.* Plato, I believe, is saying that laws are the instruments and results of persuasion, *par excellence.* It is not merely that laws are introduced by persuasive reasoned preambles and concluded with coercive penalties; they live, and move, and teach in an ambience of persuasion and consent. I hold that this doctrine is still valid and enlightening throughout politics.

There are many kinds of law precipitated out of the ubiquitous processes of persuasion. We should not forget customary law, of which we have been persuaded by the long mysterious rhetoric of experience and tradition; the case can be made that no other laws would be effective in the absence of this unwritten corpus. Then there is common law which is made out of customs by the addition of the reasoning of the courts. There are statutes made by legislatures as the outcome of deliberation and debate among the people and their representatives. There is constitutional law formed by the habits that accompany procedures of persuasion, drafted by conventions, and ratified by the people. But the experience with these so-called human laws, sometimes smooth but often rough, has forced men to probe deeper and higher to find persuasive reasons in natural law, divine law, and eternal law to found, support, correct, and improve the human legal effort when its persuasive energy falters or fails.

The modes of persuasion accord with moods of the verb and these moods in turn correspond to so-called divisions of power in a government. The legislature considers the wishes of the constituencies in the subjunctive and optative moods that go with hypothetical thinking. The representatives weigh and deliberate, considering interests and consequences. They make up the will of the community under the formality of the common good. When the decision has been made, the executive enters the process of persuasion in the imperative mood; he issues commands, enlists consent, and hopes for obedience. But the law is not certified in the consent of the governed until the courts hand down their indicative categorical judgments. They announce that the community is of a settled persuasion that such and such is the case. The rhetoric of talk and action has passed through the dialectic of deliberation and trial decree to the logic of the situation.

It is somewhat of a mystery how apparently infinitely complicated persuasions result in laws. Some of the mystery is clarified by observing the procedures and styles of the legislature and the executive, but the courts of law supply the stage, the scenery, the *dramatis personae,* the chorus, and the playwright for a full dramatic epitome of the process. The furniture of the courtroom opposes adversaries, the judge, the plaintiff or prosecutor, and the defendant. Attorneys are assigned to the parties and they put facts and arguments in briefs. They call witnesses and present real evidence according to procedural rules enforced by judges. When there is a jury, the whole case is delivered to them by the attorneys and the judge in proper form. Indefinite time is allowed for the deliberation of the jury so that persuasion and consent may come to a unanimous decision. Failing unanimity, a new trial is ordered. Even when there is unanimity, there can be an appeal to a higher court, up to the supreme court. It should be added that laws as well as persons are being dramatized and scrutinized in the various judicial institutions. The pleadings may force judicial legislation or even later legislative review.

There are crises in all three divisions of government when the conflicts of wills, the pressures of persuasions, and the puzzles of dialectic force the actors in these legal dramas to searching or ecstatic contemplation. In such crises the law appears to have an independent life of its own, majestic, luminous, brooding. In wonder men call it reason, natural law, divine law, eternal law. It is apotheosized and its persuasion is momentarily absolute. Scholars often see historic or foreign systems of law in this light. It can be an object of contemplation for the common man, as many religious cults have discovered. Law at the summit can be the great persuader and teacher.

Some of the Greek tragedies are celebrations of this moment in law. The Aeschylean trilogy, the *Oresteia,* presents the epitome of an indefinitely long period of violent dialectical persuasion during which the wrongs within one family were dealt with by feud and vendetta. An eye for an eye, and a tooth for a tooth, went to the limit of a life for a life. The guilt of generations was distilled and concentrated in the mind of one man, Orestes. Aeschylus used the dramatic form of tragedy to lift this man to an heroic type, and focused the situation in a court of law, improvised and presided over by Apollo. The Furies prosecuted; Athena was assigned to the defense. In their pleadings they pushed the mind of Apollo to the discovery of a new law and the establishment of a new legal institution. Extreme injuries done to and by individuals under a rule of vengeance became crimes against the state, to be indicted, prosecuted, and judged by the whole community through its courts. The malevolent Furies became the deputies of Apollo presiding over and protecting the rule of law in the courts of Athena's city. These plays were repeatedly performed in Athens to celebrate the discovery of law, and to teach the citizens jurisprudence. It was one of the teachings that made Athens the school of Hellas.

Aeschylus allowed the intervention of the gods in order to explain and celebrate the apotheosis of law. The case of Oedipus in the style of Sophocles is perhaps simpler and clearer. Oedipus, the King, is disturbed by the plague in the city of Thebes. He pledges himself to discover the cause and to take whatever measures are necessary to cleanse the city. As he investigates and indicts, it appears that he himself is under suspicion. Undeterred, he traces the evidence until it proves him guilty of the crimes of regicide, patricide, and incest. As judge he condemns himself to exile. Here there is no divine interven-

tion in the end; the law itself judges on the evidence, and it is justice
and freedom for the consenting man. In this play the King plays all
the roles of the courtroom. He is prosecutor, defendant, judge, jury, and
witness for and against himself. He persuades, persuades himself, and
is persuaded, thus personifying the logic of self-government.

Aristotle says that the purpose or end of tragedy is purgation and
recognition, the purgation of passions and the recognition of reason.
Tragedy achieves these ends by the unrelenting development of the
processes of persuasion. More often than not, the tragic pattern is an
imitation of the law court in which both the chronic and the acute ills
of the body politic are purged and the essential character of law is made
plain. It is not exaggeration to say that tragedy and politics have the
same essence.

It is a bit quaint that I should be reciting to you a lesson in Greek
grammar and making literary allusions to Greek tragedy. The verbal
foibles of the tiny city-state of Athens twenty-four centuries ago, even
when they are decked out with similar examples from the modern na-
tion-state, can have little bearing on the gigantic issues of the twentieth
century. Perhaps the ancient Greeks talked too much, as we certainly do
in our propaganda through world-wide systems of communication. Perhaps their tragedies unnerved them, as even the thought of our immi-
nent tragedy unnerves us today. But truly our world is a stage on which
a tragedy is being enacted, and the action is comprehended by the word,
persuasion. The hard terms of the agon are power and law embedded
in the rhetoric and illusions of half a dozen utopias and realisms, em-
bellished with propaganda and ideologies. And this rhetoric is struggling to come to terms with a new world of labor, technology, and
corporate industry; internationally of industrial development, war, and
revolution. Persuasion is taking place relentlessly at the UN; in a hundred and one parliaments; in thousands of law courts; in millions of
executive offices, both business and governmental; in the voluntary
labor, violence, and passive resistance of individuals. The end of this
tragic spectacle is the purgation of the pity and terror of the illusions
and the recognition of reason in world law. I was struck by this vision
on a recent reading of Mr. E. H. Carr's *Twenty Years of Crisis, 1919–
1939*. As choragus, watching and commenting on the action of the
drama, he is saying that law and power are both illusions if they are
not rooted in politics. My footnote here is that the life of politics is persuasion.

Part Two

The Past and

Future

of Humanistic

Education

1

The Dilemmas

of Humanistic

Education in

the United States

O. Meredith Wilson

A few years ago a colleague and I interviewed eight or ten selected members of the Sioux tribes, using William Fire Thunder as interpreter. Our purpose was to learn as much as we could of the value systems undergirding the Sioux culture, and to test, if possible, the view that antithetical value patterns blocked the successful assimilation of that Indian community by the United States. It was not easy to phrase questions that yielded anything but platitudinous responses, and finally in desperation I asked Mr. Fire Thunder to inquire of them what there was about the white man's culture that they disliked, my assumption being that by testing negative values some insight might result. Again the responses were disappointingly stereotyped, until finally, a handsomely cragged old man, who so far had listened in silence, indicated his desire to speak. His remarks as interpreted were about as follows: "I know that white men's ways are not all bad, for many good men are raised among them. But—I cannot explain why—many things about the white man seem strange to me. What I dislike most about him is that he is so cruel to his children."

These were the words of Charley Owns-the-Battle, the very prototype of the wise old chieftain; and they were delivered in sorrow and wonder. The built-in paradox was a surprise, but the value of his insight was not to be denied. Obviously, it is disconcerting to hear, even from the wisest old Indian, too often still referred to as savage, an indictment of our culture as cruel, and worst of all, as cruel to our own children.

Yet he was wise in his own ways and observant of ours. In his value system a child is a sovereign creature with its own pattern for growth. It is a natural thing best allowed to come to its full flower according to the dictates of its own internal nature. As a result of such an attitude the child was to be nurtured, but not molded, encouraged but not directed; while with us, as he observed, the natural spirit of the child is constantly pinched and cramped: he is required to develop regular, but not natural habits; to be at school at fixed hours, to practice the trumpet or piano against his will in order to become what he would not be, and, indeed, what nature had not intended him to be.

I am sure that a longer interview with Charley Owns-the-Battle would have yielded an educational philosophy quite different from our own, because his view of man and of man's purpose was so at variance with ours. But in even these few remarks he had inserted a troublesome doubt into my mind. If the flowering of a child's inner potential be the appropriate goal of the educative forces in life, then the efforts of the white man's educational system are all stultifying and perverse, for they aim to mold and direct character and behavior in the way the experience and judgment of the race have found to be good. The good life to Charley Owns-the-Battle is the product of the outblooming of inner forces; to the white man, of the molding or forming to society's preconception of good.

Which is the education for the free man, Charley's or our own? Clearly, I would not be a schoolman if I agreed with Charley. My difference with him, however, is not unmingled with sympathy and respect. His view is consistent with his conception of man. To him man is a part of nature, destined to happiness if he can learn to love and live in it. What nature intended him to be, he should become, without the interfering manipulative influences of tradition or his elders. He is a creature of intuition and of spirit commingled with countless other creatures in a rich and awesome nature. His role is not to transform nature, but to use and endure it.

Our own education is not always so consistent with our concept of man. But then, of course, we are a complex culture here in the Western World and do not have a consensus about the nature of man; and, failing that, the creation of a method for education which has both uniformity and integrity is not easy. To talk of a method of educating the young without some judgment as to what the young should become is folly; and to talk as though, because there is not complete consensus, there is no agreement at all in Western society is also foolish. Ortega's simple phrase, "Europe is intelligence," joined with the observation of John Wise, the colonial American pastor of Ipswich, that man is the most favored of all animals under Heaven because part of God's image, namely reason, is born in him, identifies the distinguishing characteristic of man as seen in the Western World. Reason and intelligence in man set him apart from Charley Owns-the-Battle's nature; it is the possession of them that makes this creature, man, the most favored of animals, and therefore, presumably makes him subject to different rules and responsibilities than are other creatures of field and forest. They are also the qualities within him that are human. Their development is the goal of Western culture, for they maximize the man, increase his dignity, and further set him free from the hunger, appetite, passion, and instinct that grip all other life to which he is so closely kin.

Though Plato could talk of a sound mind in a sound body, the interests expressed were not equal interests. The overriding concern of humanistic education has been the cultivation of the powers of the intellect. The interest in the sound body has become prudential. "Let's not hazard the loss of so precious a thing as a sound mind, by neglecting the body which nurtures it." Humanistic education has been engrossed with the problem of how best to sharpen the intellect. By what means do we help our child to fulfill his "human potential"? At this point the interest is as much in bringing to full flower the powers within the child as was Charley Owns-the-Battle's interest in the natural development of his young braves. Only our different goal for man and our perhaps halting and imperfect method of leading or directing him there have made our education seem cruel to my old Indian sage.

At this distance nothing seems more humane, or more attractive, or more intellectually exciting than the Socratic conversations. They were an exercise in precision and clarification, a release from self-deception, and an earnest search for truth and beauty. They were, given the limits of knowledge and the state of the technology in ancient Greece, a near-perfect example of humanistic education.

The state of technical refinement had not improved when the medieval universities emerged. Their first purposes were religious, and therefore they were less completely committed to the intellectual in man, yet their means to spiritual ends were largely rational. And the problems that arose between them and the Church were largely born of collision between reason on the one hand and tradition-conditioned faith on the other.

The universities caught up in a single stream of instruction and inquiry the Greek and the Hebrew-Christian cultures. The language of literature, including the New Testament, was Greek. The language of polite discourse was Latin. From wherever one came to sit at the feet of an Erasmus or an Abelard, Latin to listen to, Greek and Latin to read, were required. Books were laboriously hand copied. Mistakes enough of transcription occurred without further errors of translation. As a result, no one could be educated who had not mastered Greek and Latin, though there were men of pretense then, as now, who tried to convey the impression of learning with "little Latin and less Greek." Education, being the most conservative of all professions, continued to identify learning with the mastery of classical languages long after printing had made generally available carefully translated editions of the best books and long after much of great importance that had been written originally in a vulgar modern idiom had been added to the humane tradition.

An even more important circumstance that conditioned early humanistic education is to be discovered in the phrase "liberal education." It originally meant education appropriate to free men. But the phrase "free men" needs to be historically interpreted. They were not Jefferson's "free men all," but rather men of substance and aristocracy; men as distinguished from slaves; or men as distinguished from the rude creatures of pre-revolutionary France, described by polite writers as having the shape of man, but who dug with rude tools in the hard soil, etc. In Voltaire's words: "The people will always remain stupid and barbaric; they are oxen that need the yoke, whip and hay"—not education. Free men were men of substance and status to whom education was not important as a means to livelihood, or as a key to office. With these endowments they were born. They were born rulers; from pride in their manhood they would rule well. They were born lords and free men; they would live and lord with grace. Obviously, to such men a liberal education was not vocational, though if it could make them wise, they would fulfill their calling or vocation with greater dignity. The importance of education was the promise it gave of increasing the intrinsic worth of the man. Greater usefulness, if derived, would come, happily, as a by-product.

The violence of the assault of environmental forces on the classical tradition and on this aristocratic conception of liberal education that gripped humanistic education at the opening of the nineteenth century varied from country to country. But it could scarcely have been more intense than it was in the United States.

The ancient concept of freedom and therefore of education appropriate to free men was completely overturned. In a country where all men are created equal, no man is born to a station; he must win it and hold it through his natural talents. There is planted, therefore, the idea of a natural aristocracy, which Jefferson identified as an aristocracy of talents. Now the whole role of education is invested with utilitarian expectations. Society expects it to ensure that precious human talents are not wasted, and that no future Gray shall have occasion to write of us in an elegy:

> But Knowledge to their eyes her ample page
> Rich with the spoils of time did ne'er unroll;
> Chill Penury repressed their noble rage,
> And froze the genial current of the soul.

Society could not then afford the luxury of a "mute inglorious Milton"; neither can it now. For the individual, education means the possibility of upward mobility. The free man no longer seeks education because, born to station, he would in pride like to acquit himself well, thus to be a credit to family name, and at the same time to achieve whatever of intrinsic worth is latently within him. Rather, today the free man is aspiring to station; he has latent talents; he is not born wise, but perhaps is potentially so, and by means of education he may achieve station above the dreams of his father or any of his prior kin.

In such an environment, even the search for wisdom may seem vocational. The impatient son of the new freedom is unacquainted with the old tradition; less interested in the badges and ornaments of the venerable past than in the practical means to upward mobility. Moreover, the founders and leaders of our new republic were forced to encourage the change. After 1775 the common man in America had to become the maker of public policy. Though he was born free, he was not born wise. He was not born with a sense of public responsibility or with the enlarged spirit of an enlightened and dedicated aristocrat. He could not remain ignorant and continue free. In the language of Madison, our fourth President, "popular government without popular education is prelude to a farce or a tragedy."

For good public and private reasons, education was a first need, a matter of greatest practical utility. With this change in emphasis dictated by circumstance, educational tradition was swept into the nineteenth and twentieth centuries of scientific experiment and industrial expansion. It may only be coincidental that Adam Smith published his *Wealth of Nations* in the second year of our revolution, the year of our independence. There may be no cause and effect, but Smith's celebration and popularization of the values of division of labor are congruent with the compulsive drive toward specialization which characterizes our professions, our industry, and our educational institutions as they emerge at this end of nearly two hundred years of torrential cultural change; a current fed from tributary floods of utilitarianism, pragmatism, and empiricism.

The details of change in American education simply confirm the trend. Jefferson proposed that every child have a three-year education —not much it appears now, but a revolutionary promise when he outlined his program to John Adams. Not for twenty years thereafter was the promise fulfilled, and then at first only in Philadelphia after the strongest political efforts of the labor unions and of Thaddeus Stevens. But already in 1785 land grants were authorized to assure public instruction and they were extended to support collegiate work in 1862 and 1890. The significance of the Morrill Act (1862) was not so much the Federal support of agricultural and mechanical colleges it provided, but rather the public endorsement of the idea that children of rural homes, and of laboring and mechanical origins, should aspire to higher education. Those land grant institutions were not immediately institutions of the highest class. Thorstein Veblen describes their origin accurately in his *Higher Learning in America* (1918):

> The greater number of these state schools are not, or are not yet, universities except in name. These establishments have been

founded, commonly, with a professed utilitarian purpose, and have started out with professional training as their chief avowed aim. The purpose made most of in their establishment has commonly been to train young men for proficiency in some gainful occupation; along with this have gone many half-articulate professions of solicitude for cultural interests to be taken care of by the same means. They have been installed by politicians looking for popular acclaim, rather than by men of scholarly or scientific insight, and their management has not infrequently been entrusted to political masters of intrigue, with scant academic qualifications; their foundations have been the work of practical politicians with a view to conciliate the good will of a lay constituency clamouring for things tangibly "useful"—that is to say, pecuniarily gainful. So these experts in short-term political prestige have made provision for schools of a "practical" character; but they have named these establishments "universities" because the name carries an air of scholarly repute, of a higher, more substantial kind than any naked avowal of material practicality would give. Yet, in those instances where the passage of time has allowed the readjustment to take place, these quasi-"universities," installed by men of affairs, of a crass "practicality," and in response to the utilitarian demands of an unlearned political constituency, have in the long run taken on more and more of an academic, non-utilitarian character, and have been gradually falling into line as universities claiming a place among the seminaries of the higher learning. The long-term drift of modern cultural ideals leaves these schools no final resting place short of the university type, however far short of such a consummation the greater number of them may still be found.

They were an invitation to all classes, in part because initially they were ready to pitch their curriculum at a level that the rural boy or girl could safely try. Since that day the public universities have achieved a stature worthy of the respect of education everywhere and men and women from every social origin attend them. But their emergence has not been without price to the liberal concept of education.

They were particularly vulnerable to the appeals for utility. Much of the wonder of American productivity can be traced to their devotion to "the improvement of man's estate." The legislatures of these states measured them, not by the subtle improvements in men and women, but by their effect upon the economy; and funds were requested and defended because of improved wheat harvests, the development of hybrid corns, the introduction of new and marketable crops such as soybeans, the strengthening of strains in raspberries, or the perfection of profitable techniques for processing low-grade iron ores. But these claims for land grant institutions were only the most obviously utilitarian. The catalogues of the more conservative liberal arts colleges also began to show marked changes. Professional, semiprofessional, and even vocational courses were introduced, and, perhaps more to the point, liberal arts education was defended as the best preparation for a vocation. To be sure, liberal education remained the best means to self-fulfillment, but to sell it, it had, like honesty, to be established as the best policy.

Meanwhile, experimental science had become so spectacularly successful in reshaping our lives that failure to understand and appreciate it became tantamount to rejecting the key to our culture. The new science is not merely natural history and natural philosophy, and its methods are not documentary and descriptive. Its inclusion in the curriculum required marked changes in the balance of the college instruction, and even as a part of the general education with no pretensions to specialization, it makes heroic demands on the time and energy of the student. Collegiate statesmen were only adjusting to these new demands (science as a creative aspect of life was now regarded almost as another expression of the humanities) and were taking elaborate pains to find a new liberal arts curriculum when the late great War burst upon them. Curriculum makers were swept off their feet and have never since regained their equilibrium. Breath-taking advances in the understanding of the nature of matter and perhaps of life were made possible because our interests of security and military power coincided with that moment's most daring scientific speculations. The availability of war budgets to sponsor scientific breakthroughs transformed technical development. The best scientists became absorbed in the new wonders, and few good scientists were content to develop elementary, though liberating programs for undergraduate nonspecialists. Indeed, at the pace their disciplines were changing, caution about materials for science instruction may well have been indicated.

What began as a two-billion-dollar federal gamble on atomic fission, became the motivation for strengthening science, *qua* science, wherever possible. The National Science Foundation, the Atomic Energy Commission, the National Institutes of Health, even the Office of Education, through the National Defense Education Act in its second form, poured money into scientific research and into the defense-related programs of the colleges and universities. Grants were available to sponsor research, to develop graduate programs, to provide inducements for almost any activity except undergraduate instruction which is the lifeblood of humanistic education.

The relevance of educational institutions to national security, national government and policy, and the Gross National Product has created public and private support for our higher educational institutions. The result has, on balance, been good, and strengthened budgets may save our educational enterprise. But one can hardly fail to observe that the former poor but dedicated scholar, once fixed in academic appointment, developed an attachment to his college. He lived and breathed its problems. He took pride in its curriculum and its contribution to its new generation of students. With the growing number of students, the rising value of professorial services, and the increased dollars available to tempt scholars to new or different grooves of learning a difference has become observable. The already strong disposition to specialization, endemic in our culture, has been reinforced by the development of professional societies. And the young professor is as likely to identify himself with the American Historical Association or the American Chemical Society as with old Main, and he is likely to feel that he can serve in his professional role one place as well as another.

The double impact of ultimate specialization and the existence of grant funds, available directly to the professor from sources external to his university, has sharply affected the sense of organic integrity of the modern multipurpose university within which, at present, a large share of the young men and women of college age are getting or failing to get the humanistic education appropriate to their lives and time. One is reminded of the Story of the Third Calendar in the *Thousand and One Nights,* in which one is told of the magnetic mountain which destroyed ships that came too close by pulling out all their nails. Occasionally, one has the feeling that our universities have come too close to such a mountain and that what we need is our own Agib ben Khesib to deliver us. But scientific advance is precious to us, and it might well be the beautiful young boy sacrificed if we decide that we are being pulled apart by federal grants, and therefore reject them. After all, scientific inquiry has value not for security only, but because the creative curiosity of man must be cultivated and encouraged. In this age the plasma of creativity flows as richly in veins of scientists as in those of poets and the achievements of either are peculiarly and exclusively human and humanistic.

Our problem is not that specialists disavow the importance of humanistic education. They share our despair at the growing imbalance in support between science and nonscience. They are not infrequently the first to recognize that the most important appointment in a university is the liberal arts dean. What happens in the education of a young undergraduate is of primary importance to them, and they wish they could play their part; perhaps they will soon, but first this grant or that graduate student must claim attention. If this sounds cynical, it is not so intended. If it appears an attack on science, it is misunderstood. The same commitment to specialization, to professionalization, to the graduate student is reproducible in every corner of the campus. Only the grants are unequally distributed, and they are not unequally coveted.

It would be unfair to infer that there are not devoted and diligent committees among faculties determined to restore balance. And where faculties are at work I, at least, sustain hope. But the conditions of American life have so fostered utilitarian virtues that the solution that will work must take account of them. And of the habits of academic administration as well! Harper, Wilbur, and Hutchins, to name three, tilted with educational habit in the hope that the traditions of reason were more deep-rooted than the habits of administration. Their success in this respect, if measured by persisting changes in educational organization, was not great. Experiments with early admission to college and with advance placements have had some lasting effect on the academic ecology. Each of these efforts was premised on the judgment that specialization was here, a social imperative not to be ignored, but that our age needed wisdom and balance even more. By these devices time might be gained, so that the virtues of humanistic education could be assured and, usually, so that it could precede professional concentration. Each is important and should be encouraged. But early admission and advanced placement illustrate our concern for time, and they point to the greatest time resource available to us—the first twelve years of public instruction. We take a larger percentage of our children through twelve years than do any other people. But we also take them less far. In the past six years marked changes in secondary education have taken place, usually more the result of lifting our expectations than of modifying curricula. Hints of the possibility of programmed learning and comparisons with achievements in British preparatory schools both justify hope of much greater gains. Perhaps within the tyranny of accepted educational time cycles great gains for humanistic education are still possible.

Even so, the role of the college and the university in humanistic education cannot be abandoned. The higher the pinnacle of academic specialization, the more crying becomes the need to establish relevance to man and all his life processes. No principle grows on me more clearly than the need for an ultimate experience in synthesis for the man who has spent a lifetime in specialization. The need is recognized by distinguished specialists in medical education; it is responsible for voluntary return to adult classes in hundreds of institutions, it is product of a hunger to understand oneself, which is not assuaged by increased refinement of analysis. Moreover, the need for wisdom—indeed, the need to find some men with the courage to try to be wise—is greater than the need for strength which dictated the two-billion-dollar gamble and precipitated the resulting frenetic developments of our scientific age.

The future of humanistic education, from these pages, may be accounted grim. Yet, if we make due allowance for our utilitarian souls and take full advantage of our natural hunger for self-understanding, if we are willing to increase both social and parental expectations for our precollegiate young, I am not without hope. My children, after all, do seem better educated than was I at their age; and they are products of these, our schools. A primary characteristic of our productive economy is the division of labor which we have developed and exploited until being a specialist is a highly valued status symbol among us. There is no doubt in my mind that a faculty of specialists, properly coordinated in their efforts, can provide an integrated educational program that will polish, sharpen, and improve the head of the young scholar, just as in Adam Smith's pin factory more pins, better polished and properly headed were manufactured by the technique of division of labor. But it is not possible if the chief polisher is only partially committed to the enterprise, and is off putting a new brilliant in a pin for the goddess of war at the moment he is most needed for the shaping of some local heads. A faculty of dedicated specialists, I say, can succeed, but they need the lesson of the preacher in Ecclesiastes to ensure that there is a future for humanistic education. For the preacher said:

There was a little city, and few men within it; and there came a great king against it, . . .

Now there was found in it a poor wise man, and he by his wisdom delivered the city; yet no man remembered that same poor man.

Then said I, Wisdom *is* better than strength: . . .

2

Humanistic

Education

in

India

Humayun Kabir

It is a truism that science is as old as human civilization. Even in the earliest stages of his development, man drew upon his knowledge of the ways in which nature behaves for survival and tried to influence them to suit his own purposes. The discovery of agriculture was in itself a giant step forward in scientific knowledge. Some unusually perceptive individual—very probably a woman—noticed plants sprouting in a place where corn had fallen. The discovery of a connection between fallen corn and sprouting plants was the beginning of agriculture. In course of time, agricultural knowledge expanded and deepened and led to the manufacture of implements and tools, the improvement of seed and stock and the use of irrigation on an increasing scale.

Primitive science also led to the discovery that man could protect himself against heat or cold by the use of suitable material. Skins or leaves sewed together protected him against the cold. A sunshade sheltered him from the scorching rays of the sun. In these simple things, we already have the beginning of arts which depend on our knowledge of the nature and properties of things in the outside world. Similarly, knowledge of natural materials and their use for human purposes enabled man to construct houses. Soon came a stage when he was no longer content to eat raw food and began to cook in order to improve on the gifts of nature.

Rudimentary science is thus as old as human civilization itself. All the sciences depend on curiosity and inquisitiveness. These are qualities which men share with other animals, but science has in addition a specifically human element. All scientific knowledge depends on man's capacity to draw general principles from particular instances. This capacity to generalize developed very early in human history and enabled him to draw upon past experiences in order to face the unknown future in a far more effective way than any other living being. Through the method of trial and error, he continually improved upon his past performance. Even in what we call primitive societies, there grew a vast accumulation of essentially scientific knowledge though it was often expressed in an unscientific form through customs, totems, and taboos. The knowledge gained was invariably passed from one generation to another through traditions that helped in the survival of the community.

While scientific knowledge has been implicit thus in human society from the earliest times, it is only in the last few centuries that science has attained a separate and independent status in the corpus of human knowledge. Primitive societies had hardly any place for knowledge as a separate discipline. Theories were imbedded in practice and practice was transmitted from one generation to another by the direct impact of example and experience. As society developed, the situation changed and theories were gradually separated from practice. As man became conscious of the value of generalization, abstract ideas assumed an increasing power over him. It was under the impact of the separation of theory and practice that education became a distinct discipline in human life and developed its own institutions and instruments. Since this development was due to the recognition of the power of the abstract idea, it was perhaps inevitable that early education was almost exclusively concerned with philosophy which was man's earliest attempt to understand himself and the world around in intellectual terms.

From the dawn of civilization up to the modern age, there was a sharp distinction between formal education, which concerned itself mainly with abstract concepts and general principles, and practical training, which transmitted from one generation to another the technical skills needed for the survival of the community. The techniques of such operations were generally handed down from father to son, but this was not regarded as education in the accepted sense. Even in the case of crafts and industries where skills were transmitted from one generation to another through methods of apprenticeship, the transfer of skills remained outside the broad concept of education. Knowledge was confined to intellectual disciplines like philosophy, literature, and religion—in a word to activities not directly concerned with the production or distribution of goods needed for human survival and welfare.

This restricted attitude toward knowledge and education was not surprising. With the limited technological resources available to them, the vast majority of men required all their time and energy for producing the essential goods needed to keep the community going. It was only a fortunate few who had the leisure to reflect upon the principles and processes that guide human society. They were a privileged class set apart from the vast numbers of the ordinary members of society. Their function was to rule others or to provide rules for their conduct and guidance. Philosophers like Plato and Aristotle justified the existence of such leisured classes by pointing out that they alone could contribute to human civilization and culture.

With this background, it is not difficult to understand why education for a long time remained primarily literary and academic in both East and West. In the East, scholastic and literary education was until recent years almost the only pattern of education that enjoyed social respectability. In ancient India, the highest value was given to intellectual pursuits. Royal power and military might were given a secondary place, while members of society whose primary concern was the production of wealth were placed third in the social category. The position of the actual worker was lower still. In fact, the worker engaged in socially useful but uncongenial work like scavenging or tannery was often of the untouchables. The fate of the helot in the Greco-Roman world or of the serf in medieval Europe proves that this picture was largely true of almost all earlier civilizations.

In the ancient and medieval periods, the pattern of education throughout the world was therefore literary, intellectual, and scholastic. It is true that attempts at broadening this concept of education are found in ancient India. There are references to arts like archery or metallurgy as fit subjects for study by priests and kings. Even erotica became a subject for detailed study. By and large, education nevertheless remained intellectual, literary, and humanist. With minor variations, the same situation obtained in other civilizations of ancient times.

It is true that the advent of Islam in the beginning of the middle ages brought about some change in the social evaluation of different types of education. With its insistence on the equality of all men, Islam helped to break the stratification of society based on differences of work. This increasingly led to the recognition of the value of different professions and crafts. From this followed the first hesitating recognition of technical training as education. In India the first technical schools were established by a Muslim king, Ferozshah Tughlak. Nevertheless, the bias for literary and scholastic education continued. The highest positions were occupied by theologians and priests in spite of Islam's explicit repudiation of the priestly class. It is interesting to note that the technical schools started by Ferozshah Tughlak were given the name of *karkhanas* or factories and thus by implication denied the status and dignity of proper academic institutions. One may, indeed, regard these *karkhanas* or technical institutions as a more organized form of the apprenticeship training which was in vogue in large parts of the world. The only difference was that other apprentices were trained in a family or by a guild while these *karkhanas* had some semblance of a regular educational establishment.

The real change in man's attitude toward the knowledge of practical skills began only after the great scientific discoveries of seventeenth-century Europe opened out new prospects of prosperity and welfare for the common man. As scientific knowledge increased and led to the development of new technologies, there was an immediate and unprecedented expansion in the scale of production of almost every type of material goods. Trade and commerce also expanded enormously. Very soon, countries started producing not for a limited home market but for the entire world. This brought in competition on an international scale which in its turn led to search for new and improved techniques. It was also increasingly recognized that such improvements in technique could result only from increased knowledge of the secrets of nature. In other words, the study of the natural sciences began to compete with the study of the intellectual disciplines centering around the humanities.

In this connection it is interesting to note that scientific studies grew within the protective cover of the humanities and were for a long time indistinguishable from the study of disciplines like philosophy or ethics.

In ancient times, Aristotle, for instance, had recognized no distinction between physics and mathematics. The same held true for some of the great scholars of the Renaissance. In the beginning of the modern age, Europe also described what we today call the natural sciences as natural philosophy.

Both the humanities and the natural sciences had long employed the deductive method, being primarily concerned with elaborating general principles from individual instances. Nevertheless, the distinction between them became more and more marked as the experimental method became increasingly an instrument for the advancement of natural science. The use of the experimental method gave such studies an immediate practical turn: it also introduced a novel element into the body of human knowledge. An experiment proves or disproves a theory with a fair degree of certainty. In the case of many metaphysical speculations, there was and is no way of definitely proving or disproving a stated position. In the case of science, a single experiment could lead to a final rejection of a theory. In many cases, it could also lead to its acceptance with categorical certainty.

This concern with experiment and proof gave a practical bias to most scientific speculation. More important still, it helped to turn the attention of scientists to the world here and now. Philosophy had in earlier times almost imperceptibly merged into theology. The result was that much of philosophy was spiritual, if not otherworldly. As opposed to this speculative, theoretical, and nonmaterialistic attitude of philosophy, experimental science became more and more practical, pragmatic, and secular. Its phenomenal success in advancing the frontiers of knowledge and simultaneously leading to technologies which promised to transform human society confirmed this tendency and also gave it added respectability.

Education in the Western world changed under the impact of the Scientific Revolution. At first theoretical and later applied science and technology played an increasing role in education at all levels. In the older countries of Europe, science had to compete with the humanities, but in the newer world of America, science and technology soon assumed a dominant position. After the Soviet Revolution, a similar process began in Russia and other socialist countries. In fact, it was the study of the humanities which had to struggle for survival in some of these newly developed countries.

With its traditions of scholastic and literary education, it is not surprising that even after the British established dominion in India, the pattern of education did not change for a long time. Humanistic education remained predominant, but from the end of the last century, theoretical science started gaining a foothold in the educational system. In fact, at the beginning of the British connection, there was an enhancement of the role of pure academics. The Indian caste system had placed a higher value on abstract thought than on practical affairs. The British class structure reinforced the Indian distaste for manual labor and exaggerated the importance of purely intellectual activities.

The advance of science and technology had, however, introduced a new element whose importance could not be ignored. The striking development of industries in the Western world and the consequent rise in the living standard of the average man offered a challenge which the Indian people could not overlook. The importance of scientific education began to be increasingly recognized. This is a most welcome development from all points of view, but unfortunately, the increasing emphasis on science and technology has at times led to a neglect of the humanities. The course of educational development in India in the last hundred years offers an interesting comment on the way in which social attitudes here have changed.

Modern education in India began with the establishment in 1857 of the three universities of Calcutta, Madras, and Bombay. They marked a break from the previous educational tradition of the country and initiated a new era of secular education available to anyone who could satisfy certain general conditions. Education did not become universal, but it moved forward in that direction. All earlier limitations on access to education based on birth or status were largely removed. In ancient India, education was the prerogative of the privileged classes. Those who were not entitled to an education could try to acquire it only at great risk. During the middle ages, these bars largely disappeared, but education still remained the monopoly of a privileged few. For economic and social reasons, the vast majority could not even think of receiving anything except the most elementary education. After the establishment of the three universities in 1857, these restrictions largely disappeared. Pupils from every class and caste and from every part of the country began to enter the portals of higher education.

The first Indian universities were modeled largely after the London University and provided the same type of mainly humanistic and academic education. Philosophy, literature, and history were the major items in the curriculum. Some simple science was taught, but it was given only a secondary importance. One may say that for almost thirty years after the establishment of the first three Indian universities, the majority of able and ambitious students concentrated on the study of philosophy and the humanities.

A change began in the last decades of the nineteenth century. Some among the more enterprising students took to the study of mathematics, but here also the emphasis was on its value as a means to gainful employment. Indian industry was underdeveloped and offered hardly any scope for the application of science and technology. Service under the government or a few professional careers were the only avenues open to men of talent. The majority preferred government service and it was only when they failed to secure such employment that they took to professions like medicine or the law. It was generally held that for employment by the government or for the practice of law, the intellectual discipline of mathematics gave students a marked advantage. This, perhaps, explains the popularity of mathematics as a subject for study during these decades.

The first decades of the twentieth century saw the growth of interest in purely scientific subjects. Nevertheless, the major emphasis continued for some time to be on philosophy and literature. For more than two decades of the present century, the ablest students took to the study of English language and literature both for their educational value and their utility as a means to profitable employment. The position of English was, however, steadily challenged by the growing social sciences. In the two decades following the First World War, economics gradually became the most important subject of study in the Indian universities. In the meantime, interest in the sciences continually increased. The achievement of Indian scientists like Raman, Bose, and Saha in the twenties gave added impetus to this tendency. By the time war broke out in 1939, the study of science had become the most important field in almost all Indian universities.

Since the attainment of independence, the emphasis on science has continued, but there has been a shift from its theoretical study to its practical application. Engineering and technology have become the most popular subjects of study during the last fifteen years. Today, there is a risk that even pure science may be neglected because of the attractions of applied science and technology. In the process, all the humanistic disciplines have suffered. The order of preference of the ablest students appears to be professional studies like engineering, technology, and medicine followed by pure science with physics, chemistry, and biology in that order. The social sciences are still struggling to maintain a position among favored subjects, but purely humanistic disciplines like philosophy, literature, and languages are today struggling for minimal survival. The paradox of Indian universities is that the number of students in these humanistic subjects has enormously increased, but their quality has declined in a marked manner.

One can understand the concern with the applied and professional studies in an impoverished country like India. Indian agriculture remained static for over three thousand years and it is only in the last decade that the application of science has started a process of change and progress. The position was still worse with Indian industry. It did not even remain static but suffered a decline over the last two or three centuries. Since independence, there has been a tremendous effort at revival and expansion of industrial activities in all fields. All programs for the expansion and improvement of industry, however, depend on the application of science and technology. Since technology itself must ultimately depend on steady scientific development, the study of pure science is thus able to attract some of the abler students. The more immediate prizes offered by technology, however, lure away many who could have done outstanding work in purely theoretical study.

There is growing recognition among all sections of enlightened opinion in India as elsewhere that these trends may pose a danger for the future. While the importance of technology and science cannot and must not be minimized, we have also to recognize that undue concentration on science and technology may impair our sense of values. Without a deeper understanding of the nature of man and an acceptance of the ideals which have held societies together throughout the ages, a mere increase in scientific and technical knowledge may threaten the very survival of man. There is also a danger that neglect of the humanities may lead to the development of a sectional and narrow outlook among vast numbers of the members of society. Science and technology are essentially selective. If, therefore, the younger generations are engrossed only with science and technology, we may ultimately get a society of men and women with highly specialized skills in narrow fields but without the broad human perspective and the larger sympathies which alone can bind society together.

Great scientists have themselves recognized the need of preserving the humanist tradition in the study of science and technology. The Technological University of Berlin, perhaps the earliest institution of higher studies based on science and technology, included in its curriculum from its very inception the study of literature, history, and other humanities. In the United States the Massachusetts Institute of Technology has been one of the pioneers in insisting that a balanced development of personality demands the study of humanities side by side with that of science and technology. In the Union of Soviet Socialist Republics, students of engineering and technology are now required to solve problems arising out of the study of literature and philosophy. In India, also, students at its various institutes of technology are now obliged to take courses in literature and the social sciences. There is thus increasing recognition throughout the world that neglect of the study of the humanities will impoverish human experience and may in the end lead to the defeat of science itself.

In India, the tradition of the study of the humanities has always been strong. In both the Hindu and the Muslim social outlook, emphasis has been placed on the attainment of spiritual excellence rather than the achievement of worldly success. Sometimes the emphasis has been exaggerated and the contemporary Indian preoccupation with material needs may be regarded as a reaction against their former neglect. Once the gross deficiencies in the material standards of life have been removed, one may look forward to the reassertion of the moral and intellectual values which have characterized the Indian outlook in the past.

3

Principles
and Particulars
in Liberal
Education

F. Champion Ward

Robert M. Hutchins must view the present educational scene in America with a certain irony. A number of his ideas appear to be in style. The reasons for espousing them are not always his, and there is little acknowledgment of his advocacy of them thirty years ago. Nevertheless, early entrants to college, once consigned to the children's crusade at the University of Chicago, have been passing through some of the nation's most reassuring portals without loosening the ivy; colleges now give advanced standing to entering students of superior preparation and competence; the rhetoric of educators, politicians, and even admirals is full of such severe terms as "excellence," "the disciplines," and "independent study"; any communication with anyone is called a "dialogue"; the three R's are popular, even in California; the gifted child and the superior student have been discovered; more and more teachers are being educated as well as trained; and the legions of John Dewey are thinned and still.

With austerity and purpose thus apparently restored to the schools and colleges, why not conclude that the reforming task which engaged the leaders of education in the thirties and forties has been successfully completed? A closer look at the current scene will show how miscellaneous have been the changes noted above. As an example of this phenomenon, I propose to examine the recent fortunes of general, liberal education, which was advocated so vigorously by Mr. Hutchins and many others as a means of restoring rigor and coherence to collegiate education in America.

In 1950, as Dean of the College of the University of Chicago, I was rash enough to proclaim in print that "In the nation, 'general education' is at last in vogue. Its principles bid fair to become the operative educational theory of the remainder of this century."[1] This act of *hubris* was soon avenged. Three years later, on the darkling plain of the University's inter-faculty council, my colleagues and I found ourselves struggling to salvage some part of the University's curriculum of general studies and some degree of authority over what remained. I had not yet understood the peculiar mixture of shallowness and volatility which marks the discussion and practice of education in America. George Santayana, in describing the academic tone at Harvard at the turn of the century, had seen how deeply rooted is this characteristic. "You might think what you liked, but you must consecrate your belief or your unbelief to the common task of encouraging everybody and helping everything on."[2] In mid-century, conformity is still preferred to agreement; tasks are undertaken before they are defined; ideas are forgotten before they are tested; problems are replaced before they are solved; and battles are lost which never were joined.

Mr. Hutchins' dissent from this tradition made the University of Chicago uniquely interesting, and strenuous. Declining the accepted presidential role of gregarious referee, he retained to the end of his tenure a quixotic interest in education. He insisted upon the potential importance of education to the achievement of such national goals as the proper exercise of citizenship and the right uses of leisure and freedom. He had a tenacious belief that educational ideas should be stated sharply and pursued doggedly until their powers and limitations were plain for all to see. And he seemed to feel guilty when swimming downstream.

---

[1] F. Champion Ward (ed.), *The Idea and Practice of General Education*, University of Chicago Press (Chicago: 1950), Preface.

[2] George Santayana, *Character and Opinion in the United States*, W. W. Norton and Company, Inc. (New York: 1920), p. 59.

The College of the University of Chicago was an unusually thoroughgoing effort to realize a set of ideas concerning the nature of general, liberal education and its place in the education of Americans. As such, it is worth recollecting, in comparative tranquility, a decade after the restoration of the conventional undergraduate program at the University of Chicago. For the problems which the College sought to resolve continue to plague American education, with no relief in sight.

Such a review would not be instructive if the demise of the College had been unambiguous. However, the "debate" concerning its future centered, not in its educational performance, but in the presumptive cost to the University of Chicago of continuing to be different. Indeed, several reassuring studies of the performance of the College's graduates in national examinations, in postgraduate studies, and in the awarding of fellowships and other academic honors, were in hand as the debate began. The students of the College were strong and clear in their support of the education they were receiving, and their teachers risked the loss of their union cards to defend it. As a result, like a burial at sea, the College sank to a chorus of praise, much of it sincere, mixed with laments that so fair a thing should have proved so frail.

The College offered a balanced and prescribed program of studies in the humanities, social sciences, natural sciences, mathematics, and languages, with culminating efforts to employ history and philosophy as means of "integration." Students were admitted to this program after ten, eleven, or twelve years of schooling, and they were placed in it at a level appropriate to their preparation and competence; therefore, they completed it in varying lengths of time. Three years (aye, there was the rub) proved to be the time required of most students. Upon completion of this course of study, the University of Chicago's Bachelor of Arts degree was awarded.

This curriculum was developed and taught by an autonomous faculty of the University, grouped in divisional staffs but without the conventional departments offering "majors" in single subjects. These teachers had the usual academic credentials in specialized fields. Some also belonged to departments of the University's graduate faculties; some did not. Advancement in the College faculty was based upon teaching and upon contributions to the improvement of the curriculum. Therefore, it was not possible to ruin the reputation of a member of the College faculty by "spreading the nasty rumor" that he was a good teacher.

The principal materials employed in the College were original works or selections therefrom ("Great Snippets"), rather than textbooks, and the principal method of teaching was by discussion of these materials in preparation for examinations not set by the instructor.[3] Contrary to a number of widespread impressions, there was no master list of Great Books; most of the selections were modern in date; the medieval period was on the whole neglected; selections were changed more rapidly from year to year than in most courses in charge of individual teachers; and two years of laboratory work were required in the three-year natural-sciences sequence.

The over-all end of this education was to teach students "how to think." In a free and increasingly complex society, men and women are confronted constantly by diverse statements purporting to be true, by alternative courses of action claiming their adherence, and by individual works of art inviting their admiration. The College sought to give students the knowledge and intellectual competence required to choose wisely and live well in such a society.

Although the curriculum was integral, it proved not to be terminal for most of the College's graduates, who continued beyond the College in large numbers, to pursue specialized and professional courses.

The course of study just described embodied the notion that a liberal education should constitute a single whole, whereas most colleges in America will be seen to have two foci or principles of unity, variously called "general" and "specialized" education, "distribution" and "concentration," "lower" and "upper," "introductory" and "advanced," *et cetera*. These two foci coexist plausibly enough in college catalogues, but in the actual education of individual students they are clumsily and uneasily conjoined.

The bifocal curriculum is subject to characteristic lapses and strains which do not appear to have gone away in recent years. Because the program culminates in "majors" in single subjects for which academic departments are made responsible, these departments become the principal points of attachment for both students and faculty. As a result, when thus placed in a single degree program with specialized education,

---

[3] The relative reliability of textbooks and of the sources from which they are directly or remotely constructed is sometimes not clear to students who have been confined to the former. "Thucydides was right about that battle," a student once assured a class of mine, "I looked it up in a history book."

general education contracts "to fill the time available." Theoretically, there may be an even division of the four-year course into two halves, but close examination of the half devoted to general education reveals that the two years of work of which it is composed becomes a *pastiche* of survey courses for "non-majors," prerequisites required or suggested by departments and professional associations, and introductions to single subjects. It is almost inevitable that members of a faculty appointed and advanced by departments will give pride of place to departmental interests and expectations. It is predictable, also, that as between general and departmental requirements for a single degree, students will slight the former.[4]

When they are attempted at all within the bifocal curriculum, interdisciplinary courses are commonly designed and maintained by virtue of complex and precarious treaties among departments which are natural rivals for "student time." Thus, a distinguished professor in one leading university once told me, "I have only one injunction from my department as their representative in this survey—'Maximize the segment devoted to sociology.'" Pedagogy, too, is shaped by bifocal organization. Particularly in the very large universities, departmental introductory courses are apt to be taught by means of lectures by senior professors, "followed-up" by sections in charge of distracted and evergreen graduate students who give quizzes and conduct discussions designed to "clear up the points made in the lectures." (The resemblance of this procedure to that of the high-school textbook, with its chapters of exposition followed by review questions, must be depressing to new and still-hopeful university students.) The lectures enable the university to proclaim the interest of its senior faculty in undergraduate teaching, and the employment of graduate students as "section men" enables the younger to support the older students with a minimum of educational "overhead."

The present location of the Bachelor of Arts degree, marking as it does the completion of a departmental "major," leads many colleges and universities to maintain one or more bargain-basement departments, in which undergraduates of marginal ability can both "major" and survive. Nor (such are the frailties of tests and measurements)

[4] Particularly if, as in at least one university, certain departments require of prospective "majors" an average grade in their general studies "closer to C than to D." Intending "majors" may perhaps be forgiven if they elect to qualify with an average closer to C than to B.

is this incorporation of mediocrity avoided altogether by the form of preventive detention now employed by at least one university, which maintains, on a kind of siding, a separate college to which may be shunted students considered upon entry to be incapable of "majoring."

By contrast, blessed with serious students and rejoicing in the good opinion of the graduate schools, stronger colleges are tempted to turn into forcing beds for specialists. The chairman of the department of chemistry in one of the nation's most impressive colleges told me that his honors graduates, on arriving at Harvard, regularly took and passed examinations for the degree of Doctor of Philosophy, which left them with only a thesis to complete. "Do you think we may be neglecting their general education?", he asked, but did not wait for an answer.

It is my impression that the last decade has seen an exacerbation of these structural tensions. Scholars and scientists hope not to teach, and students hope not to be taught. Certainly, the scholarly teacher who cultivated wide intellectual interests and was encouraged to do so, and who showed a concern for the whole impact of his college upon its students, appears to be in retreat. He is being replaced by the professional with a packed suitcase. To retain the latter, colleges raise salaries, lower teaching "loads," and encourage conventional research, only to find themselves engaged in a losing competition with the universities which, in their turn, aspire to the condition of postdoctoral institutes. Meanwhile, the best undergraduate students appear to be expecting more from their education than their teachers have time or inclination to supply.

Apart from the sciences, where this tendency is most advanced, the situation is unsatisfactory but hardly disastrous. In the sciences, there is a danger that scientists, subsidized and distracted by industry and government, may fail to reproduce their kind. This drift was visible ten years ago. I remember a meeting at the University of Chicago at which the dean of the physical sciences division joined me in exhorting members of that faculty to teach in the College. A young chemist sitting next to me listened with solicitude but did not enlist. "I'd like to help you," he murmured, "but my faculty pays off for research."

Here and there, noting the fragmentation of their students' education, college faculties get up a special interdepartmental course, designed to "draw together" each senior's knowledge as he leaves the college. But since by that time each senior has exercised to the full his right to ignorance and the free abuse thereof, he presents an unique mosaic of what he knows and what he has elected not to know. "Wholeness," in such circumstances, must be sought at a dangerously abstract and banal level. Other colleges have sought a belated intellectual community for their seniors by departing altogether from the curriculum to deal with "Vital Issues of the Day" in a series of public lectures for credit.

Most colleges long since gave up the search for common intellectual topics and pursuits deriving from the curriculum. They have tried to substitute an extracurricular community of the grandstand, the dance floor, and the visiting speaker.

The lack of a shared intellectual life in most American colleges is not surprising when it is recalled that only American undergraduates and their teachers attempt to realize two primary purposes within a single degree course. Students of law, medicine, and engineering pursue coherent courses of study which their faculties do not hesitate to prescribe. The professional students of a university, pursuing courses of study together, form with their teachers educational communities with a capacity to generate intellectual topics and activities within and outside the classroom which is often the envy of the undergraduate division of the same university. The success of the College at Chicago in achieving an unusual degree of shared intellectual life suggests that such an achievement does not depend upon the age and vocational interest of students, but upon a common curriculum realizing a single educational end.

The chief loser in all this is the student who seeks to acquire the knowledge and competence which "everyone ought to have." But his deprivation is not caused solely by elements in the bifocal college which are indifferent or hostile to general education. Many practitioners of "general education" have themselves contributed to its lowered estate. For every sound and thoughtful effort, there has been at least one discreditable venture in breathless "coverage" or loose philosophizing. Moreover, there has been a paradoxical confusion concerning the constituency for general education. I have already cited one university which provides a general education for students considered incapable of "majoring." In other universities, the opposite view is taken, and only selected students are thought to be capable of engaging in "directed liberal studies" or of profiting from an interdepartmental senior seminar.

Tensions have been heightened further by a rhetoric of mutual deprecation. Charges of narrowness and superficiality are exchanged between "generalists" and "specialists," "dilettantes" and "pedants." I believe that both parties to these exchanges have failed to look closely enough at the relationship between principles and particulars which ought to obtain within a liberal education. To paraphrase Kant, principles without particulars are empty; particulars without principles are blind. Liberal education is not a vaguely inspirational exposure to ideas; nor is it an engorgement of the student by blocks of facts and conclusions, tidied up for easy commitment to memory. Liberal education should induce in students the habit of being general and the habit of being particular, but these are not separable ends to be served by two separate parts of their education. Even where working distinctions are drawn between them, general education need not be an education in generalities, and specialized education should issue in a grasp of principles.

Paradoxically, attempts to use "distribution" requirements in single subjects in order to avoid loose generalizing in interdisciplinary courses (or to avoid the effort required to make such courses rigorous) may defeat themselves. There is nothing more vacuous and misleading than those preambles on the "five steps of the scientific method," "the nature of social science," *et cetera,* which preface "distribution" courses. It is only superficially true that one science or art is a surrogate for other sciences or arts. Ask an economist if he really believes that sociology or political science is interchangeable with economics as an exemplar of social science. Ask a physicist if biology illustrates his science. Or ask an architect if he regards architecture as "frozen music." It is a hard truth that the student who does not study economics will not understand an economy, and that if economics is the only social science he studies, he may not understand the difference between an economy and a society. This is why general education takes time.

The casual Platonizing which proposes the substitution of "distribution" requirements for prescribed courses dealing comparatively with related but distinct subject matters and methods, is in contrast with the "Aristotelianism" of the College curriculum at Chicago. In shaping a program designed to keep principles and particulars in tandem, to provide a grasp of both the unity and diversity of the world of knowledge, and to instill in students balanced habits of relevant judgment, Aristotle was a useful guide. Aristotle was a born dean. His distinction among knowing, doing, and making; his respect for both the general and the specific; and his care in holding each mode of inquiry to its proper end, subject matter, degree of precision, and order of generality, were all reflected in the curriculum of the College. This Aristotelianism was not doctrinal. (The College was never able to digest a Thomist.) Its educational bearing is indicated broadly in the preface to what a College student is alleged to have called, by an understandable and happy error, the *"Nico-McKeon Ethics"*: ". . . It is the mark of an educated man to look for precision in each class of things just so far as the nature of the subject admits; it is evidently foolish to accept probable reasoning from a mathematician and to demand from a rhetorician scientific proofs."

"Now each man judges well the things he knows, and of these he is a good judge. And so the man who has been educated in a subject is a good judge of that subject, and the man who has received an all-round education is a good judge in general."[5]

If this essay is to adhere to its own premises, including these pregnant truisms of Aristotle, some account of what was done *in concreto* in the College should be added to the general principles, descriptive outlines, and strictures on alternatives which have been advanced up to now. Since it was most familiar to me, I will describe the three-year sequence in the humanities, first placing it in relation to the other two major sequences in the natural and social sciences and then giving some account of its internal details.[6]

A chemical treatise, a study of the business cycle, and a work of literary criticism are all products of the disciplined intellectual activity of men, but there is an increasing affinity between the practitioner and his subject matter as one passes from nature to society and art. Nature is not of human making, and the austere and abstract kind of knowledge sought by the natural scientist reflects this fact. Society is partially of human making and partially the product of impersonal and

---

[5] *The Basic Works of Aristotle*, Richard P. McKeon ed.; Random House (New York: 1941), p. 936.

[6] In this account, I shall use the past tense, from ignorance of the exact modifications in length, form, content, or accessibility to students which these courses may have undergone in recent years. A reading of the current *Announcements* of the University of Chicago suggests that many of the general courses are extant, but that the relation of many of these to the actual programs of students is now *à la carte*. I shall be borrowing freely from an account of the humanities sequence originally written for *The Literary Criterion*, edited by Professor C. D. Narasimhaiah, at the University of Mysore, Mysore, India. It appeared in the summer issue, in 1954.

extra-conscious forces, and the chronic debate about the place of values and action in social science reflects this fact. Works of art are essentially of human making. From this fact derive the autonomy and importance of the humanities, and the special characteristics of the College "humanities sequence."

Broadly speaking, the first year's work in the humanities was directed to acquiring a grasp of what might be called the "grammar" of the arts; the second year, to analysis of literary works; and the third year, to criticism. These levels of acquaintance, analysis, and criticism were sought to be achieved through examination of many individual examples of musical, visual, and literary art, and, in the last year, of critical works dealing with the nature of one or more arts and the means by which they may be appraised intelligently.

To take only the example of literature, the student was asked in the first year to read and discuss a number of novels, plays, and lyric poems with a view to grasping the elements which compose them, the forms imposed on those elements, the artistic purposes of their authors, and the external (cultural, social) and internal (stylistic, conventional) factors which gave them their final character. Biographies of authors, histories of literature, philosophizing about art, and other forms of secondhand acquaintance with literary works, were rather severely repressed in favor of developing competence to grasp and enjoy the works themselves.

In the second year, the student attempted to learn how to read different kinds of books. More difficult texts were chosen, and these were examined more intensively. The *genres* were histories (*e.g.*, by Thucydides, Gibbon, Tawney), rhetorical writings (Pericles, Lincoln, Burke), dramatic works (Shakespeare, Sophocles, Chekhov, Shaw), novels (Flaubert, Fielding, Tolstoi, James), and philosophical texts (Aristotle, Plato, Hume, Dewey). Attention was concentrated upon the purpose and structure of these literary constructions. In addition to the detailed study of individual texts, there was explicit consideration of the literary kinds to which they belonged and of the similarities and differences which obtain among these kinds. The intention was to enable the student to know what to expect, and what not to expect, from a work of rhetoric, as against a work of historical narration; to recognize that such an issue as the struggle between human and divine law may be put to quite different uses in a play by Sophocles and in a philosophical argument by Fichte; in general, to have a heightened consciousness of what is going on in the books he reads.

A word needs to be said about the time allotted to the analysis of individual works or topics in "general" and in "specialized" courses. It is often assumed that a general course must be a hurried series of rapid reading assignments, culminating, *faute de mieux,* in attempts to cope with such examination topics as, "Trace the Idea of Fate from Sophocles to Nietzsche (illustrate)." This assumption was rejected in the College, in favor of fewer works read carefully enough to establish a capacity to read more. A single course in Sophocles will take up more of his plays than will a course in Greek drama, and the latter will take up more than a general course in literature or in the humanities. But all of these courses may give the same amount and kind of attention to *Oedipus Rex.* I once discussed this question with a dean of Columbia College. We agreed to differ when we realized that Columbia assigned many texts because, as the Dean pointed out, "the students haven't read anything," and Chicago assigned few texts, because "the students don't know how to read."

Appraisal by the student of the merits of works of art is, of course, inevitable at each of these levels of experience with humanistic works. But deliberate attention to the problems which criticism of the arts entails was withheld until the third and final year of the course. In that year, the student continued to read individual literary works (there were "variants" of the course which centered in music and the visual arts), but he also read a series of texts which proposed a number of different bases for criticism of works of art. Such works as Aristotle's *Poetics,* Plato's *Phaedrus,* Hume's *On the Standard of Taste,* and Tolstoi's *What Is Art?,* as well as examples of contemporary criticism of particular works of art, were read in order to become familiar with the variety of premises upon which appraisals of individual works may rest and with the variety of estimates of a given work to which different premises may lead. The object was not to make an esthetician of the student or to pull him away from a primary concern with individual works of art. Rather, it was hoped that he would come to understand what a critic is doing when he praises or denigrates a work, and would be able to give some account of his own critical assumptions. It was hoped, also, that he would know what a critic is *not* doing when he places a given work in one finite perspective among the many which might be employed to disclose its full nature. He would thus be protected from the wooden and sometimes fanatical insistence upon a single standard of criticism which has often hampered the proper business of criticism, which is simply to help us understand and enjoy individual works of art.

In 1953, at a student rally designed to protest the impending reduction of the College curriculum to two years, a College student is said to have vowed that without the last-year courses he would have been "only a man of parts." He was quite right. The tripartite division of the College curriculum left him little wiser concerning possible interrelationships among the disciplined activities of men, including theories of those interrelationships which could call that very division into question. Explicit attention was paid to this matter in two "integration" courses, one a course in the history of Western civilization, the other an examination of various "organizations, methods, and principles of knowledge." In these courses, materials, ideas, methods, and works which the student had first encountered in his separate studies of nature, society, and art were brought under a number of historical and philosophical purviews. The aim was not to equip the student with a single synthesis of human knowledge or to assign a single meaning to human history. Rather, it was to enable him to use the disciplines of history and philosophy (particularity and generality in their most inclusive embodiments) in the search for knowledge and wisdom which every civilized man should carry on throughout his life.

The foregoing account cannot be said to have stressed the imperfections of the College course of study. The College was, in fact, slow to exploit certain of its own capacities: for eliciting sufficient written work from its students, for varying its pedagogy adequately in consonance with diverse subjects and learning tasks, for insuring that "placement" did not have the effect of exempting students altogether from what they could do best, for finding ways to incorporate more use of foreign languages and mathematics in the substantive sequences. These deficiencies were not structural; indeed, a number of them were at least partially removed as experience accumulated. A more drastic possible flaw ought to be cited. It may be that the most general assumptions of the College about the nature of intellectual work and its proper subjects were too "Hellenic," in that materials not easily subjected to analytic treatment tended to be left out. However, this is perhaps a generic trait of Western education, which is going to be subjected to some new and interesting strains as colleges now attempt to include in their curricula "non-Western" materials on which the light of Hellas never shone.[7]

Even with these imperfections on its head, I believe that the College was able to show that a collegiate program of general, liberal education must have a degree of substance, coherence, and rigor not attainable in less than three years of serious study; that such a program should be the responsibility of a single faculty of scholarly teachers, individually expert but not insulated from each other in conventional departments; and that the intellectual attainment of the graduates of such a program is worthy of the award of the Bachelor of Arts degree.

The reader will not have mistaken these probable reasonings for scientific proofs. However, the substance claimed above for the College curriculum, and the appropriateness of awarding the Bachelor of Arts degree for its completion, received a certain degree of validation when, in 1952, a representative third of the last-year students of the College took the Graduate Record Examinations. Each student took all the Tests of General Education and two Advanced Tests, selected from six of the latter. In the General Education Index, which averages the performance in the eight Tests of General Education, 99 per cent of the College students exceeded the 70th percentile of senior students from other colleges included in the national norms, and 73 per cent exceeded the 90th percentile. It would have been distinctly disturbing if they had not, since the business of the College was to provide a superior general education.

Less predictable were the results attained in the Advanced Tests, which are designed as a measure of the achievement of college "majors" in individual subjects. In biology, sociology, philosophy, literature, and history, 100, 95, 94, 80 and 80 per cent respectively, of the College students exceeded the median of senior students "majoring" in those subjects elsewhere. Norms were not available in the case of the

---

[7] At least one wise and trenchant American educator, Professor Jacques Barzun, appears to view the mysteries of the East as an unclear but present danger to the Western "house of intellect," already gnawed by all manner of home-grown termites. Far from assigning any limitations to Western education, he seems to be ready to man the barricades. (See his *The House of Intellect*, Harper & Brothers (New York: 1959), p. 25 ff. Elsewhere, I have tried to show how a "universal curriculum" might be developed without self-destruction on the part of Western teachers and students; but the proof, if forthcoming at all, will be in the pudding. ("Toward a Universal Curriculum," Proceedings of the Seventeenth Annual Meeting of the American Conference of Academic Deans.)

sixth test, psychology. It should be pointed out that the six advanced tests made available were not selected at random but because of their relevance to subject matters judged to be most pervasively treated in the College curriculum. Also, in the case of the test in biology, half of the students who took it had done work, in addition to what was required in the College, which was judged relevant to their performance.[8]

Granting these qualifications, these results appear to show that if a prescribed and cumulative course of general studies is pursued beyond introductory levels by able students and teachers, and if it does not confine itself to "principles without particulars," a respectable quantum of knowledge of individual subjects will be acquired.[9] I do not believe that the converse is true and that selected single subjects may be studied in such a way as to yield a general education. The "flower in the crannied wall" theory on which this possibility is predicated has been discussed in connection with the resort by many colleges to "distribution" requirements in lieu of required general courses.

If three years of work in a single program are essential to a sound general education, where is the third year to be found? Experience at Chicago and elsewhere suggests strongly that it is the twelfth year of schooling, a year now usually spent in high school. This assertion requires some defense, both in respect of the more drastic original assumption of the College at Chicago, that general, higher education should begin after ten years of schooling, and in respect of a current impression that the high schools have been improving so sharply as to be able to keep even their ablest students fully "challenged" through their twelfth year of school.

It is true that studies of able students admitted after ten years of schooling to the University of Chicago's College, and subsequently to other colleges, have shown that they were capable of college work and did not suffer, either academically or socially, from their "early

[8] Further details concerning the performance of College students are reported in an article entitled "The Chicago Bachelor of Arts Degree after Ten Years," by Professor B. S. Bloom and the writer, in the December, 1952, issue of the *Journal of Higher Education*.

[9] But there are limits to the range of individual subjects, as well as to the amount of knowledge, which can be expected to be acquired in the course of a general education. For example, no College student could have achieved that knowledge of the Norwegian language which the University of Chicago now requires of its undergraduate "majors" in that subject.

entrance." However, it seems to me unlikely that the mass of American parents of future college students will support quite so early a removal of their children from the home and from inexpensive public education. And I see no reason why what might be called the "grammar" of collegiate studies cannot be instilled successfully by the high schools. I have in mind such competences as "reading a page of French or English with precise understanding, knowing where Malaya is or when the Republican party was founded, understanding a statistical statement, and expressing one's thought in clear prose."[10] A school and high-school program addressed seriously to the establishment of these competences in college-bound students could, I believe, accomplish its purpose in eleven years.[11]

On the other hand, it is unlikely that most of our high schools will be able to extend the education of their better students effectively beyond this level. The sheer mass of high-school students, two-thirds of whom are not destined for college; the unscholarly atmosphere surrounding public education; and the increasing precocity and restiveness of urban students, all suggests that the American student bound for college is now held a year too long in the American high school. He should complete his schooling in eleven years and spend the next three years in a single program of general, higher education leading to the Bachelor of Arts degree.

It is sometimes said that the lycees, gymnasiums, and public schools of Europe succeed in providing an impressive general education and that, therefore, American high schools can do the same and thus free American colleges and universities to concentrate, as in Europe, on specialized study. The differences in clientele, staff, and social role which distinguish these European schools from American high schools seem to me to be very great, and ineradicable within the foreseeable future. Moreover, as secondary education spreads to a wide range of schools and students in Europe, the European universities are finding their students deficient in "general culture." In any case, English students, for example, do "Sixth Form" work during the same years here proposed as appropriate for general study in American colleges; there-

10 Editorial comment, *The Journal of General Education,* July, 1952.

11 It is interesting that when the University of Chicago changed its undergraduate program in 1953, the "laboratory school" of the University shifted from a total duration of ten years to one of eleven, not twelve, years.

fore, higher specialized study would begin at the same age for both groups.

Which existing American institutions might provide such an education for those students capable of profiting from it? I see a variety of prospects, divided into two principal groups: those which would confine themselves to general education and those which would also provide further courses of study. In the first group, I would include two-year junior colleges, which would admit students to a three-year curriculum following eleven years of schooling; liberal arts colleges having limited resources for specialized work; and the strongest preparatory schools.

In the second group, I would include the stronger liberal arts colleges, which would provide both general studies leading to the Bachelor of Arts degree and, with special attention to the preparation of teachers, specialized courses leading to the master's degree; and universities, which would give primary emphasis to higher degrees but would carry on some college work in general education as a stimulus and model to outlying efforts.

There are able students who do not plan to pursue higher studies beyond the bachelor's degree, but who would benefit from an added year of work in which they were required to undertake an individual task suggested by ideas and topics encountered in their general studies. Independent liberal arts colleges and university colleges could offer the Bachelor's degree with honors to such students.

Able students completing their programs of general studies at any of the foregoing types of institutions would be ready to undertake intensive and well-planned courses of study leading, normally in three years, to the Master's degree, or to begin work in a professional school. This essay has been concerned with that stage in the education of intelligent Americans when they should all acquire a liberal education. The task has been to specify those conditions of preparation, time, and organization under which a liberal education can be most effectively provided. In such a discussion, it is easy to convey a false impression that one regards advanced, specialized education as a marginal concern. In fact, the benefits to specialized education of the scheme here proposed would be considerable. Eleven years of schooling, followed by two three-year programs, the first establishing a common intellectual base for all students, the second providing intensive courses of specialized study for the abler products of the first, are surely superior to the present arrangement of twelve years of schooling, followed by two fragmented years of "lower division" work, followed, for able and mediocre students alike, by two years of undergraduate "concentration," followed by one or two years of "master's" work, often under new management. On the basis of what I believe to be instructive experience, the differences between eleven and twelve years of schooling, between a two- and a three-year program of general education, and between a divided and a unified master's course, provide an optimal division of function and effort within a fixed stretch of educational time, and can make "all the difference" to the quality of what is achieved.

Whenever a scheme for American education as a whole is proposed, two contrary "dangers" are sure to be cited. There is first the apparent danger of agreement upon a national curriculum. In spite of the example of the French, educational uniformity is believed by most Americans to be incompatible with political democracy. Indeed, any attempt at searching discussion of education in America can be nipped in the bud by pointing out that further progress toward agreement would endanger the pluralism of the system. Given this national conviction, the risk of excessive uniformity may perhaps be dismissed. The contrary danger is more substantial. It is the danger that diversity will simply be a euphemism for uneven quality in the actual performance of different educational institutions purporting to be engaged in the same task. It is not enough to say that this is now the case and there isn't much to lose. An attempt should be made to keep general, higher education at a good standard, while respecting pluralism. I believe that the answer lies in a limited pluralism. The number of inventive minds and superior educational settings is limited at any given time and is likely to remain so. Therefore, there should be deliberate exploitation of superior minds and settings for the purpose of developing new forms of general education, devising standards of achievement for college students, and giving special stimulus and training to teachers in isolated situations. As state systems of higher education multiply and deploy their constituent colleges more and more widely, at least one light-source of the type suggested should be maintained and exploited for the benefit of each system as a whole.

During the war and in the nation's first postwar response to the compulsions and alarms of international politics, general, liberal education was a natural casualty. Not even humanists escaped "processing." In the first year of the war, I heard a brisk university executive promise the Pentagon "a steady stream of humanistic know-how." The mood has been useful in many ways, in exposing educational flabbiness, increasing facilities, and strengthening the education of engineers. But if free men and women are reduced to "skilled manpower" and invested in as "human resources," their freedom will be no more than a collective sovereignty. In the absence of a shared wisdom, experts will not understand each other, nor will their fellow citizens know what specialists and managers are trying to do. As the need for wisdom is felt as well as seen, we may hope that the deliberate nurturing of "good judges in general" will find its full place in American higher education.

4

"A Connected

View

of

Things"

Rexford G. Tugwell

Anyone who is a parent, or anyone who even pays taxes must sometimes ask himself what education is for. And if he has any feeling for his associates on earth, any view of the future, or even any common sense, he must come up with something beyond self-improvement. Yet we have built a vast system with not much more than this as an intention—to keep young people at it until their position in the world is assured.

This is corollary to the economic motives we depend on: each individual is to try to get the best of every other. And how can he do it unless he has the training? The absurdity of such an expectation is shown in actual results. A monopolized and regulated industry somehow allows us to keep our theory while we escape from its governance. But departures are frowned on in other areas, education being one; children and young people are held to fiercely competitive regimes in which Mill's "connected view of things" has only an incidental part.

It is curious—and rather wonderful, I think—that into education, as into competitive business, other influences are always creeping.

Other ends are always being sought. Men try to help each other in spite of feeling sheepish about it. And culture infiltrates education, too, although usually disguised as an improving endeavor. Even when educators argue that physicians, lawyers, engineers, and other specialized people ought to have some "liberal" college years before they enter professional school, they feel forced to say it will make better professionals of them. But what they really have deep in their minds is something entirely different: an ambition to produce, somehow, an improved generation, one better read, less attracted to time-wasting activities, more tolerant and reasonable, with an active sense of responsibility, and with some knowledge of the whole environment, not just of some of its parts.

Mill on the Rounded Man

Can anything deserve the name of good education that does not include literature and science too? . . . Is not anyone a poor, maimed, lopsided fragment of humanity who is deficient in either? Short as life is, and shorter as we make it by the time we waste on things which are neither business, nor meditation, nor pleasure, we are not so badly off that our scholars need be ignorant of the laws and properties of the world they live in, or our scientific men destitute of poetic feeling and artistic cultivation.[1]

This dichotomy has given our system its curious ambivalent character. But it is important not to overlook the hidden purpose and its consequences. And there is one noncompetitive resolution that is simple, direct, open, and admirable. We admit a commitment to democracy. This heritage, at least, has been left to us as a result of our ancestors' fierce struggle for liberty and equality. The influence is perhaps limited; but it is pervasive. Every voter, it is agreed, must be able to read, else he cannot defend his equal status.

It is not by any means agreed that all must be provided with the knowledge—through education—that will enable him to use the franchise in such ways as will advance the interests of the Republic. Perhaps this is because the calculation of what this would involve is so appalling.

Jefferson, defending universal suffrage, relied on the argument that

[1] John Stuart Mill, Inaugural Address at St. Andrews, 1867.

the more voters there were, the less likely it was that all of them could be bought. He thus implied that honesty was enough; and that any person, however ignorant or prejudiced, had a contribution to make. But Jefferson was surely as wrong as others who argue in this way. Moreover, he knew how lame the contention was. The more there are who do not know what they are doing, the vaster the catastrophe they invite—hence the University he was so proud of. The cult of practicality even in his time was following close on the literal equality he defended. The higher education of those who could qualify—and those alone— was an untenable extrapolation from his premise.

Administrators of our educational system even today are suffering from the general demand for practicality. They argue desperately that "cultural" studies will turn out to be useful in the end; and sometimes they are believed by those they have to convince that something beyond the three R's is desirable. But what a strain!

Nicholas Murray Butler once defined the practical man in a devastating phrase: "He is," he said, "one who neither knows what he is doing nor why he is doing it." This, in our day of colossal organizations run by professional administrators, calls up a picture of behemoths blundering about in the powerhouses of civilization destroying as much as they create. Such devotion to practicality could ruin us overnight and conceivably it may; yet if there is one word more honored than another among those who control our educational system it is certainly "practical."

We are, actually, not all that devoted to it; but we cling to the pretense that we are, and are thus committed to defending something that neither exists nor is really believed in.

Still it is difficult to see what conditions would allow a more forthright development of humanistic studies. Europeans, who lay claim to superior systems of education, are actually even more devoted than we to professionalism. The single-minded plunge that their young people are required to make into medicine, law, engineering, and the civil service excludes everything not strictly preparatory. They are bred and groomed like show animals to a single narrow career. True, the British have shown resistance on behalf of a few privileged individuals; but the cost seems to involve lingering in enclaves where only the classic languages or studies of the past are cultivated. The choice of this as against the offerings of American universities is not one we would care to make. Say what you will, it must be admitted that there is hardly a university campus in the United States where a preprofessional student cannot find a professor and a group of students who are considering important episodes in intellectual history or the accomplishments of the masters in all the philosophies and arts. This refreshment may not be required, and it would be better if it were systematized, but it is available. He *can* acquire the sophistication of the learned, touch the great minds of the past, gain some view of the future, and be guided to an appreciation of the arts—if he is spared the time, has the energy left over from his central interests, and if he wants to. Not a great many want to; but then we do have adult reading and discussion, cultivated by talented teachers and made available to many. There is a considerable recognition of the education that goes on and on throughout life.

It is hard to understand how anyone can take a fresh look at our American educational establishment—the whole of it—without being impressed with its sheer size; and not only its size, really, but the variety and scope of its offerings, and sometimes its excellence. Much less than a century ago hardly anyone could get what we call a liberal education; yet we are now close to making one available to every young person who can make use of it. The trouble is not availability; it is that we do not show young people why it should be wanted.[2]

What impulse has so steadily and massively supported this diversion of resources from other and more immediate projects—such, for instance, as roads, hospitals, and public utilities, to say nothing of industrial expansion?

The system has mostly been paid for in taxes, and businessmen and property owners hate taxes with special virulence. Yet there has been a continuous growth; and this is made more impressive by knowing that the schools and even the universities have been largely public

[2] I avoid for the moment the problem of limited youths who cannot go beyond some level short of that needed for participation in cultural activities. They furnish the familiar drop-outs who so often become at best social debtors and at worst delinquents. This is largely because of neglect. There are ways to employ those who cannot find places in ordinary employment. They can at least be kept out of mischief; and very often they make a contribution, sometimes a valuable one. But our massive educational effort ought to comprehend rather than merely to discard them. They will never be adequately educated; but they will always be present and always challenge the system that will not accept them.

undertakings supported mostly by local or state funds. So it was not a concerted matter; it was something each community decided must be done.

Why was this? Plainly not just for the reasons usually offered. Was it to qualify the coming generations for participation in a technological revolution since they would otherwise not get on in the world? Was it a matter of status: each family trying to surpass neighboring ones? Had it something to do with the civic sense: with the conception of our organized life together?

We all know that one of the centers of controversy in every village and city, rising occasionally to bitter exchanges, has been the school. Self-appointed representatives of taxpayers have denounced the extravagance of proposed expenditures; and these have as ardently been defended by friends of the schools. There have always been those who were certain that they knew better than educators what children should and should not be asked to learn. At the worst this has developed into cults whose members terrorize the institutions within their reach. Education is never sufficiently narrow and—by their definition—orthodox to meet their demands. And the same sort of pressure has often been exerted on legislative committees.

Educators dread the ordeal of defense against fanatics of this sort. They naturally feel that they are specially equipped to determine what ought to be taught and how it ought to be done. Generally speaking they have prevailed. Harassments do die out, even if they leave problems to be dealt with. The educators remain on the job. They may have compromised; but perhaps only for the time.

There is a defense to be made for interferences, of course. It is not the privilege of the teacher or school administrator to define civic purposes; nor may they tell adults what their children ought to be like when grown. But there is one part of their function that they are entitled to defend from any and all outsiders. They are the guardians of children's liberties, the openers of doors, the cultivators of free minds. If the definition of purpose belongs to the electorate, the educators are in charge of its continual renewal. As so often, there is here the difficulty that so many adults are apt to oppose open minds for their children. There is a strong impulse to perpetuate tradition and even prejudice. The educators in this part of their duty are most vulnerable and most apt to compromise. Yet the system itself has grown so massive and educators so numerous and so bulwarked by traditions of their own that outside impacts are less and less effective.

What is effective is the cultural climate. This climate has gradually grown more favorable to technique—how to make all kinds of mechanisms run, how to improve them, and how to make them widely available. The cultural climate has also become favorably disposed to social machinery, too. It has gradually shaped the whole educational process to preoccupation with a preference for an amplitude of smoothly operating devices. The recognition is very general that a child must have first of all the knowledges and skills necessary to participation in the making and running of things.

The question of qualification for participation is a difficult one. What shall be done about children who cannot get far in mathematics or any of the sciences, who resist reading, or who cannot remember history? Of course if the weakness is general such young people become drop-outs; but often it is not general but selective. A line of A's in every subject but one turns up occasionally; so does the reverse. The brightest student in chemistry may have a dismal record in English or history. And even when he is nevertheless admitted to college, there is the further problem of deciding whether to temporize with newly appearing disabilities—for they continue to show up at every higher level—or whether to close out the educational career once for all.

A young graduate of Columbia College was telling me recently about meeting again a friend with whom he had gone to school. They had separated; and the friend had made a brilliant record in science, had graduated into a well-paying job, and was getting ahead with what seemed fantastic rapidity. "But," said my informant, "he seems to have missed out on education. There's hardly anything I can talk to him about. He might as well be from another planet."

This exchange might be the theme of a discourse on the weakness of our system. Two young men, trying to renew a friendship, and frustrated because they could communicate about nothing but old associations! Inquiry showed that the scientific major had been *exposed* to social studies, history, and literature, as of course he must have been at Johns Hopkins. He simply had not absorbed them. And consequently he was a nonparticipant in all contemporary discussions and activities outside his very narrow interest.

Indifferent instruction might go some way to account for instances of this sort. Those who themselves are allergic to all knowledge except their own specialty, who use texts written by others of their own sort, or even those who demand more than an appropriate share of students' time and energy, will attract the willing attention only of those intending to become specialists, too. Others will show their reluctance in various degrees.

But this has forced the acknowledgment that if students are required to take subjects quite outside their interest, it must be because these subjects contribute to the orientation of one who must live in today's environment and ought not to live in it more ignorantly than his abilities determine. He ought to be able to give and to receive—to communicate, "to know what he is doing and why he is doing it." And the courses he is asked to take ought to be shaped to this intention. If they are not, he will have a piecemeal education, a good part of it resentfully pursued; and he may very well turn out to be half educated, as the young Hopkins scientist was. He may even be one of those anti-intellectuals the intellectual classes so often produce.

He will dislike the city and long for the wilderness; he will have a house full of hideous art objects merely because they are not machine made; he will drive a foreign car under the impression that in buying it he is striking against industrialism; he will sneer at political processes, disparage bureaucrats, and perhaps even vote Republican because the Republicans are reputed to be reactionary. At any rate he will show some highly developed sign of withdrawal from a civilization he finds strange and unfriendly because he cannot understand or really participate in its activities.

Among the teachers who most often resist shaping their knowledge to the young people who are not going to be their professional successors but who ought to understand what is going on, scientists have been quite as much at fault as the classicists so effectively indicted by T. H. Huxley far back in the nineteenth century for not respecting science. It seemed outrageous to Huxley that the most honored intellectuals were not in any recognizable sense educated at all. Their attitudes and opinions about subjects other than their own were grossly uninformed and sometimes fantastic. Even then the life of a humanist scholar, in a world run by industrialists and politicians, was one long protest. He was apt to express himself volubly on many matters; and he was often amazed that distinction in his field did not gain respect for his lucubrations.

Precisely the same observation can be made in these later days. Specialists are often ignorant, opinionated, and tend so often to reaction or withdrawal that it can almost be said to be an occupational neurosis. But the classicists have nearly disappeared; and it is now the scientists who offend. They are slow to give way, having reason to believe that their minds are superior. The common run of people cannot understand their subject and the run of students cannot or will not follow into the esoteric sector of their explorations. Their demonstrated superiority, they are apt to feel, must extend to the simple matters of managing industrial affairs and running the country. About this weakness, I like to use the example of Frederick Soddy, the distinguished chemist, who felt that, by giving some incidental attention to matters the economists managed so unsuccessfully, he could straighten them out.

Soddy was an interesting instance of the singular obtuseness apt to characterize the brilliant scientific mind. He turned, rather late in life—or, at least, after a scientific career had been fully developed—to economics. He was as distinguished in chemistry as anyone in his generation (he was born in 1877 and lived until 1956). He was not only a creative experimenter but a noted expositor; and in 1921 was awarded a Nobel prize. It was in the same year that he lectured to the Student Union at Birkbeck College and The London School of Economics on a subject he chose to call "Cartesian Economics." He was, he said, bringing to bear "the existing knowledge of the physical sciences on economics." It seemed to him so simple that plainly the economists could have fumbled so badly only because they had not studied the scientific method. He ended by saying that Utopia could be reached by "curbing the demon of debt which masquerades among the ignorant as wealth," a simplification that appalled those economists whose attention he caught. He advanced beyond this during the next decade; and in 1932 published a small book called *Money and Man*. He was now every bit as assured that money management was the cure for society's ills. He thereafter formed, and gave a good deal of time to, an association for propagating his ideas. He was much offended because his recommendations were so universally ignored.

This is an exaggerated case. There have been others of milder sorts among the scientists. But it must be said that the classicists who were Huxley's earlier target have remained about as they were then—urbane, superior, and exclusive. When, occasionally, they emerge from their towers, with instruction for responsible officials and pontifical opinions about issues puzzling to lifelong students of politics, they are no more helpful than Soddy was.

Financial independence gave many of the early colleges a certain immunity from the controversies that began almost as soon as the academies and high schools began to be organized. If they had independent Boards of Trustees (usually self-perpetuating), they could define their own duties; or if they were denominational institutions, their biases and dogmas were known and no one had to attend them unwillingly.

It was different when higher education became a public responsibility. State universities, and even more, community colleges, encountered many of the same problems local schools had had to solve. They were besought to teach this and that—or not to teach this or that—and they had to go to an elective body for funds. Those with some interest other than education often had to be recognized. And demand always outran facilities of all kinds, including teachers.

But it went on, and as it did, the impulse to serve all and all alike that had enlarged the elementary school system first and then the high schools, reached higher education. And here new differences about the nature of education complicated the old argument about what children should be taught. No one doubted that there were certain tools a child must acquire in his first years of schooling. Beginning with the three R's this easily extended to advanced mathematics, certain of the sciences, history, the literatures, and the languages. There was some reluctance to recognize that aptitudes were becoming important in high school. But, however belated, recognition came and brought with it a corps of testers, analyzers, and counselors. These, it is true, at first thought themselves responsible for directing students in the way they should go to attain the traditional ends—success and position, mostly. But also they helped in the better adjustment to the purposes they gradually came to understand. The community colleges inherited the civic responsibilities of the high schools, and found them much enlarged.

This was an enormous relief to the universities. It kept away from the already overgrown campuses a threatened flood of students who would not go on to higher levels but would end with no more than an introduction to higher education. The universities could cultivate the more advanced studies, emphasize research, and regain the depth of measured reflection.

But for the colleges there was superhuman work to do. As in the high schools, it had to be recognized that there were the differences between those who would go on and those who would not—the one to be prepared for advanced studies, and the other to find an occupation. But also there was a responsibility to make each group in its degree useful in more than a training sense.

In this interest, and with this duty, educators more and more insist that technical training give way—be put off or limited—until civilization is understood in some depth and breadth. They must find ways of bringing young people into adulthood with their capacities freed, and their cultural and civic responsibilities prepared for, as well as their talents sharpened and exercised.

Fitting such a comprehensive curriculum into one single developing life, not necessarily single-minded about learning, is a technique that will be mastered only by experience and patience. One part of the effort must be that of making the material digestible; and digestibility depends much on method of teaching.

T. H. Huxley on Education

Suppose it were perfectly certain that the life and fortune of every one of us would, one day or other, depend upon his winning or losing a game at chess. . . . Do you not think that we should look with a disapprobation amounting to scorn, upon the father who allowed his son, or the state which allowed its members, to grow up without knowing a pawn from a knight?

Yet, it is a very plain and elementary truth that the life, the fortune, and the happiness of every one of us, and, more or less, of those who are connected with us, do depend upon our knowing something of the rules . . . of a game which has been played for untold ages, every man and woman of us being one of the two players in a game of his or her own. The chess-board is the world, the pieces are the phenomena of the universe, the rules of the game are what we call the laws of nature. The player on the other side is hidden from us. We know that his play is always fair, just, and patient. But also we know, to our cost, that he never overlooks a mistake, or makes the smallest allowance for ignorance. To the man who plays well, the highest stakes are paid, with that sort of overflowing generosity with which the strong shows delight in strength. And one who plays ill is checkmated—without haste, but without remorse.[3]

It seems to me strange that right here a serious quarrel among educators should have developed. As members of a democratic society very few would admit to a set of aims that those on the other side of the controversy do not also hold. But the heat of the exchanges has tended to rise and its smoke to obscure the elements both claim to accept.

The quarrel centers in the region where students are considered ready to enter the preliminary training for engineering, law, medicine, or the other professions. And it has to do with the control of these preprofessional years. The engineers would like to reach down into the colleges and say what will prepare their applicants for success in their schools; so would the medical professors, the lawyers, and even the faculties of schools of administration, journalism, social work, and, if you please, teaching.

The college authorities generally feel the pressure when engineers prescribe a severe regime of mathematics, chemistry, and physics, and physicians one of biology and chemistry. Those faculties are where the Nobel prize winners are and even those not so distinguished as this have formidable prestige. But curriculum makers have their sticking points. Asking themselves what they are there for, they cannot say that it is to prepare students only to be effective professionals. They balk at seeing their educational plans confined in such ways.

It is difficult. Quite clearly, a student who has come through high school and is eighteen, say, and shows a talent of some sort, ought not to be denied the chance to begin the work he feels may be his for life. But college people have seen too many specialists who obviously had no conception of either the need to generalize professionalism or to stay in communication with the rest of society. In fact, they are used to continual harassment in university councils by these insistent colleagues.

But, assuming educators to have carried their point that theirs is a responsibility to the entire society that authorizes their existence,

---

[3] "A Liberal Education: And Where to Find It," *Lay Sermons, Addresses, and Reviews,* D. Appleton & Co., Inc. (New York: 1870). The quotation is from the opening address at the South London Workingmen's College.

and not alone to its professions, they still have the problem of making communicants out of reluctant students who can hardly wait to get into a laboratory or law library, as the young man I spoke of could not. This forces as many compromises as the insistence of the specialized faculties.

The scientists and engineers are not their only problems either. There are students among the freshmen and sophomores who have other talents and different ambitions. They have a literary bent; or their easy familiarity with the philosophers is an obvious indication of their intellectual futures. This might be thought to make participation and communication easier; but every experienced educator has known literary students with a superior talent who are as indifferent to general cultural values as any engineer. Incredible as it may seem to others of their cult, philosophers can also be lost in contemplation of their books, and quite willing to let the rest of the world go its way.

There are those who suggest, following a famous mentor, that the only way to secure our future existence is to foster the development of a governing class. Its practitioners would have acquired the necessary skills from studying the history of governmental institutions, the administration of public bodies (which can become a full course in itself if it goes on to accounting, budgeting, personnel management, the making of legislation, and so on), and the careers of statesmen.

Perhaps we shall come to some variety of civic elite. But there are reasons for thinking it might be as unsatisfactory as letting the engineers take control. Anyone who recalls, or has read about, the tragicomic confrontation of the politicians and the scientists when argument arose about the control of nuclear energy will realize what is meant. Here something that would revolutionize man's relation to nature had come upon a legislative body entirely unaware that it might happen. Hardly one of those who had to deal with it understood where its most spectacular manifestation—the bomb—had come from. And naturally their fear of what it might do was blind and paralyzing. They had no more comprehension of its peaceful potentialities.

The first impulse was concealment so that its potential should be exclusive. The scientists said over and over that, since the nuclear explosion was no more than a last step in a progression reaching far back into the history of science, it could not be monopolized. Science was universal, not national. That last step could be taken by any people in time—the time depending on its system of education and its willingness to commit resources. This, however, was an inadmissible thought.

The politicians did gradually come to some sort of accommodation with the monster in their midst. But the choices given them were all unwelcome. They could try to stop its further progress; they could turn its development and control over to the scientists; they could ask the military to take the responsibility. There was one other—they could set up a public body, responsible to themselves, to go on with its development. This is what they did. They imposed secrecy, regardless of the warnings, and hoped the scientists were wrong.

But the subsequent history was not good. The legislators could demand reports and make policy decisions; but they could never do so with any confidence that they knew what they were doing. The technicians tended to sneer at them; and they resented the sneering. Altogether it was an unhappy affair.

It is fair to ask whether this was a failure of the educational system. Certainly many of the scientists, all through the years of adjustment, made efforts to reach the politicians' minds, often ending by being convinced that they could manage public affairs far better than those in charge of them, and sometimes attempting to convince the public that this was so. And the politicians tended to turn sullen, to belittle amateurs' interference in political matters about which they were hopelessly ignorant.

When the Russians reached the point of perfecting a bomb, too, all the security measures, all the restrictions, were shown to be as ridiculous as the inventors had been saying all along that they were. The only effect of these measures was to deprive the nation of exchanges with others whose knowledge could well have been used to advantage.

Ought we to have developed scientists who not only could make a bomb but could communicate about it with public authorities? And ought we to have provided ourselves with public men who understood that it could neither be suppressed nor controlled by the clumsy means they attempted to use? I should like to urge that if an improved educational system cannot do this we are lost. This incident was so plain a lesson and its consequences so momentous that if we cannot learn from it, we cannot learn from anything.

But there are those in the educational world—and they seem still to be in the majority—who have remained unconvinced, and many even unaffected. They desire to cultivate their professions; and have the highest aims for their perfection. But the spectacle of ignorance confronting revolutionary science is something they have missed. Indeed, they are blind to it.

Mill on the University's Function

The proper function of a University in national education is tolerably well understood. At least there is a tolerably general agreement about what a University is not. It is not a place of professional education. Universities are not intended to teach the knowledge required to fit men for some special mode of gaining their livelihood. It is very right that there should be public facilities for the study of the professions. . . . But these things are not part of what every generation owes to the next, as that on which its civilization and worth will principally depend. . . .

Education makes a man a more intelligent shoemaker, if that be his occupation, but not by teaching him to make shoes. . . .[4]

This is perhaps because educators habitually think of politicians—and this includes all those with public powers—as inferior in intelligence, comic fellows, largely windy, hypocritical, and even often corrupt. But educators are not concerned to do anything about it. There is still a tendency to regard politicians as unimportant.

Buchanan and McKinley let wars happen that might have been stopped; a depression nearly ruined the economy not too long ago and public policy is known to have been crucial in its onset and its deepening. Politicians were Commanders-in-Chief in two World Wars and made the peace for us.

No, it is not a tenable position that the dialogue between the governing establishment and the technical and managerial elite is unimportant. It is vital. Indeed, it can be argued that the survival of our civilization is dependent on the establishment of communications between the movers and shapers and the planners and managers—just as Mill said it was.

Sir Charles P. Snow has been talking around this subject in a kind of baffled way for some time. The particular value of his concern

[4] John Stuart Mill, Inaugural Address at St. Andrews, 1867.

is that he is at least listened to by both "cultures" as he calls them. When he used the illustration of Professor Lindemann to show the dangers of scientific obtuseness, he caused some temperatures to rise. But on the whole the controversy is much less excited and intense than that between the scientists and the theologues in the post-Darwinian period. This may be because T. H. Huxley and Bishop Wilberforce were laboring over men's immortal souls and the Snow-Lindemann controversy concerned only their mortal bodies.

Snow on Communication

There have been plenty of days when I have spent the working hours with scientists and then gone off at night with some literary colleagues. I mean that literally. I have, of course, intimate friends among both scientists and writers. . . . Constantly I felt I was moving among two groups—comparable in intelligence, identical in race, not grossly different in social origin, earning about the same incomes, who had almost ceased to communicate at all, who in intellectual, moral and psychological climate had so little in common that instead of going from Burlington House or South Kensington to Chelsea, one might have crossed an ocean.[5]

I am reminded by Sir Charles' reminiscence of an incident told me by a busy Governor. A priest came to remonstrate with him about a policy that, the father said, would be permanently damaging to the Commonwealth. The Governor had to tell him that their definitions of permanence might be quite different. The Governor, telling me about his reply to the clergyman, was obviously pleased with himself; but he did add what I considered a defensive line. "I do have to think of the next election." What he did not say was whether his answer had given other satisfaction than that he himself felt. I am sure it had not; but perhaps there had been a significant communication. And that is what is really important.

Snow defines the difficulty with the emphasis of simplicity. The practitioners of the two cultures do not have to agree; but they ought to understand each other's arguments. Above all they ought to respect each other's activities. Even when these are beyond our comprehension,

[5] *The Two Cultures and the Scientific Revolution*, The Rede Lecture, Cambridge University Press (New York: 1959).

their effect can be a matter for discussion. The two intellectual coteries, Sir Charles is afraid, have grown farther apart, less tolerant of each other, more exclusive. The scientists talk to each other in symbols and the literary folk simply ignore the existence of the individuals who are changing the environment. Literature, as a result, keeps to old and simple themes; and the scientists regard writers as having had an arrested development.

Aldous Huxley has more recently addressed himself to this literary-scientific lack of communication, and done it somewhat more cogently than Snow. His demonstration of how to write a modern poem about a nightingale shows how glaring the ignorance of literateurs has been and what they must know to meet his criterion. "If . . . art is inept, our experience will be vulgarized and corrupted," he says. "Along with unrealistic philosophy and religious superstition, bad art is a crime against society." Being himself a descendant of T. H. Huxley and familiar with ecology, he used the nightingale to illustrate his lesson.[6]

Huxley, like Snow, is concerned with *two* cultures; but surely there are three. The third includes all those who are working in a segment of learning and practice that is of at least equal importance. The social sciences seem to have been overlooked; and these include public law and politics, economics, sociology, and anthropology. I do not know how to classify history, but certainly it is neither a science nor an exclusively literary art; it belongs to literature only a little more than to science.

The system of mutual understanding here is just as badly in need of repair as that failure Snow has been dwelling on. Some decades ago economists began to be chided for not having brought into their discipline the developments in industry that were revolutionizing productive activities and making communication and transportation swifter. These were raising the *standards* of living, but not rapidly enough the *levels* of living, and economists were not being helpful in closing the gap.[7]

Science was responsible, but only partly, for the rush of developments during the decades of the World Wars—unless, of course, planning and management are called sciences; and Snow certainly has not meant to include them. The rapid changes and wrenching adjustments

[6] Aldous Huxley, "How to Write a Modern Poem about a Nightingale," *Science and Literature*, Harper & Row (New York: 1963).

[7] Cf. *The Trend of Economics*, Alfred A. Knopf (New York: 1924), a symposium; and the author's *Industry's Coming of Age*, Harcourt, Brace & Co. (New York: 1927).

all through society presented problems for government at all levels, bringing a need for reorganizations political theorists were not eager to tackle.[8] And sociologists had a whole new corpus of material to organize. Historians were presented with demands for explanation that their older brethren had not provided. And there began what can only be described as a new kind of history, that devoted to social, economic, and political issues rather than to the chronicles of public affairs so familiar to the student of other days.

The historians did more to explain the social sciences to their contemporaries than scholars from the other disciplines were able to do. They often had something of the novelist's or poet's arts; and they were better able to communicate than economists or political scholars. They even had some recognition for this talent from the literary critics, grudging and meager, but perhaps growing. The situation today is that the critics I speak of would certainly look at, or perhaps read, the works of Schlesinger, Commager, Nevins, Johnson, Boorstin, and Hofstadter (there are so many creative historians alive and writing now that I am reluctant to mention names because of many I would forget). But I should be surprised to hear that those same critics could name, much less claim to have read, the more important books of the economists, the political theorists, or the sociologists. I seldom meet one who has come further than Veblen—and they are uncertain about him, having read only his least important book (*The Theory of the Leisure Class*) many years ago.

The historians—at least those of the sort I have mentioned above— have had to inform themselves even if it meant penetrating a forbidding gloss of language peculiar to each of the disciplines. And they have very often established the communication that is so badly needed.

T. H. Huxley on the Educated Man

That man, I think, has had a liberal education who has been so trained in youth that his body is the ready servant of his will, and does with ease and pleasure all the work that, as a mechanism, it is capable of; whose intellect is a clear, cold, logic engine, with all its parts of equal strength, and in smooth working order; ready, like a steam engine, to be turned to any kind of work, and spin the gos-

[8] Cf. the author's *The Industrial Discipline and the Governmental Arts* (New York: 1933).

samers as well as forge the anchors of the mind; whose mind is stored with a knowledge of the great and fundamental truths of nature and of the laws of her operations; one who, no stunted ascetic, is full of life and fire, but whose passions are trained to come to heel by a vigorous will, the servant of a tender conscience; who has learned to love all beauty, whether of nature or of art, to hate all vileness, and to respect others as himself.[9]

Snow feels, he says, that the drifting apart he speaks of can be arrested if we will pay more attention to education. This will not be a "total solution," but without it "the West can't even begin to cope." But he does not say what kind of education, and with what devices. This is equally true if we speak of three instead of two cultures.

Concerning the mutual understanding of all three cultures, we are entitled, I think, to call attention to the effort of American colleges during the last four decades as the most hopeful, perhaps we are even allowed to say, the most successful so far undertaken. It was in the first full academic year after World War I that Columbia College began its courses in Contemporary Civilization. The movement was led by John J. Coss, of the Philosophy Department, abetted by the Dean of the College, Herbert E. Hawkes. For the elective courses in the social studies one comprehensive course was substituted and required. The intention was to raise in students' minds the issues they would be confronted with, to reach back toward their beginnings, and feel for solutions. The Departments of Philosophy, History, Government, Sociology, and Economics were represented. Each instructor had one or two groups of about thirty students; and he went through the whole year with them, meeting daily for an hour.

The intimacy of those meetings, probing issues in all the fields, had the quality of the mythical Hopkins on his end of the log and the student on the other.

The movement spread. The physical scientists were induced to prepare a course of their own. It came at a logical moment, just when even the most specialized physicists and chemists were acknowledging that old distinctions were no longer tenable. But, even more important, it was intended for the student who would never be a scientist of any

9 "A Liberal Education: and Where to Find It."

kind. It was meant to catch his interest to show him the nature of science and the inevitable direction of its unfolding.

No student who went through Columbia College in the twenties was surprised by the nuclear bomb in the forties. A good many others were not surprised either—those who had gone to colleges where similar programs were developed. They spread very rapidly; by 1930 it was exceptional for any college to have escaped the movement.[10] The University of Chicago had made notable contributions, with Harvard, slow to give up a well-fixed tradition of electives, coming along a good deal later, but making characteristic superior sounds when it did so.

But something else of importance happened at Columbia in the twenties. Students who had shown promise, and had no professional intentions, were allowed to take honors courses during their upper-class years. The method in these courses was to read and discuss selected original works—from the early classics (translated) to those at the foundation of modern civilization. John Erskine, Professor of English, took the lead in this. He also took advice; and the Great Books read by that generation of students were scientific, political, and economic as well as what is usually called literary. It was a revealing experience to discover that Descartes and Darwin, Adam Smith and Comte could actually be read just as Shakespeare or Cervantes could.

What is significant about these developments is that they proved to be the beginning of two lines of experiment. They have been extending ever since. Comprehensive courses were not so much copied from early models as taken from them as a starting place. This is a general attack on the very problem with which Snow is so concerned. It has its significance in the fact that so many of those of appropriate age in the United States are actually in college, and that the proportion is increasing. And everyone knows the impact of the Great Books idea, not only in institutions but in the enormous development of adult education.

But university people ought to consider their effort of two generations as no more than a beginning. Communications are not yet adequate. The Departments of English and those of Economics still do not share many interests; and neither understands the symbols used quite ordinarily by the scientists. None of them is carrying far enough the

[10] *Redirecting Education*, Columbia University Press (New York: 1934), edited by the author, was published in the midst of this movement. *Cf.*, also, successive editions of syllabi for the courses, as well as special readings developed for them.

preparation of their students to understand the world of technology they live in. But progress is being made.

When Theodore Roosevelt in 1881, feeling a strong but bizarre attraction, went around to the Republican Club rooms in his Assembly District of New York City and volunteered his services, friends in that silk-stocking district remonstrated. Politics, they told him, was an ignoble business carried on by inferior persons. He retorted that they seemed to govern the country; and as for him, he intended to become a member of the governing class.

There remain, perhaps, remnants of that superior attitude toward public affairs, and especially toward the activities that result in elections, but it is only a remnant. Very few professional politicians have not been through one of those collegiate educations whose most important feature is the comprehensive course. In future even those Congressional committees dealing with the impact of revolutions prepared by the scientists will be, if not wiser, certainly more knowledgeable.

The point about this is that these comprehensive courses are in constant development. As faculties become clearer about the intention, their procedures and teaching are improved. By now most of those who are in charge of these educational enterprises have themselves had experience of them as students. It may be, as Snow says, that the misunderstandings are growing worse rather than better; but there are certainly modifying circumstances.

What tends to increase differences, of course, is the progress of technology and the esoteric nature of its various practitioners. It may still be true that some of them only feel really comfortable in association with the few of their own specialty. But there have been some shocking lessons. The worst of them was undoubtedly the confrontation of the Congressional Committees with the problem of the nuclear bomb. The struggle to decide what to do about its development was a horrible one for all concerned. It may not have produced an immediate mutual understanding; but those who participated, or even watched it, were made deeply aware of the dangers underlying the immediate issue. This was clearly enough defined as the gross ignorance within each group of technologists—scientific and politico-economic—about the work of the other.

This, I believe, ought not to worry us, as committed democrats, nearly so much as another effect of progress. This is the rapid lifting of the qualifications for participation. We hear a good deal about high-school drop-outs but not so much about the collegiate ones. Not more than half of those who begin college manage to finish. At all levels it is a problem of the same nature if not of the same serious consequences. A hundred years ago, a young person who could learn to read and write and cipher could have a life almost undistinguishable from those of others in his generation. Those same young people today are turned back to their parents unable to participate in any general activity going on around them. They are not allowed to work until they have reached a minimum age; and then they are often baffled by requirements they cannot meet. The number grows in proportion to the population because technology reaches more and more activities. Those who really cannot participate in any meaningful way in modern life may already have reached a majority if all those above fifteen years are considered.

These millions will never have any interest in the activities of the elite. And because they are not useful, the elite tends to ignore the problem they pose. This is progressive. At each level of qualification those who are eliminated fall into a distressed and neglected class. It has long since begun to haunt society. It produces, at its lower reach, juvenile delinquents and, at its upper one, the resentful nonparticipant who at the least becomes anti-intellectual.

I must confess that communication among the three cultures worries me far less than the nonparticipation of those we have no use for. What is it that we see as our future in this democracy? Its rewards cannot conceivably be, like the Heaven of some sects, reserved for the elect. For each of us, according to our qualifications, there must be a place. If we may not be participants of one sort, we surely can be of another. There are some of us who can recall an America without any such problem. In the village life of my youth there was a gradual settling down, in each generation, to the work and enjoyments of our choice. They may not have been as exciting as those of a later technological world, but they were more comprehensive. It is not beyond our wit or our sympathy to substitute for the devices of the village, ones as satisfactory for the metropoli most of us live in. We ought to be more seriously concerned about it. This is not to say that we ought not to go on with productive progress, and progress, too, in communication; but looking at both problems, it is really hard to choose the more demanding.

5

The

Liberating Arts

and the

Humanizing Arts

in Education

Richard P. McKeon

"The liberal arts are the arts of freedom," Robert M. Hutchins reminded us twenty years ago. "To be free a man must understand the arts of freedom." In much the same fashion the humanities are the arts of humanity. To be human a man must understand what has been accomplished and what can be accomplished by the arts of man. The liberating and the humanizing arts are as interdependent as the possibility of doing and knowing and the power of doing and knowing. The history of education has been an interplay between conceptions of freedom and conceptions of value. In Plato's *Republic* the education of the guardians was designed to make them "artisans of the freedom of the city," and they built their guardhouse for the exercise of this art in "culture." (The fact that "music" no longer conveys what Plato meant by *mousike* is in itself a capsule history of "culture" and the "humanities.") Twenty-five hundred years later "general education" was the name given to a revolution in education designed to rediscover the arts to make men free and the arts to discern and understand the problems men must face and the values they might achieve.

In a free culture the humanizing arts would be the liberating arts; man would become a man by becoming a free man. Yet in the history of education the liberal arts have undergone cumulative divisions into philological and scientific techniques by which to investigate various kinds of expressions or forms and various kinds of things or processes, and in the history of those segmentations, conflicts are periodically discovered between two or three or more cultures, such as the humanities, science, religion, the social sciences. Education in the humanities has therefore tended to divide the fine arts from the mechanical and the intellectual arts to investigate the commonplaces and styles of "periods" and "cultures," and in the process conflicts are discovered between two or more cultures, such as elite and mass cultures, civilized and barbarian cultures, Western and Eastern cultures.

If one speculates concerning the future of humanistic education in the light of its past, the problem of identifying and relating the liberal arts and the humanistic arts is at the center of all other problems. The history of humanistic education is a series of conflicts and segregations; the stages of the history have been the discovery, step by step, that the separations were unwarranted and unprofitable; but in the development of the new integrated humanism the same separations and oppositions made their reappearance in modified form. There have been many "battles of the books" which have set "ancient" in opposition to "modern" and "tradition" in opposition to "innovation." The programs of education arrayed in each skirmish were unmistakably different, but a refined dialectic is needed to show the senses in which they might be thought to contribute to "liberal" education, until hostilities were reconciled in an innovation based on the common tradition they defended. There have been recurrent battles of "practical" and "theoretical," which have set "education of character" in opposition to "education of thought" and the "whole man" in opposition to the "intellect." The programs of vocational and academic education set students performing different exercises, but they had no bearing on humanity or human conduct except at those moments of renovation when human experience and ordering principles of human action were brought into relation with each other. We are engaged in the same disputes today. Whether we hope to learn from experience or from invention, an examination of the ways in which like controversies have been resolved or forgotten in the past is relevant to our present efforts to determine what arts liberate and humanize, and how tradition and innovation may be used to influence character and thought in ways which increase men's freedom and humanity.

The ancient Romans have provided us with an influential model of these oppositions as well as with vocabularies to express the differences and with precepts and facts to fix their meanings. The Romans were suspicious of the refinements and pedantry of education based on the Greek classics; they also invented the term *Humanitas* and they canonized and enumerated the *artes liberales*. *Humanitas* has followed the historical trend to fragmentation, first, by becoming a comparative adjective attached to "letters" in *litterae humaniores* and, then, by becoming a plural substantive in "the humanities" which preserves the plurality of subjects but obliterates the last trace of reference to humanity. The liberal arts underwent a like evolution becoming at the outset, seven arts (three of words and four of things) in which the investigation of principles gives way to the investigation of terms and experience and, then, becoming the subject matter of the "arts and sciences" taught in "liberal arts colleges" in which the multiplicity and fixity of facts are adjusted to freedom by instituting the rules of a game and the rules of a language.

The delicacies and subtleties of Greek literature and learning were thought to be a danger to the native Roman virtues on which the greatness of Rome was nourished. Greek rhetoricians and philosophers were expelled from Rome in 161 B.C., and Latin schools of rhetoric were closed in 92 B.C. The opposition to the study of alien, that is, Greek, classics is stated early and forcefully by Cato the Elder. Athens had been found guilty of an act of aggression against a neighboring town, Oropus, and had been fined 500 talents. To appeal the fine the Athenians used the shrewd device of sending an embassy composed of the heads of three philosophic schools—the Peripatetics, the Stoics, and the Academics—to Rome in 156 B.C. The philosophers used the leisure of their visit to give lectures to Roman audiences. Cato, doubtless alarmed in particular by Carneades' skeptical lectures concerning justice, moved in the Senate that the business on which the Athenian envoys had come to Rome be concluded as expeditiously as possible in order that the envoys might return to their classes in Athens, leaving the youth of Rome to seek their instruction as before from the wise conversation and example of her public men. Cato also contributed positively to the formation of an education for Roman character based on Roman tradition. He wrote a book of guidance for his son, *Praecepta ad Filium,* in which he warned him against Greek physicians and Greek literature which he said was worthy of inspection but not of study, and a set of maxims for everyday life in verse, *Carmen de Moribus*. His *Origines* is the first history of Rome, and his *De Agricultura* is the earliest extant Latin prose work, and therefore destined to become a subject in later humanistic studies based on Latin as well as Greek classics, and a reminder of the link between the culture of the mind, the cult of God, and the cultivation of fields and flocks.

The same art of rhetoric was employed to argue no less cogently that Roman modes of life and thought stood in need of the foundation, ordering, and embellishment provided by the Greek arts. The group of men Scipio Africanus the younger gathered about him, which has come to be known as the "Scipionic circle," included historians, philosophers, poets, soldiers, statesmen, and men of affairs. Cicero gives a dramatic presentation of their manner of inquiry and discussion in the *De Re Publica;* practical men, adherents of different philosophic schools, go to Roman experience to improve on Greek political theory. Cicero also uses the words *humanitas* and *artes liberales* in the characteristic meanings they assume when the arts are used to advance humanity and freedom. He conceived of humanity not in terms of bodily mechanisms or psychic sensitivities but in terms of the arts, and he held that all the arts which pertain to humanity are held together by a common bond and kinship. Later Latin writers elaborated this idea and argued that humanity is known best by study of the great achievements of the arts, that the word *humanitas* is a translation of the Greek *paideia* and means, not "philanthropy," but "education," "learning," "culture." The liberal arts likewise were the arts of the free man and therefore contrasted to the vulgar or mechanical arts, but the emphasis was not on the contrast between intellectual and manual but on the disciplines by which knowledge is applied to statement and action. The earliest enumeration of the liberal arts in Varro's *Disciplinarum Libri Novem* lists nine arts, the seven which were to constitute the mediaeval trivium and quadrivium—grammar, logic, rhetoric, geometry, arithmetic, astronomy, and music—plus medicine and architecture. The liberal arts constituted a cycle or circle of learning to which the Romans applied the Greek phrase *enkuklios paideia*. Like the conception of humanity, the conception of encyclopaedic learning is a Roman adaptation of *paideia*.

The contribution of the Romans to the formation of the liberal and humanistic arts may be used as a key to understanding later problems of the humanities and the arts. The arts were not invented or systematized by the Romans. They were invented, for the most part, by ancient Greek philosophers. They were elaborated and schematized in handbooks of rules and collections of materials by Hellenistic scholars. The Roman transformation is determined by their use of one of the arts, rhetoric, and by their consequent attention to communication, invention, commonplaces. They did not conceive of the liberal arts as methods of systematizing philosophy or organizing erudition but as preprofessional education and as compendia of information. The rare occurrences of the phrase *enkuklios paideia* are symptomatic. Vitruvius and Quintilian use it in describing the education a man should have if he wishes to become an architect or an orator or lawyer. Pliny the Elder uses it to explain his organization and presentation of facts in the *Natural History*. The circle of learning was put to practical uses and concrete applications. Roman education and learning reflect the Roman rhetorical tendency to adapt tradition to innovation and to simplify theory to practical uses. Invention is one of the basic parts of rhetoric; Cicero's *De Inventione* has been a widely used and influential textbook, and later speculations concerning the discovery of arguments, of things, and of arts repeat and adapt its distinctions. Education in the arts proceeded in three stages based on the distinction rhetoricians made of natural ability, practice or experience (guided by a model of excellence), and the principles or rules of the art. Both tendencies, that based on nature and that based on invention, are translated without distortion into the terms in which modern concerns are expressed. Nature was recognized in aptitudes, experience in achievements, art in ability to apply principles; and all three were measured by invention or creativity.

The seven liberal arts, the trivium and the quadrivium, underwent during the Middle Ages a diversified history of development which we tend still to reduce to the simplicities of the ancient oppositions: we set the "dark ages" of illiberal and antihumanistic apriorisms and verbalisms described by the humanists as the slumber preceding their Renaissance against the numerous recent scholarly reports concerning mediaeval humanisms and renaissances. In all three monotheistic religions, those who feared the pagan arts and learning as distractions from the good life or as sources of error were opposed to those who sought to use human knowledge to supplement and support human formulations of divine wisdom. In all three traditions, as knowledge of the pagan arts and learning increased the opposition became one between those who made philosophy the handmaiden of theology and those who distinguished two independent but noncontradictory ways in the method of theology and the method of philosophy. Finally, with the increase of "secularism" it became an opposition between Christian philosophy and philosophies which sought to adapt scientific methods to the solution of philosophic problems. If there have been conflicts between religion and the humanities, religion has also laid foundations for a new humanism and has given new extensions to the arts of freedom, and what has survived of the pagan classics owes its preservation to the interests and industry of Christian, Muslim, and Jewish scribes and priests.

In all the religious traditions which came into contact with the culture of Greece and Rome, the development of the liberal arts and the humanities was related to the interpretation of the law. Similar problems were faced in the course of those evolutions, and the high Middle Ages was one of the periods of rare intellectual communication when the learned men of Islam, Judaism, and Christianity were able to borrow distinctions, engage in disputation, and hope to reach agreement by argument. Nonetheless the course of the evolution and of the disputation was different in each culture. In Western Christianity, the liberal arts were strongly influenced by the development of canon law, in the institutional framework of the Church, in which rhetorical methods were used to work out the concordance of discordant canons in law and by the adaptation of those devices in the scholastic method to work out the resolution of questions in theology and philosophy. In Eastern Christianity, the liberal arts were based on the methods of the interpretation of texts and worked out the grammar of dogmatic and heretical ideological positions. In Islam, the liberal arts were elaborated to relate the various branches of science to the discourse of revelation or the *kalam:* the Mu'tazilites, the first speculative theologians of Islam, used reason in the interpretation of revelation, arguing that reason is a natural light and that both religion and the world are rational, while the Ash'arites argued that God's freedom cannot be constrained by prior laws of reason. Mohammedan philosophers—Alkindi, Alfarabi, Avicenna, and Averroes—unlike Christian philosophers, were not theologians, while orthodox theologians limited themselves to borrowing arguments against the philosophers from the Stoics and the Skeptics but without committing themselves to materialism or skepticism. Algazali came to the defense of orthodoxy in the *Restoration of Religious Knowledge,* and he attacked the philosophers in a work known during the Middle Ages as *The Destruction of the Philosophers* (a more accurate translation of its title is *The Incoherence of the Philosophers*), the last section of which deals with the confusions of the philosophers in the natural sciences. Averroes answered Algazali's arguments in *The Destruction of the Destruction* (or *The Incoherence of the Incoherence*). This mode of opposition is resumed eight hundred years later, with appropriate changes of the opponent to philosophy from theology to economics, when Marx answered Proudhon's *The Philosophy of Poverty* (or *The Philosophy of Misery*) with *The Poverty of Philosophy* (or *The Misery of Philosophy*). In Judaism, the liberal arts elaborated the Talmudic methods of interpreting and applying the Torah with devices adapted from Plato's dialectic (which Plato was alleged to have borrowed from Moses) until Maimonides recodified the law in his *Mishneh Torah* (*Repetition of the Law*) and brought metaphysics to the support of revelation in his *Guide of the Perplexed.*

Culture and science in the West grew out of the development of the seven liberal arts of the trivium (grammar, rhetoric, and logic) and the quadrivium (arithmetic, geometry, astronomy, and music). When translations from the Arabic, like Domingo Gundisalvo's translation of Alfarabi's *De Scientiis* or his longer presentation in the *De Divisione Philosophiae,* began to appear in the twelfth century, new sciences like algebra, statics (or the science of weights) and perspective (or optics) were fitted easily into the familiar framework, and the system of the liberal arts, in its Arabic development as method and system of the sciences was one of the instrumentalities used by the Latin World in ordering the enormous educational and cultural changes which resulted when the Aristotelian sciences and scientific method became available for the first time in the West in the thirteenth century. The application of the liberal arts to this new body of scientific material once again took two directions which were developed in controversial opposition: Bonaventura in his *Reduction of the Arts to Theology* and Roger Bacon in his formulation of the method of "experimental science" sought to unify the methods of science and theology; Albertus Magnus and Thomas Aquinas sought to distinguish the methods, objectives, and subject matters of theology from those of the sciences and applied the distinction to theology itself to separate the *a priori* propositions of revealed theology from the *a posteriori* inquiry of natural theology. We have only recently begun to study again the rich developments in logic under the influence of Raymond Lully, Duns Scotus, and William of Ockham because modern scholars could continue to repeat Renaissance criticisms of the verbalism and eristic subtlety of late Mediaeval logic until developments in symbolic logic and mathematical physics awakened us to an awareness of the meaning and relevance of fourteenth-century logical innovations.

The transformation of the liberal arts during the Renaissance and the effects of those transformations on the seventeenth and eighteenth centuries have blunted our appreciation of the long history of changing interpretations and applications of the liberal arts. The Renaissance transformation was strongly influenced by Cicero; his attachment to the arts of humanity was modified in humanism to an attachment to the study of Greek and Latin classics; and his topics for the discovery of arguments were applied to experience for the discovery of all manners of things. The art of rhetoric provided the instrumentalities for the transition from words and arguments to things and facts. Rudolph Agricola sought to remedy the errors of Scholastic logic by recourse to invention in his *De Inventione Dialectica,* and he related philological studies and the whole man in education in his *De Formando Studio.* Peter Ramus reformulated the liberal arts with a like emphasis on rhetoric and dialectic. Marius Nizolius attacked pseudo-philosophers and found the true method of philosophizing in rhetoric in his *De Veris Principiis et Vera Ratione Philosophandi contra Pseudophilosophos* (a work which Leibniz later edited). Francis Bacon turned from the commonplaces of rhetoric to establish the proper places of a new instrument, a *Novum Organum,* for the discovery of things and of arts. Innovation is not unambiguously separate from tradition in the new sciences or the new education. Copernicus begins the exposition of his new theory in the *De Revolutionibus Orbium Caelestium* by discussing the place of the study of the stars among the disciplines of letters and arts (*literarum artiumque studia*), judging it a divine rather than a human science (*divina haec magis quam humana scientia*) because of its subject matter; and he passes ancient theories in review, remarking in his Preface that he first read in Cicero that Nicetus thought the earth moved and later learned in Plutarch that others shared this opinion. Fermat established a new approach to number theory by writing equations in the margins of his copy of Diophantus. Descartes moved from algebra (which Alfarabi described as one of the sciences—"Mucabala" is another—which combine the treatment of number and geometry) and devised analytic geometry to resolve problems of Pappus and Apollonius. As a final twist to the paradox, the art of discovery was sought in different directions, in the places and tables of inductive logic which Ramus and Bacon borrowed from rhetoric and in the deductions of Euclidean geometry which Descartes and Huygens used as a heuristic method.

As in previous cases of opposition in the development of the arts the terms in which the opposition is formulated are ambiguous, but although either side might claim "innovation" or "tradition," "the whole man" or "mind," a new humanities, a new science, and a new education emerged without ambiguity from the transformation. The nature of the difference between the mediaeval liberal and humanistic arts and the modern liberal and humanistic arts is already apparent in the Renaissance treatises of erudition, education, and information, to which the term "encyclopaedia" was applied indifferently. A great many treatises, letters, and orations were written on the nature or the order of studies, such as Lionardo Bruni's *De Studiis et Literis,* Erasmus's *De Ratione Studii,* and Joachim Fortius Ringelbergh's work of the same name, which was often published with Erasmus's essay. All three reappear among the twenty-four essays published under the title *H. Grotii et Aliorum Dissertationes de Studiis Instituendis* in 1645, some of which are included in a collection published under the title *Gerardi Io. Vossii et Aliorum Dissertationes de Studiis bene Instituendis* in 1658, and in the collections edited by Thomas Crenius, *De Philologia, Studiis Liberalis Doctrinae, Informatione et Educatione Litteraria Generosorum Adolescentum* in 1696 and *De Eruditione Comparanda* in 1699. The nature and causes of the changes in the arts are given many expositions of which one of the most elaborate is set forth by Juan Luis Vives in twenty books *On the Disciplines* (1531) which he divided into three parts, seven books on the causes of the decay of the arts, five on the disciplines to be inculcated or on Christian instruction, and eight on expounding the disciplines. In the oscillation between emphasis on method and on facts the restoration of the liberal arts was sought in facts which might be found in the cultivation of religion, in the study of letters, or in the investigation of nature. The continuing paradox is that it is both true that the method of reading Scriptures, Classics, and the Book of Nature are similar, since God geometrized, and also that religious, humanistic, and scientific education and erudition are set in opposition to one another.

Throughout the history of the liberal and the humanistic arts there has been an interplay between consideration of disciplines or methods suited to the treatment of subject matters or problems and consideration of data or facts which depend on methods of interpretation, use, and ordering. During the Middle Ages the organization of the arts was by disciplines; after the Renaissance they were reorganized according to subject matters. During the Middle Ages "literature" was not a liberal art; the methods for the study of letters were found in grammar or rhetoric; Cassiodorus divided his *Institutiones* into two parts, one concerned with *divinae litterae* devoted to the arts of interpreting Scripture and the other concerned with *saeculares litterae* devoted to the seven liberal arts, and in the later Middle Ages "poetics" became a part of logic. Philology in Martianus Cappella's *Marriage of Mercury and Philology* was the "love of reason" and Mercury was "eloquence." During the Middle Ages, this satura contributed to the interpretation of three sisters, Philology, Philosophy, and Philocaly—Love of Reason, Love of Wisdom, and Love of Beauty. After the Renaissance, philology became one of the basic studies of the new erudition, in which the science and history of literature made their beginning. During the Middle Ages history made use of the methods of the liberal arts, particularly those of rhetoric; after Jean Bodin the method of history was given special consideration and the materials and parts of history were examined by historical methods. In the same fashion, philosophy, which had been the sum of the liberal arts, the discipline of disciplines, became one discipline among disciplines; the history and organization of philosophy had a modern beginning. The mediaeval quadrivium was the sciences of things as distinguished from the sciences of words; the modern sciences took their beginnings in applications of those mathematical sciences to processes and phenomena by use of methods of discovery elaborated from rhetoric and methods of analysis borrowed from sophistic.

Literature, history, and philosophy were involved in a new form of the ancient controversies in their modern development. From the seventeenth century to the present the issue between those who sought to use the methods of the sciences and those who sought to develop distinctive and supplementary methods for knowledge of nature and humane knowledge has run through many stages. The sciences of society and of man, the social and behavioral sciences, came into separate being in time to become involved in a particularization of that dispute in the opposition of those who argue that the sciences of man have not kept pace with the sciences of nature and those who show that the natural sciences have not been adjusted to the values of man and society.

The liberal arts as subject matters have continued the process of discrimination and division which was initiated in the identification of their fields. Literature, history, and philosophy were divided into ancient and modern; each was subdivided according to periods and places; and finally literary criticism was separated from the history of literature, philosophizing was freed from the encumbrance of the history of philosophy, and history dispensed of any need to consider values of art or principles of philosophy before explaining both away as parts or consequences of history. Physical science, biological science, and social science went through like processes of division and subdivision according to subject matters and problems. It is a process which has come to be known as the "fragmentation" of knowledge, and the remedies proposed for it have general appellations appropriate to this diagnosis, such as "interdisciplinary cooperation," "cross-fertilization," and "unification of the sciences," but they have had little effect on the separation of sciences except occasionally to add a new independent intermediary science to the list, or to specialize the study of cultures to "areas."

We have been led to believe by humanistic critics that the mediaeval liberal arts went to seed as educational methods because in their emphasis on discipline, method, and artifice they became verbal, logic-chopping, and abstract, and lost all relevance to the processes of nature and the operations of human life. We have been led to believe by critics of the separation and conflict of cultures that the modern liberal arts —as letters and science, or as human, social, and natural sciences—have become sterile educational material because in their emphasis on subject matter, experience, and nature they have become factual, pragmatic, and technical and have lost the communication with each other and the over-all intelligibility which are based on common principles and conducive to co-operative use. The simplicity of the pattern of complaints about the degradation of the liberal arts is adequate to the rhetoric of controversy about the arts but throws little light on the facts of their history. However, the ordinary language of propaganda often provides the leading principles of liberating and humanizing movements. The vocabulary of the fourteenth century developed its basic terms in terministic logic, speculative grammar, speculative mathematics, and sophistical resolution. The language of practical and intellectual reform today adapts its terms to facts and data, actions and rules, experience and existence, language and history. The remedy for excessive formalism is respect for, and organization of, facts and processes. The remedy for excessive empiricism is inquiry for, and elaboration of, principles and theoretical structures. When Hutchins proclaimed the slogan "Back to Galen" the return he advocated was from exclusive reliance on factual information to recognition that the discovery of principles is essential in the revolution by which science takes the place of informed opinion and by which scientific data take the place of observed facts. He argued that all education, not medical education alone, showed the effects of forgetting the lesson of Galen. "We have witnessed a shift of emphasis throughout education from thought to information, from idea to fact." Hutchins did not convince his opponents, but the programs and methods of general education, liberal education, and higher learning have influenced the practices of universities throughout the United States and in many distant parts of the world and account for fundamental differences in education today and forty years ago.

The problems of the liberating and the humanizing arts cannot be stated adequately in the simple pattern of rhetoric about the arts. "General education" was conceived as a way of giving new effectiveness and content to "liberal education," but in the controversy concerning arts viewed as subject matters the protagonists in the debate have separated and opposed general education and liberal education. The new critics of "general education" argue that it is broad and superficial and therefore has no bearing on higher education or later life, whereas a "liberal education" must acquaint the student with what men know in particular fields and with what men do in particular communities, cultures, and circumstances. In recent stages of the debate the question seems to have become whether a liberal education consists in studying the natural sciences, the social sciences, and the humanities to acquire skills and information which apply to particular fields of knowledge or whether it consists in studying biochemistry, mathematics, sociology, or linguistics to acquire skills and information fundamental to other fields or to all fields. It is a trivial question because it suggests no criterion by which it could be answered: men have been liberally educated by general studies and by specific studies, and both varieties of studies have failed to provide a liberal education. The difference exploited in the controversy disappears when one begins to inquire concerning what disciplines and principles are common to several subject matters, or particular to one subject matter, and how they are related to each other. The controversy has a familiar form: it is similar to our formulation of the problems of community and society in our concern with conformists and eccentrics, status seekers and beatniks, as an opposition between consensus and pluralism. If that were a simple antithesis, community would be impossible, for consensus without deviation is a mechanism or a herd or a despotism, and pluralism without agreement is a chaos or a segmentation or a war of all against all.

Even a sampling of the past of humanistic education produces evidence that the continuous and multiform controversies concerning whether the disciplines of education are abstract or concrete, general or particular, have never in the long history of education thrown light on what the liberating and the humanizing arts are. The controversies are, indeed, signs of the degradation and confusion of the arts in which the trivium is employed on trivial forms of the problem of the universal and the part-whole problem. The liberating and humanizing arts are *general* disciplines for the interpretation and control of *particular* processes; they render *parts* of experience intelligible and consequential in the context of *wholes*. From the earliest stage in their evolution as *enkuklios paideia* they have found a bond or union among the arts and sciences as well as differentiations and separations, and four different aspects of generality have emerged relative to four varieties of particularity in the history of the development. They are general in the sense of applying to all subject matters and therefore in the sense of providing an approach to any particular subject matter placed in a context of other parts of information or knowledge. They are general in the sense of embracing all fundamental skills that can be acquired in education and therefore in the sense of providing a basis for any particular skill exercised to supplement or advance other processes of thought and action. They are general in the sense of bearing on the formation of the whole man and therefore in the sense of providing a model or ruling principle for any particular excellence fitted into the achievements of a good life. The fourth sense, which is implicated in these three senses, has become more explicit in recent times: they are general in the sense of being the arts of all men and therefore in the sense of providing guidance for each particular man and each particular association of men responsive to the cultures and objectives of other men and of mankind.

The arts which liberate and humanize may, like all other arts, be misused. One of the products of their misuse is a variegated host of sham substitute liberal and humanistic arts. Whatever other causes cooperate in the transformation of the arts, they contain the seeds of their own degradation, and they are changed in the changes of man and culture which result from the illiberal and inhumane uses of the arts and disciplines. Each of the characteristics of generality and particularity which make them liberal and humanistic undergoes easy mutations into less arduous and synonymous substitutes. The *enkuklios paideia* ceases to be a circle of learning and becomes an encyclopaedia or handy reference book for ready and up-to-date information. The liberal arts become compendia and textbooks of rules and specifications for discourse and calculation or compilations and handbooks of data for scholarly and scientific composition, which liberate men only in the sense of distinguishing some from others by the education attested by their years in school and their diplomas and degrees. The humanizing arts become the fine arts marked by the taste and style of an elite, and they are designed, not to humanize, but to produce humanists who are distinct not only from the mass of mankind but also from scientists, technologists, and men of affairs. The great works of man cease to be models for contemplation and edification and become vast storehouses of clichés to be discovered and polished with philological and philotechnical pedantry or to be exposed and refuted as critical prelude to innovation and discovery. Culture becomes cult, then becomes breeding, and finally becomes the pots and jars and other archaeological remains of peoples of the past and the habits, opinions, and practices of living peoples.

The restoration and cultivation of the liberal arts and humanistic education today will not be advanced by refurbishing the reputation of disciplines that were once called the liberal arts or the humanities or by propagandizing for their reinstitution. The mediaeval liberal arts are not adapted to the task of liberating men today; and the humanizing arts are not the "humanities," or the "social sciences," or the "natural sciences," or any interdisciplinary amalgam in which humanists will learn the second law of thermodynamics and responsible governmental posts will be created for scientists. Some thought must be given, first, to discovering what arts liberate and humanize in the present world situation. More thought and invention must be employed, second, to develop those arts for use in the revolution in education which will transform our schools and colleges and graduate schools during the next few decades. The education which emerges after that revolution will be put together capriciously in response to pressures and counterpressures within communities unless it is designed wisely with the aid of experience, knowledge, and the arts.

We are only beginning to explore the implications of a humanistic education suited to all men. The United States pioneered in "general education" not because of an awakened sensitivity concerning humanity and human rights but because of a large and continuing increase of students from families and environments unacquainted with the traditions of collegiate education and unadjusted to traditional prerequisites. Many of the newly liberated countries sought to construct a general education to form an independent, responsible, and deliberative body of citizens. Many of the nations with long traditions of education and civilization became interested in general education when the population explosion reached the universities and the need for trained personnel obliterated traditional class distinctions between education and training. But we have proceeded for the most part by addition and subtraction. We set up distribution requirements to be general; since they are general and superficial, we add specialization requirements to be proficient and profound. We require engineers to study the humanities and the social sciences, and we add "area" courses concerning other cultures or regions to rectify exclusive concern with the Greco-Roman or the Judaeo-Christian tradition; but we are not clear about what disciplines engineers should acquire in contact with the humanities or what disciplines are involved in learning the languages of other peoples and acquiring information about them. In these processes it is not necessary to examine the possibility of a humanistic education for all men designed to develop the arts and disciplines for living in the world community of mankind and for cultivating and advancing the values and virtues of each tradition as it has contributed to the inclusive tradition of mankind. Our writers on world culture tend to speculate on the common tenets of world religions rendered ecumenical by omission of distinctive doctrines and practices rather than to inquire into the possibility of stimulating a diversity in which common values are cultivated in different forms and in different manners, much as the virtue of a just man is recognized and esteemed by men who do not share his mores, and the art of a poem is appreciated by men who do not share the passions or pieties of the poet.

The other three characteristics of the humanizing arts are more familiar, but they have undergone comparable changes in scope. We should like a liberal education to introduce the student to all subject matters. But we complain that there is now so much to know that no man can encompass it all, forgetful in our complaints that the arts and sciences have progressed because men of genius have been inspired by how much there is to know and to do. The philosophers of Greece, the summists of the thirteenth century, the universal men of the Renaissance, and the polymaths of the eighteenth century were men of art who had learned from their art what to study and what to ignore. Our ingenuity seldom rises beyond the reductive search for one science to explain the other sciences—sociology by psychology by biology by physics, and the resultant choice between physicalism and the sociology of knowledge is only one among endless controversial pairs at war to establish the unity of the sciences.

We should like a liberal education to give the student training in all the basic skills of life and knowledge. But since techniques are now so numerous and refined it is wise to teach the young only the arts they will later use in life. We all manage to make ourselves understood, and therefore we have in education no need of normative rules of grammar, rhetoric, and logic (which, moreover, have no scientific basis), and the arts of the trivium can be particularized to use and schematized in structural grammar. Few of us use much mathematics and therefore what remains of the arts of the quadrivium can be particularized to use and schematized in set theory. But we must also remember that the modern world depends on public relations and technological skills, and that modern man must adapt himself to the media of mass communication and to a world reduced in size by interdependence and to the methods of thinking developed by science and to the world pictures formed by those methods. The methods of appreciating and knowing become indistinguishable in educational theory and practice from the methods of persuading and producing.

We should like a liberal education to contribute to the formation of a whole man prepared to integrate all interests and objectives in the growth and enrichment of a good life. But we build up the "all" of the whole man by additions and subtractions: when we have added training in other aspects of life to intellectual training, it is difficult to enumerate the parts (they are certainly not the moral and the intellectual virtues) or the whole (it is certainly not dependent on principles of moral or intellectual integration). Instead we have worked with the paradoxes of internal-external-autonomous; as we have formed men by adjusting them to their environment, we have narrowed their environment to their job, their community, and their recreations without adjustment to the environment in which they might encounter ideas, actions, and art objects at variance with the common acceptances of their local environments.

The arts that liberate and humanize must be constituted anew, as they have been reconstituted to meet new problems at various periods in their past. Their history suggests that a new formulation of the arts must be based on examination of the subject matters with which they must be concerned and of the disciplines which are adapted to accomplish their liberal and humane purposes. The lesson of history is continuity and change. It is likely that if we understand why some subjects were liberal and humanistic in the past, we may be aided in marking off the subject matters which can be treated in a like fashion today; it is unlikely that we shall be able to transform existing departmentalizations of subject matter to make one of the traditional subjects, or one combination of them, peculiarly relevant to liberation or humanity. It is likely that if we understand why some disciplines were liberal and humanistic in the past, we may be aided in constituting new arts for achieving comparable purposes today; it is unlikely that they will be the arts of any past period although they may be given names and they may adapt devices which have had a continuous history.

What are the *subject matters* of humanistic education if they are not the subject matters of the "arts" and "sciences"? Inquiry for them may profitably pursue many paths. Among possible paths is one suggested by the past of humanistic studies. We have seen that the Romans played an important part in defining and organizing the liberal arts and the humanities, and that the Renaissance put a similar emphasis on similar conceptions of arts and humanism. Both approaches were strongly influenced by rhetoric. Our own interest in communication gives our approach to the liberal arts a similar orientation. The subject matters in which we are interested reflect this orientation which traverses the arts and sciences, and they are confused by the ambiguities of controversial oppositions. They should be defined and distinguished to be used in a humanistic education relevant to the fields they cut across.

The first of these fields of humanistic education is invention, or discovery, or, as we have come to call it, "creativity." We tend to approach this field by way of psychology, but a psychology of discovery is without guiding principles without some knowledge of the world of discoveries. The traditional opposition has been between discovery and proof. During the last century a classic skirmish in that war was fought by Whewell and Mill over the possibility of a logic of discovery as well as a logic of proof. The devices of discovery should be examined as they move among rhetorical, psychological, and mathematical devices from the discovery of arguments to the discovery of things, to the discovery of arts and sciences, and they should be related to theoretic, practical, and artistic discoveries if we wish to determine the subject matter with which the student should be acquainted to acquire the humanistic art of coping with new problems.

The second of the fields of humanistic education has its preliminary definition by exclusion from the field of discovery. One can be sure that one has discovered the new only to the extent that one has recovered the old. But in a more profound sense, once controversial oppositions have been reconciled, the recovery of the old is an instrument for the discovery of the new. The Romans put the culture of Greece to Roman uses; the Renaissance built a new culture on the ancient liberal arts and humanities. A sign that the art of recovery is not to be identified with "history" is seen in the fact that all colleges have departments of history, but the histories of arts, music, literatures, institutions, sciences, and philosophy are studied in other departments. The devices of recovery should be examined as they move among grammatical, technical, and scientific devices from documents to objects, to processes, to actions, to values, to ideas, and they should be related to the objects of various activities if we wish to determine the subject matter with which the student should be acquainted to acquire the humanistic art of recognizing objective evidence.

The third of the fields of humanistic education has its preliminary definition by exclusion from the fields of discovery and recovery. What has been discovered or recovered cannot be considered unless it is presented. Whatever the audience, trained or untrained, particular or general, to which a presentation is addressed, the presentation is determined in part by the subject presented and in part by the interests and preconceptions of the presenter and of those to whom it is presented. Since science and objectivity are cognitive, we have tended to make the region of the arts and practical values noncognitive and emotive. Our broad interest in the passions is manifestation of this field, but the study of the passions needs guiding principles derived from some acquaintance with the objects of passions, preferences, and evaluations. The devices by which reason is used to affect action and art (as well as to discover truth and recover facts) should be examined as they move among rhetorical, psychological, and calculative devices of passion and knowledge in presentation from science to prudence, to agreement, to persuasion, to deception, and they should be related to what is sought and what is known, if we wish to determine the subject matter with which the student should be acquainted to acquire the humanistic art of sensitive awareness and judgment.

The fourth of the fields of humanistic education has its preliminary definition by exclusion from the fields of discovery, recovery, and presentation. We have learned a great deal about the facts of equality and about the relations of men to each other. We have used great ingenuity to adapt practice and policy to conscience, justice, and good will, balanced by equal ingenuity employed to preserve our own interests, traditions, and glories. But we lack the arts of common action and thought, and our vocabularies are too meager to express the unifications and pluralisms that would open up the intelligible meanings and practical programs which lie beyond presentations of "tolerance" of differences, "desegregation" of separations, and "one world" unified by communication and technology. There are normative elements in the process which can be introduced only by liberating and humanizing arts. Tolerance, as a social virtue, should be more than indifference to what other people do; it should be more than scientific and sympathetic study of the odd ways they act and of causes that lie behind their strange customs and modes of thought; it should also be an interest in their values, which might lead us to modify our own conception of values or to exercise the right of deciding that they do not have enough bearing on our values or on common values to deserve extended attention. Desegregation, as a social institution, should be more than removal of barriers to action and to the exercise of rights in a community; it should also be a development of freedom and responsibility. The recognition that the world is one, as social awareness, should follow not only from the calculation of interrelated needs and interdependent calamities to culminate in the possible unity of total destruction; it should also arise from the combination of interrelated interests and interdependent opportunities which make possible a community of values. Not only the devices of co-operating with each other in the satisfaction of wants but also, and more important, the devices by which each takes into account the objectives, the autonomy, and the injuries of others (without supposing that his own notions of progress, independence, and justice will do as well as or better than common understanding) should be examined as they move among logical, experimental, and practical devices from the tyrannies of opinion manipulation, merchandising advertisement, and political chicanery to the interdependences of responsible and free communities, and they should be related to the private and public consequences of action if we wish to determine the subject matter with which the student should be acquainted to acquire the humanistic art of responsible action.

What are the *disciplines* of humanistic education if they are not the "liberal arts"? Among the ways in which one may inquire concerning the new liberal arts is one which is adapted to the four fields of discovery, recovery, presentation, and action which are beginning to be recognizable in our experience as a result of the increased importance of communication, factual precision, objective valuation, and contact among peoples. Four disciplines should be developed which should be of use in each of the four fields. The old divisions of the liberal arts should be abandoned because they should be arts both of words and things; and it is doubtful whether a new rhetoric or geometry could be freed from the distortions they would inherit from the old criticisms of the new linguistics and mathematics. Yet some of the old names and devices may be used to indicate the directions which inquiry and innovation might take.

We need a discipline which might be called *canonics* to set forth the simplest and most significant forms of general expressions which determine compendent bodies of statements and to identify them without loss of generality and precision. Within any culture there are many selections of modes of expression which are applied to the same things, and many selections of varieties of things which are signified by the same expressions; in the historic succession of cultures there are many selections of basic terms and principles and many selections of significant things and values which characterize the differences among ages;

in the relations among cultures there are many selections among modes of expression and relations of things which affect communication. The art of differentiating viewpoints and of translating them for communication is the art by which *tradition* is related to *innovation* in the many frameworks in which novelty is encountered and treated.

The growing contemporary interest in *hermeneutics* should be broadened, as it has been in the past, to include not only the interpretation of documents and texts but also the interpretation of actions and facts. The art of interpretation is the art of relating *facts* and *values*. The two have been set in radical separation from each other (for what is is no indication of what ought to be, and therefore what ought to be is only the statement of someone's preference), and the realm of facts and the realm of values has developed each its own dogmatism which, in changing dogmatic combinations, renders us naïve alike concerning alleged facts and alleged values. We make the same double error in reading what men say and in reading the book of nature. Hermeneutics as the art of interpretation should bridge the gap between what is and what is desired, what is possible and what is desirable, and between the facts and laws of science and the hypotheses and methods of inquiry.

We have worked out elaborate arts to explain the sequences of discourse and even more elaborate arts to explain the consequences of occurrences, but we need a liberal art to relate the two sets of arts. The art of dealing with sequences and consequences is the art of relating *particulars* and *universals*. Since in the practice of that art intellectual assumptions and practical ends are alternatively architectonic, the new art of methods may appropriately (in pious recognition of the importance of communication) be called *homilectics*. The determination of the true depends on facts and principles, but truth is also a value, and the determination of truths, like the determination of facts and principles, depends on circumstances. The determination of the good depends on preferences and prudence (or, as the canonic art would remind us, Kantians among us would prefer to say on the hypothetical imperatives of prudence and the categorical imperatives of will), but the determination of goods must itself be a truth dependent on its proper facts and principles. We shall come to no unshakable certainties in either process, but the art which makes clear what universal considerations and what particular determination operate in the sequences and consequences encountered in what we say and in what we are talking about will provide needed guidance in the pursuit of the true and the good.

In the whole of experience there are many self-contained wholes which have proper parts indiscernible from the perspective of other wholes. In experience and art, in life and polity, in history and science, in questionings and commitments, there are systems, and an art of *systematics* is needed to achieve insight into the coherences of experience, value, and knowledge. It is an art to relate *parts* and *wholes* within each whole and among the plurality of wholes; it is an art to relate judgments and objectives, utilities and goods, knowledge and wisdom. There is a pluralism in such systematizations as well as a communication among them and a common community in which they are evolved and pursued. The art of systematics is the art of stimulating each of the pluralisms in turn to the end of advancing the systematic interrelations by which further advance in the coinfluential systems of life and thought will be initiated.

We are in the midst of extensive and profound changes in education and in the arts. They are all results of changes in circumstances. We are clear about the circumstances: education must be changed because there are more accumulations of knowledge, more arts, more choices, and more people. We are less clear about the objectives of the changes because we have no criteria for distinguishing among the kinds of knowledge or arts that might be acquired or for deciding which of them increase freedom in choice or humanity in man. We debate the changes by means of oppositions like theory and practice, abstractions and facts, and many other pairs which run in ambiguous history to the terms which the Romans borrowed from the Greeks for like disputes clustering about *facta* and *verba, phusis* and *ergon.* The Romans dropped theoretic subtlety and logical rigor from the learning they based on Greek culture; the humanists did not cultivate philosophy or logic as they were transmitted in mediaeval education; and we, on the evidence of the education that we might have received if we were a little older, decide that we live in an anti-intellectual, anti-rational, anti-humanistic age. Even the pessimistic diagnosis should have an ironically optimistic appendix. We have devised new illiberal and inhumane uses of the arts and sciences, but the tradition of the liberal arts and the influence of the great works of man continue strong, and the force of circumstances may constrain us, as has been the case in the past, to be freer, more humane, and even wiser than we have the arts to know or say. But the truly optimistic prospect should not be forgotten in the flood of competing prophecies of doom. Times of danger are times of opportunity. The subject matters and the disciplines of the new humanistic education have emerged in our experience, and what work is done to develop and apply the new arts is itself an exercise in the arts that liberate and humanize.

6

Innovation

and Reaction

in Higher

Education[1]

David Riesman

Recently Clark Kerr, President of the University of California (and, perhaps, the academic equivalent of Secretary McNamara), delivered the Godkin Lectures at Harvard. In these lectures he affirmed that there was no longer any need for giants to head American universities; indeed, he asserted, the "great man" era was well dead and buried. What was needed, he stated, were mediators—individuals who could compromise among the divergent tugs and pressures which demand that higher education serve a diversity of constituencies—mediators who could insure representation to all voices without at the same time promoting fratricide.

Certainly it would seem that the "great man" era is vanishing on the American campus. The end of ideology has occurred there, as it has been reported to have occurred in our general political life. If one thinks of the leaders of American higher education of one or two

[1] From a tape-recorded address. Work on problems dealt with herein has been facilitated by a grant from the Carnegie Corporation.

generations ago—of Woodrow Wilson, A. Lawrence Lowell, Benjamin Ide Wheeler, Clarence Cook Little, Alexander Meiklejohn, Robert M. Hutchins—most have been men who held passionate political positions in the general community and passionate ideological positions about education. There are many reasons why this kind of man is a vanishing breed. We have learned—indeed, our education has conditioned us to believe—that things are so complex that people who try to do good often end doing harm and earn no thanks for the effort. We have become cool, moderate, less ideological, and less fanatical as well.

In earlier generations, leading American educators were struggling for academic excellence in a society many sectors of which were either apathetic to their goals or actively hostile. Some were fighting what Mencken called "the booboisie," asking in Mencken's own Baltimore, for example, for a theoretically oriented institution closer to the German than to the British model. Others (as at the University of Wisconsin) were trying to adapt to the land-grant system ideas about the university as a source for social renewal and reform, igniting the hostility of vested interests, both secular and fundamentalist. (Richard Hofstadter's *Anti-Intellectualism in American Life* provides a catalogue of the range of opposition confronting academic and intellectual leaders throughout most of our history.) These battles are by no means concluded; echoes of them can still be found. But increasingly academic values are victorious, and the more advanced colleges and universities, only rarely put on the defensive, today ride the tide of success and prestige. While support for higher education even in its more esoteric aims is seldom for unmixed motives (of course, hardly anything is ever done or perhaps should be done for unmixed motives), there is at any rate less need to fight for the status of higher education when its primacy is assured by ample Federal financing, National Science Foundation grants and fellowships, and the growing demand for and repute of the intellectual—as well as the expert—in American life. Hence, it can be argued, higher education may no longer need charismatic leaders to collect on the legacy of public understanding and support established by earlier generations of leaders. And if this is the case, Clark Kerr may be right in stating, as he did in the Godkin Lectures, that great men in education might be useful in the universities of Latin America or in other underdeveloped countries where the preaffluent issues of political ideology are very much alive. What I would add to this is that great men are no longer necessary in most parts of the United States to *mobilize* support for rigorous standards of teaching and scholarship in the universities; one might, however, argue that they are as important as ever if one seeks to depart from the going model of what a big university should be like, and to start something more experimental and untried in an age when many experiments are no longer controversial and have become an accepted part of the academic landscape.

If the university president no longer dominates American education, who does? I think the answer is clear—the faculty. Professors peregrinate with their own grants, their own colleagues, and in many institutions even with their own graduate students. Poor institutions, out of the money, not in the running for these academic plums, can have the leftovers of high principles and the tyranny of their educational leadership. The fact is that an eminent faculty has its administration at its mercy. In a lecture on the administrator at the University of Chicago, Robert Hutchins once made the (tired, tart, torrid) comment that the way to get ahead in a university was to attack the administration. If a Nobel Prize winner threatens to leave unless he is given a new laboratory, the president gives in. Similarly in a good university the president is unlikely for a variety of good and bad reasons to sacrifice a member of the faculty to the protest of an aroused right-wing community, not necessarily because he believes in academic freedom himself, but because if he wants to keep a good faculty, he must protect it. Indeed, a study of academic freedom done under the auspices of the Fund for the Republic in 1955 indicated that one way to build a good faculty was to insure controversy with the community.[2]

In the long run, building what Clark Kerr called a "federal grant university" (of which there are more than a score in the United States) depends entirely upon the eminence of the faculty, because federal grants have in the past been given to individual scholars, largely on the basis of merit.[3]

Contrary to popular assumption, the administrators, the presidents, and the deans of leading universities, now come generally from the

[2] *Cf.* Paul Lazarsfeld and Wagner Thielens, Jr., with a field report by David Riesman, *The Academic Mind: Social Scientists in a Time of Crisis,* The Free Press (Glencoe: 1958).

[3] It should be noted that presently many Congressmen and Senators are insisting, contrary to the merit system, that grants be made to institutions on the basis of geography; they want grants made to the small or struggling as well as to the large and eminent academic enterprises.

faculty and share faculty values. These values are the more readily shared by the administrative hierarchy since they have been well diffused throughout the educated community in America. Today, with the rise of an educated elite, with the use of the universities as sorting stations for talent to run the society, academic values enjoy a priority which they have never had before in America.[4] This ensures that power will not be centered in the president or his administrators, but in the academic guild as such.

The academic guild is divided into departments which are national and cosmopolitan as against the institutional "home guard," which is interested in a particular college and its merits. The opinion of professional associations, such as the American Chemical Society or the American Anthropological Association, matters more to a distinguished institution than does that of the local community. The professional associations—and not the community—will be decisive in the recruitment of faculty and, to a considerable degree, of graduate students. The opinion of such associations may matter even more than that of the alumni, some of whom are no longer able to get their children into their "own" college. Other alumni will have settled comfortably on the college faculty, joining the home guard in the war against the cosmopolitans, yet prevented from fighting that war to the finish because they will want to send their best students on to leading graduate schools where admission and advancement depends on their having been trained in manners and modes of scholarship acceptable on the national market.

As a result of these developments, the rather sharp division that once separated the great undergraduate majority from the tiny minority going on with graduate studies in the arts and sciences is becoming attenuated. To insure admission to the best graduate schools, undergraduates are increasingly driven not only to secure high grades as undergraduates, but also to take the requisite courses that will demonstrate their ability in relevant fields. In my own view and that of many other educators, an undergraduate who knows that he is going on to

---

[4] For fuller consideration of this theme, see Riesman and Christopher Jencks, "The Viability of the American College," in Nevitt Sanford, editor, *The American College: a Psychological and Sociological Interpretation of the Higher Learning*, John Wiley (New York: 1962), pp. 74–192; and Riesman, "The Academic Career: Notes on Recruitment and Colleagueship," *Daedalus: Journal of The American Academy of Arts and Sciences*, Vol. 88, No. 1 (Middletown: 1959), pp. 147–169.

do graduate work in one area ought principally to explore other areas while still in college. But this freedom is jeopardized by the desire of an apparently increasing number of graduate departments to force the educational decision back into the earlier years. They do this partly so that they can judge a man's aptitude, say, in physics or economics, by the way he has performed in these precise fields as an undergraduate. But they may also wish to relieve themselves of the necessity for teaching subjects they regard as elementary, even to very bright and committed students whose preparation lies in other fields. As one psychologist to whom I protested the necessity or importance of teaching learning theory to undergraduates, replied, "I don't want to have to teach them in graduate school; I want to put them to work on projects."

How different all this is from the picture Thorstein Veblen paints of the American university and its leadership in his book *The Higher Learning in America* (1918). He assumed there that the leaders—the college and university presidents whom he termed "Captains of Erudition" —were only shrewd commercial operators, slavishly oriented to the prevailing business culture and contaminating scholarship with the values of commerce and predation. Veblen took it for granted that, if faculty members themselves ran academic institutions, they would not be so contaminated, but would be dedicated to the aims of scholarship and to what he termed "idle curiosity."[5] In more recent times, however, with faculties more powerful vis-a-vis both trustees and administrators, it has become clear that their collective conservatism is in itself a vested interest which is sometimes protective of idle curiosity and sometimes is not. Faculty government is not a highroad to academic innovation. Clark Kerr correctly observed that many professors whose political views are extremely liberal or even radical outside the campus are, in their academic "domestic" views, apt to be standpatters. This phenomenon is particularly noticeable among those campus humanists who believe themselves to be the only people fighting for the traditional values of the academy against the advancing vulgarities of mass culture—and this syndrome conduces to their being liberal in national politics and conservative in faculty politics. (One small element in this conservatism of the academy may lie in the fact that men trained in our

[5] A somewhat comparable idea has recently been put forward by Paul Goodman in *The Community of Scholars,* Random House (New York: 1962).

graduate schools increasingly have the option of pursuing their careers outside the university in the setting of a research institute; hence, if they choose to stay in the academy, they will do so in part because they have been socialized by their environment and appreciate its values. Another equally compelling motivation for remaining within the academy is an often overpowering desire for tenure, for which scholars, in search of premature security, often ask when only in their early thirties, while at the same time denouncing the "organization men" of corporate life.)

Veblen, as I have suggested, spoke about "idle curiosity" as his ideal. It is hard to find idle curiosity today, despite the fact that the Philistinism and muscular anti-intellectualism against which he fought have considerably diminished in our society. One reason is that a profession —a guild—has clients and is concerned with clients, while a learned society is concerned with colleagues. Neither the impulsion of clients nor the impulsion of colleagues provides a wholly satisfactory solution to the problem as to the sources of curiosity or as to the relevance of particular pathways of research.[6]

It is often thought that pure research is better than applied research. This is certainly the dominant opinion in sociology, where applied research is generally frowned upon. It would be necessary, however, to observe very closely to see whether the call of a client is more distracting than the call of one's colleagues. Paul Samuelson, the noted economist, in his presidential address to the American Economic Association several years ago, said that economists should work for the applause of their professional colleagues, eschewing popularity and publicity. He makes a necessary point, and yet I think this applause of one's colleagues can be as dangerous as the applause of the public, for neither constituency possesses the key to understanding what we already know (but often, because of its very mammoth quality and compartmentalization, lack access to) or to the discovery of new questions and new knowledge, or to the application in dialectical fashion of what we know to what we do. The purity Mr. Samuelson commends is often the purity of snobbery or of forced simplicity.

Veblen was also mistakenly persuaded that the young faculty members were better than the old—part of a continuous romanticism with the young that is common to most radicals. The fact is that present-day

---

[6] This is an observation which I owe, like much else in this talk, to the work of Professor Everett C. Hughes. See for example his essay on the professions in *Daedalus*.

young academicians seem to me to be academically more conservative than many of their elders. One reason for this, if I am correct in my observation, is that an older generation entered academic life when it offered less in the way of prestige and emoluments than it does now. Hence, in an earlier era dominated by business values, teaching and research offered opportunities to those who rejected business, whether to pursue knowledge or erudition or to escape the competition of the marketplace. In this setting, some very notable men found in the cause of science a countervailing power to prevailing evangelical attitudes; for instance, sociology was once notable for the number of ministers' sons who undertook to carry on a crusade quite unlike their fathers' in appearance, although, beneath the anticlerical passion for science, often resembling it in underlying attitudes. As with a nation, so with a discipline: affluence and success bring new problems of inwardness and meaning. We can see, for example, the shift in the recruitment of psychoanalysts in America from the first generation of Freud's followers (or the followers of his leading dissidents), who entered a career at odds with the established medical and cultural order, to the present generation of analysts, who pursue what Allen Wheelis speaks of as the quest for identity from the vantage point of a more established but also less adventurous profession.

But this is not the whole story. One also finds that the disciplines of scholarship were much less developed in this country a generation ago, and the excitement to be found in various border or frontier areas of study was considerably less than at present. If earlier professors enlisted in a crusade on behalf of science in general, today the causes that excite enthusiasm are more intramural, involving, for example, the battle for mathematical economics against descriptive or institutional economics, or the newer molecular biology as against the older natural-history sorts of biology, or psycho-linguistics as against philology, and so on across the academic map. With the usual mixture of motives, all sorts of new sub-disciplines are being formed, eliciting at once crusaders and careerists; but the newer battles are waged, less against the whole society than against older definitions of one's subject, or against competing methodologies, or in terms of oligopolistic competition among a small, though growing, number of leading institutions. It is characteristic of the present situation that, according to the *Princeton Alumni Weekly,* the average Princeton professor in the natural sciences controls an annual budget of a hundred and twenty thousand dollars, of which at least 50 per cent comes from the Federal Government. An academic man with this kind of operation under his control is in a very different situation from that of the older type of college teacher; moreover, he is very likely to be younger (although he may be retired, as physicists go, at the age of thirty or so).

These developments seems to me to have cast doubt on Veblen's view that the Young Turks will be more rebellious and innovative than their predecessors, now "Old Turks." Even if this was so in his day and up through the 1930's, it may be questioned whether it is so today when the young are better trained, better equipped, and economically and professionally more secure than their elders were at the same age. All this may sound as if I am looking back nostalgically, as many people are inclined to do, to a Golden Age of dedicated teachers and wide-ranging humanists in American academic life. I do not, however, regard the old times as better. They were different. Each epoch has its grandeurs and its miseries. In general I would say that American academic culture is a more vital enterprise now than it was at any previous time. In the earlier day, when it attracted more crusading spirits in search of an unconventional career, it also attracted many dreary, unambitious men for whom the ministry was not suitable and who were seeking shelter from the world, less because of their desire for cultivation and reflection than because the colleges offered a respectable way toward the pinched, genteel, white-collar world of poverty that Veblen described in *The Theory of the Leisure Class*.

The task of education today is not to look back and exalt earlier times, but to see what problems and opportunities are being created for the modern academy by the victory of the academic. It is a victory won over earlier anti-intellectual trends in America; and the danger is that this very victory of the academic may foreshadow a victory not only over the anti-intellectual but also over the intellectual. The danger of the triumph is that instead of cultivating further discovery in diversity of talent, the successful academic guild tends to encourage the reproduction of itself, the training of its own stereotype, and the consequent limitation of its continued growth and development.

Now that I have stated and no doubt overstated certain general contours of the present academic scene, I want to turn to a few experiments recently begun in elite, residential, private colleges which have attempted in various ways to counter prevailing trends. I shall devote most of my observations to an experiment at Harvard College in which I participated.[7]

The first experiment I shall mention is now only on the drawing boards; the plans exist, but not the reality. This is the plan at Bowdoin College to establish a Senior Center in which all seniors will be required to live and in which, while also pursuing specialized study, they will share a common intellectual program. The idea behind the Senior Center, as I understand it, is based upon the assumption that by their final year students of high initial promise will have "had it" in their fraternities, in their other collegiate rituals, and in some measure perhaps even in their academic departments. (Almost all Bowdoin students pledge, as freshmen, one or another of the residential fraternities.)

Before I say more about the plan itself, let me point out that it is an example of innovation (like the Meiji Restoration in Japan) which came from the top down, rather than upward from the (younger) faculty. Indeed, it is my impression that it took the President of Bowdoin many years to persuade his faculty to permit the experiment to be made, and many of the senior men resisted as home-guard conservatives, while younger itinerants came and went in pursuit primarily of academic, but not pedagogic, opportunity.

This is not to deny that the Bowdoin Senior Center plan raises serious and difficult questions concerning the timing of general education. It is generally thought that general education should come at the beginning of one's academic career and that only later should a student specialize. But many students come to college today headstrong and eager to prove themselves adequate in the field in which they excelled in high school. If they are prevented from following this program, if they are obliged to slow down in their freshman year and spend some time in courses of a general nature, their recalcitrance and unco-operativeness is often tantamount to sabotage. Putting general education in the last years says to the student, in effect: "Agreed, that you have now proved that you can do good work in your special field; you have proved that you can run your fraternity and be sufficiently bored after three years; you have even proved, perhaps, that you can

[7] For a discussion of two unusually interesting experiments in public commuter colleges in the state of Michigan, see my comments in "Proceedings of the Symposium on Undergraduate Environment," Bowdoin College, October 18–19, 1962.

manage with the opposite sex; now relax and learn something before you graduate." That, at least, seems to be the idea.

The problem of this approach is that, having been exposed at the end of one's education to new possibilities and even to the desirability of changing one's career, time has run out in which to prepare for the change. And the fact that this may be so—or that students in their anxiety and conservatism may regard it as so even if it is not—may cast its shadow before, and make a student reluctant to explore the possibility that he may have chosen the wrong occupational niche for himself.

The idea of the Senior Center seems to me, nevertheless, one worth trying out. Whether Bowdoin itself, however, is an optimal locale for such an experiment is another story. No doubt it is good to wean the student back from their fraternities, but it may also be asked whether a student should spend four years in a small, liberal arts men's college in Brunswick, Maine. Is one not ready by twenty-one for a wider human diet than one could cope with at seventeen or eighteen? In the huge universities, human scale has long been lost. In such institutions, as in the metropolis, students may retreat from massiveness into little villages. Some of these are based on mutually shared interests, whether academic or extracurricular. But the most common "solution" to the problem of being lost is the fraternity: instead of being with a group of twenty-five thousand, one is with a group of twenty brothers of one's own class and perhaps sixty brothers in all. But sixty is too few. Rather, it seems to me, the responses to the problem of scale ought to shift as a person becomes older. One way to do this is not to move the college but to move the student. Something of this sort happens in a rather unplanned way in California where some able students attend the junior colleges or the smaller branches of the University of California, such as those at Davis or Riverside, then moving on in the junior year to Berkeley or UCLA.

The Harvard Freshman Seminar program, in one of its aspects, addresses itself to the question of scale, but it is pertinent at the outset to describe how this innovation came about and what some critical problems in such innovation are.

Throughout its recent history, the administration of Harvard has been concerned with the University and with research and professional training, and also with the undergraduate College and the quality and scope of undergraduate teaching; but the emphasis on one or another of these poles has tended to shift with the times, with administrative incumbents, and with opportunity. Thus, it could be said that Presiden Charles Eliot moved away from the collegiate in the direction of more specialized and graduate education, and that President A. Lawrence Lowell sought to re-emphasize the college, while his successor, President James B. Conant again emphasized research and professional training. These shifts have always been matters of balance and emphasis. In the present era, President Nathan Pusey and the former Dean, McGeorge Bundy (now Special Assistant to the President for National Security Affairs), have naturally been concerned to preserve undergraduate education against centrifugal pressures arising from research commitments and professional affiliations among the faculty. Harvard professors do not think of undergraduates, as they are thought of at many great state universities, as a kind of nuisance or at best an unexplored wilderness. Since Harvard undergraduates are bright and attractive, readily regarded as future leaders in academic and other work, many Harvard faculty members are not allergic to the young. Part of Harvard's success—a relative success, of course—in advancing both the academic guilds and the somewhat less specialized areas of undergraduate education is the fruit of its comparative affluence; because its laboratories and libraries are not starved for funds, money spent on undergraduate education does not arouse the combative and hungry appetites of faculty members, as might be the case in institutions equally ambitious but more impecunious.

The Harvard House plan, the product of earlier munificence, divides undergraduates in their upper three years into Houses, each with some 400 members; each House has affiliated with it a number of tutors, mostly young, as well as senior faculty Associates. Thus the Houses help to maintain ties, all too tenuous in some cases, between undergraduates and faculty members, permitting the latter to gain a somewhat less distorted understanding of students' problems.

Among both members of the Administration and some of the faculty, there has been increasing preoccupation with the problem of the freshman year, defined in very different ways, as I shall indicate in a moment. There had been suggestions that something like a freshman seminar program would be a good idea. Some of these suggestions had come from young administrators and had received a small amount of faculty support. It may be doubted, however, if much would have come of this had an outside donor not come along and said he would give money for freshmen—but not for anything else. The donor's restrictive caveat legitimated the concern of a handful of administrators and faculty with freshman education and provided a partial solution to the problem of finding the necessary resources without having to undertake a battle for the expenditure of general funds.[8]

Money, however, did not answer the question as to what, if anything, was wrong with the freshman year. Thus, for example, there were some members of the faculty who were making what might be called an Admiral Rickover judgment: that because we were in the Cold War, that because we needed excellence, that because students were too slack, and because they wasted their high-school education on driver training and such like courses, that now we should move them along faster and get them into advanced work right away in the freshman year. This comes close to being a "manpower approach" to education.

There was a very different, but somewhat overlapping, concern arising from what came to be called at Harvard the "Exeter syndrome." Exeter and Andover together send a hundred students to Harvard every year, among them many who believe that when they come to Harvard that they've already had it, that they are already too mature for the fare offered them. An increasing number of these students move directly into advanced sophomore standing. When I came to Harvard, I decided to interview a number of these students in order to find out why they desired to escape the freshman year, because in very many cases they could certainly have afforded to remain the full four years, without eliding their freshman year. Sometimes they said, "I'm going on to medical school" or "I'm going into biochemistry" or whatever, "and I don't want to waste unnecessary time in school." In other cases, they said, with brutal frankness, "I want to get out of all that freshman General Education drivel." The motivation of such students was often to convince faculty members that the feshman year they wished to accomplish. The impact of these very articulate students was often to convince faculty members that the freshman year

---

[8] In the spring of 1963, following a fairly detailed review of the Seminar Program after its four first years, the Faculty voted hereafter to support the Program from general funds. The donor's money had acted, as is often the case, to start something that could then continue on its own.

was too dreary academically and intellectually for the best students—not because they had to be accelerated for the sake of advanced study or for the sake of the "manpower" crisis, but rather that they had to be given more interesting experiences as freshmen if they were going to become or remain freshmen at all.

Beyond these considerations, there was still another feeling, already alluded to earlier, when I spoke of the problem of scale: Harvard is not a huge university, but it is big. There are twelve hundred undergraduate men and three hundred undergraduate women in the first year. Many entering students are leaving home for the first time and, by now, nearly 60 per cent of Harvard undergraduates come from public schools and a decreasing proportion from boarding schools. These public-high-school graduates, coming in the great majority of cases as the only representatives of their school, find at Harvard a competitive and impersonal situation. This impersonality besets them, moreover, in an epoch in which people increasingly feel that impersonality is unendurably cold and that only the small group is "human."

On the faculty side, in addition to the diverse judgments cited as to what some of the problems of the freshman year were, there were various motives for wanting to experiment with a freshman seminar. Some had made the exciting discovery, especially notable in mathematics and the natural sciences (see, for example, the writings of Jerome Bruner) that, to put the matter in its most extreme terms, one can teach anything to anybody at any age; such men believed that freshmen could do advanced work, just as some high-school students have been doing. Moreover, while freshmen may be permitted to enroll in upper-class courses, ordinarily, in order to teach freshmen, one must offer a large General Education course, involving not only a very heavy commitment of time and energy over a considerable period, but also requiring the approval of the Committee on General Education. In comparison, offering a freshman seminar was a much more informal enterprise which committed one to a good deal less. In the same way, a faculty member might offer as a Freshman Seminar a course which his own department might not want to sponsor—although in general at Harvard, as at other leading institutions, faculty members have a great deal of freedom in choosing what they will teach.

At the same time, as one might expect, there was opposition. There was some feeling that, if the seminars were right, then large lectures were wrong. Since Harvard was committed to large lectures, this objection was framed in the form of a polarity. It meant that seminars must be wrong since Harvard couldn't—and shouldn't—give up large lectures. Dean Bundy, in a characteristic, unideological understatement, said that the Freshman Seminar Program was not the fight of right against wrong, but an experiment with something different though not necessarily better. However, earlier, I think it may have been felt by some of the faculty that this *was* a fight between the right and the wrong precisely because of the guilt that many research-minded scholars feel because they devote so little of their energy to teaching undergraduates. (To be sure, a number of such men do devote themselves, in spite of competing pressures, to undergradute teaching.) At the same time the pressure on senior faculty members at Harvard to spend all their time on research that will enhance the national and international fame of the institution may be somewhat less than is the case with institutions presently less eminent and consequently more eager to become visible in the academic marketplace. (To be sure, it would have to be added that men at Harvard are under a rather subtle pressure to justify their being there, and "permanent" tenure is as little likely there as at other places to lead to relaxation and an easy life!)

With this all too cursory sketch of the general political and pedagogical atmosphere out of which the Harvard Freshman Seminar emerged, I should like to add a few words about the Seminar which I conducted during the first year of the experiment. It was untypical. Most of the seminars took very small groups: five, six, eight, or ten students, often previously selected on the basis of the talent their high-school records evidenced for the specific subject matter. For instance, Oscar Handlin, the historian, took a number of students who had done well in history or social studies at good high schools and tried to put them to work on historical research. Dean Bundy himself led a seminar on national policy in Southeast Asia based on readings from the Congressional Record, taking students who might be inclined in the direction of a foreign-service career or academic work in the field of international relations. Some members of the science faculty took into the laboratories students who had already exhibited energy and talent at schools such as the Bronx High School of Science in New York.

In my own case, I felt it already well established that one could move especially gifted and selected freshmen into proto-graduate work in a good many fields. It appeared to me, therefore, that a truer and more taxing experiment would involve taking a group large and heterogeneous enough to be something like a cross section of the Harvard student body—a group which, of course, by national norms might be especially talented, but not by Harvard norms. Consequently, in the catalogue sent to freshmen listing the seminars that were offered, I offered one which was not labeled under any of the three fields—natural sciences, humanities, or social sciences—making clear that it was not intended for specialists, and accepting those who applied on a first-come-first-served basis.

Sixty students (forty young men and twenty young women) were accepted. These were divided into four sub-groups to work separately with my colleagues, Dorothy Lee, Kenneth Keniston, and Susanne Rudolph. As I went over the applicants' records, I tried to see in what way they differed from a cross section of the whole Harvard-Radcliffe freshman student body. They seemed to differ primarily in the fact that they had *chosen* to come to Harvard; that is, they had not automatically come to Harvard, as a boy from St. Marks, or a boy from Boston Latin, might have to make a decision *not* to come to Harvard. We didn't get such boys. We got a boy from, let us say, Choate who had not gone to Yale, or from Southwest High School in Kansas City, who had not gone to the University of Kansas, or a girl from Woodrow Wilson High School in Washington, D.C., who had gone to Radcliffe and not to Goucher, and so on. We got the students who chose a novel seminar rather than doing what the Harvard student had done in the past. We got the more venturesome students, although in fact they were a cross section in terms of aptitudes, predicted grades, and other readily measurable qualities. We also got a group who, having chosen to come to Harvard, could also choose more readily than the average to leave Harvard (as a matter of fact, one of the criticisms made of the seminar I led was that a considerable number of its students did choose to drop out for a year or so). In other words, these students did not think the world began and ended at Harvard.

What my colleagues and I were trying to accomplish in the seminar is apparent from the fact that we opened it with a reading of C. P. Snow's *The Two Cultures,* which had just appeared. At that time, I said to the students: "I expect that each of you comes from one or leans toward one of these two cultures. I see that half of you, like half the Harvard student body, are headed toward science (or medicine) and intend to major in science or mathematics; and only a third or so of you are in the humanities, while the social sciences are under-represented, as they are in high school. I want each of you in this year to look across the cultural divide, to redefine yourselves, to see if you really want to stay in that one of the two sub-cultures that you have been brought up in so far. We are not trying to make any converts; we are not interested what becomes of you in academic terms; we are only interested that you have another look around."

My colleagues and I required each student who came into the seminar to take the most difficult and demanding "new criticism" course offered for freshmen in the General Education program in the humanities, knowing full well that many of the students, the majority certainly of those headed for the sciences, would not have dreamt of taking such a course; in fact, would not have been admitted to it. By reassuring them of our compassion and our participation in the ardors of the experience, the Seminar became a kind of home base. I would have done the same thing with a natural-science course if the faculty had permitted this, but some of them thought our seminar was being too "monopolistic" as it was. What I could do instead was to suggest to students who had, for instance, a pronounced tropism toward literature or government and away from science, that they not seek out a General Education course in the natural sciences which had the reputation of being a "gut," but rather take one which would really allow them to test and discover their capacity in that area as well as to confront science in one of its more contemporary and more demanding versions.

The Seminar sought not only to create a kind of cross-disciplinary common culture but also, and equally important, to create a common culture from a group of very diverse people with very different aptitudes. We had in the seminar students who were at the very top, at the eight hundred ceiling in their College Board scores, but we also had students at very much lower levels whose admission to Harvard represented a gamble by the Admissions Office in its efforts to avoid concentration on excellence as already defined in a "meritocratic" way and hence to widen the doors of opportunity. Thus, the admission of students with low scores was often based on the feeling that they had come from poor high schools, that they hadn't had a chance, and that, partly in order to mix the breeds, Harvard should give them a chance.

This is admirable from the point of view of Harvard. It is often admirable as well from the point of view of the student who, with a bit of help, can move readily into a new intellectual league, and develop capacities greater than he might have realized, for example, at a community college. But the individual student can, of course, suffer if Harvard takes a chance on him (and some students, fearing this, refuse Harvard's admission and go to a college they hope will be less demanding). Some who come with inadequate preparation were nevertheless the valedictorians in their local high schools; they enter a Harvard seething with five hundred other valedictorians, often from better schools; when such a student gets his first one or two C's, he suffers an academic defeat which obliges him to realize that he is in a new world where he may no longer be able to distinguish himself in the accustomed way. The effect can be traumatic for him, for he may begin to define himself as "mediocre"—first at Harvard, and later on, throughout his life. Such redefinition is not new, but the escape from the label of academic mediocrity into peer-approved careers as a playboy, an aesthete, a student-body politician, or even an athlete is increasingly deprecated and under pressure.

Each seminar subgroup met once or twice a week for several hours for discussion of specific topics; and, as a total group, we met every Monday night for a dinner at which we had placecards, so that everyone would be mixed, the young men with the young women, the high scorers with the low scorers, the science students with the humanities students, and the seminar's faculty with its guests. During the course of several months each of the students would have met all the others and (usually) talked.

One evening I sat with a student who had come from a small town in North Dakota where his father ran a gas station. He had been the top chemistry student in his high school, and he had been advised, on coming to Harvard, to take the elementary chemistry course in which there were many students who had never before had a chemistry course. The assumption was that he would excel; however, three or four weeks after the term had begun, he was behind the others. I said I thought maybe he had come to the wrong college, and he said, "Yes, I know I have, but I can't go back again. The band played when I left home. I was the first student in my high school to go East to college." I think the Seminar may have supported this boy in a situation which was difficult at best.

The Seminar was also very helpful to some of the most talented, because we said to them, as I have already implied, that the Seminar afforded them the chance to play from weakness rather than from strength. The absence of grading in the seminars allowed us to encourage students to take chances and emphasize areas of study where they had felt or feared themselves to be inadequate. There were, of course, some students disinclined to take much of a chance; if they took an ungraded seminar, they had one less shot at an "A," and therefore they avoided the prospect. Other students did take this chance. Our Monday evening meetings gave us the opportunity to explore the whole problem of careers—to consider whether one has to go on in life doing what the culture has defined as important and even what one has defined in external terms, independently of personal pleasure and satisfaction, as doing one's "best."

Many people do well in subjects they don't enjoy (or about which they do not know what they feel), while they may in academic terms do slightly less well in subjects they do enjoy. It is my conviction that in a rich society it is important to discover what real work tastes like. It is one of the most important discoveries one can make in college. What is it that one relates to in work? What is it one really enjoys, quite apart from where one's future may be thought to lie? In order to facilitate this discovery I ran within the Seminar a program in which we brought people from both inside and outside the academy to talk to the students. From outside, there were an inventive and civic-minded businessman, an ambassador, a missionary, an inventor-entrepreneur, a state hospital psychiatrist; from inside, men and women in philosophy, history, government, clinical and social psychology, anthropology, Indian and Far East studies, biology, theoretical physics, English literature, and so on. These visitors were asked to tell the students how they came to be working on the problems which concerned them at the moment, and what their careers in college had to do with them? It was striking how often the college career had been in a different field from what the person was working on presently. In scheduling these visitors, we made an effort to map the vocational and academic areas to which many of the students had had no or minimal exposure, and thus to widen the range of their possible choices.

In this vein one of the things we tried to do for that half of the students who were not headed for science careers (but also for the students who were already in science) was to present them with science as an intellectual adventure—a rather different view of science from that in which they had commonly been exposed in high school. Science at its most abstract and speculative, I suggested to them, can have a poetic, freewheeling quality. Many of these students regarded science (either in its attraction or repulsion for them) as monolithic, rigorous in definition and in self-definition—a kind of two-gun, slide-rule affair. It was not my intention to urge the students to suspend their career concerns; I was not suggesting that they sacrifice their futures on the altar of some vague definition of the "whole man"; and I was far from holding that specialization portended alienation. Instead, I sought to encourage the students to acquire a more realistic view of the risks that they might be taking in altering their career plans and to make the best of their undergraduate experience while still keeping an eye on postgraduate opportunities and requirements. I had often seen students exaggerate the danger of taking very small risks—perhaps because, by doing so, they avoided any questioning of their own objectives.

One of the surprises for many of the faculty members who gave seminars within the Freshman Seminar Program was how hard the students worked in them despite the absence of grades. It should be remembered that these were students who were already, as the term goes, "highly motivated"; at other, less high-pressure institutions than Harvard, absence of grades might not encourage comparable dedication. Indeed, given the milieu of grade-getting in which many of these students had grown up, taking away the incentive of grades allowed a very small number to exploit the Program, made others anxious with the absence of metrical or numerical feedback, and for the majority served to decontaminate the Program because one did not worry that one's work reflected only one's being a mark-hound. So, too, it was astonishing to me that students who were strangers to each other outside of the Seminar (which occupied a quarter of their total freshman program) gained the sense of solidarity that similar groups did. Our group of sixty began to call themselves "the Seminarians" and, as I suggested earlier, they regarded the Seminar as home base—a conclusion facilitated by the fact that the Seminar Program had taken over an old house near the Yard as its headquarters. The students were not competing with each other for grades; they could share their troubles; they could share both their criticisms of Harvard—which were many—and their equally numerous discoveries of Harvard. The considerateness and camaraderie which developed, comparable in some ways perhaps to that of an athletic team, were especially striking against the background of the individualistic and even at times solipsistic culture that is more characteristic of Harvard.

A follow-up study of seminar members disclosed that those students who had been in a freshman seminar felt better acquainted with faculty members (even outside their own seminar leaders) than did other Harvard students. Despite the great variation in the conduct of seminars, this study showed that they had helped their students to adjust to Harvard, and do better there, in academic terms, than a control group with apparently comparable backgrounds and aptitudes.[9] Hence in the faculty review of the program during the spring of 1963, the experiment was pronounced a success—even by many skeptics who had resisted it at the outset. One of the reasons for this is that almost any experiment is a success by definition. This is the so-called "Hawthorne effect"—if you study human subjects and take them seriously, they are apt to like it, and respond to the very enthusiasm of the enterprise itself—which means that no such experiment is in any sense a strict experiment. The control is never a true control because the experimental subject, being party to the experiment, responds better. The control is influenced by the fact that somebody pays attention. The people who were in the freshman seminars, when compared with their controls of similar entering academic prowess, did more things and did them better.

But many problems remain. Some faculty, myself included, found giving a seminar extremely demanding and time-consuming. Some students found that the rest of Harvard didn't always live up to the billing. This is frequently the "problem" of innovation—it creates discontent with what comes later—and this, I think, is on the whole a good thing. Moreover, the problem that I referred to in my discussion of the Bowdoin Senior Center—namely, where should general education be located?—was not solved. It was clear that freshmen could do the work, and this gave them a confidence which was cumulative. It led them to do other work, but whether it would have been better to take a group of seniors and work with them is, of course, still not known.

[9] See the report of Byron Stookey, Jr., Associate Director of the Freshman Seminar Program, Harvard College, "The Freshman Seminar Program: A Report to the Faculty of Arts and Sciences," (mimeographed), February, 1963.

What can be learned from the Harvard Freshman Seminars? Any effort in a major university to encourage research-minded faculty members to devote themselves, in an experimental and hence often taxing way, to undergraduate teaching has to find ways of maintaining the research opportunities of those who do devote themselves to teaching undergraduates, especially freshmen and sophomores and those who are not majoring in the professor's own field. One way is to cut down the total amount of teaching required of all faculty members (which may well improve the quality of the remaining teaching), while at the same time being chary of handing out research professorships which require no teaching whatever (save perhaps of post-doctoral fellows); and there may be instances where it will be wise for an institution to insist that everyone do some undergraduate as well as graduate teaching. Of course it is a help if the students are themselves responsive, not simply a captive audience, and if faculty members are encouraged to experiment with ways of teaching which are nonroutine. I believe that many graduate students shy away from teaching, not because they are primarily careerists, single-mindedly devoted to publishable research, but because they are afraid that they will not be good teachers and that they have had no coaching or other opportunity to become good teachers.[10] On the other side of the divide, those who teach only undergraduates run considerable risks, not only to their careers but also to their teaching mission itself, as may happen with many missionaries who have no other outlet than the "natives" to whom they are assigned. Hence I think it important to give frequent sabbaticals to teachers so that they can do research or other scholarly or creative work uninterrupted by teaching.

Beyond questions concerning the tactics of educational innovation are fundamental questions of educational philosophy which I have touched upon, thus far, only by implication. One must ask: What does a faculty want of its students? Does it want the students to resemble itself, and if so, in what aspect—in its vocational commitment or in more general respects? One has to ask whether the ideals held by different

[10] This is so because the schools and departments of education are so fiercely deprecated in the graduate schools of arts and sciences that perhaps any effort to teach college and university teachers how to teach is bound to be thought *infra dig*. To be sure, many men who teach graduate students do make an effort to induct them into teaching as well as into research.

groups of faculty members are merely snobbish. Do the faculty members speak for a particular heritage, generally European-classical, and for a particular social class? Is not our ideal of excellence also snobbish, meritocratic and achievement-oriented rather than aristocratic and birth-and-breeding-oriented? Isn't it true that many faculty members seek for their students not so much specific accomplishments as an introduction to a somewhat intangible cultural style—critical and skeptical, uncommitted yet tasteful? (This style is an advance over parochialism and traditional moralizing, as cultural relativism is an advance over ethnocentrism, but this outlook of the men whom one of my colleagues has termed "atheists for Reinhold Niebuhr," when it becomes a fashion, reveals what I regard as serious limitations.) Or do faculty members want their students to have what they themselves have missed, as parents often want their children to have what they have missed? For example, do faculty members want their students to act out their own unfulfilled rebellions while resenting their students' greater self-indulgence and their higher starting salaries?

Some faculty members, as I suggested earlier, see the young as manpower for the Cold War, and as expensively trained for requirements already set. I think the trouble with this view, or one of many troubles, is that nobody knows what it is that an advanced society really needs, or even what the concept of "needs" means. Indeed, the students are among those more privileged members of society who can help us discover what is missing in our prevailing versions of the good life and what other versions may be more satisfying.

To speak now for myself in conclusion, I would like students to become more fully what they are potentially. This is implicitly a theory of human nature. If people are not alienated, if they are not discouraged from becoming committed, if they are allowed to remain human, they will respond to the needs of society. As they invent those needs, they will not be irrelevant to what the society needs, but the relation will be oblique, tangential. I would like to see students realize what they are capable of becoming, because I see them as potentially individuated and yet able, as happened with many in the Seminar, to develop a sense of compassion and solidarity with people less well endowed—and not only those within their own guild or nation.

I would also like to see, as I suggested, students discovering their potentialities by giving themselves a wider choice both in their calling and in their nonworking life. This, I think, comes about if students gain in college a sense that they can master something new, including an awareness of how specialists, in whatever field, actually work. This requires gaining a feeling for competing vocabularies and languages and the means of translating these into yet other languages and it also involves a sense of the social processes and technical momentum of science, and hence of society as continually recreating itself. If the student achieves this complement of sensibilities he comes to understand that his life's ticket is not handed to him by nature, but can be rewritten by will, intelligence, and resourcefulness.

No conceivable educational system is going to bridge the gap between what society thinks it needs and demands and what individual destiny asks of those who are subject to it. But as I have suggested before, we are only in part an underdeveloped society (although in considerable part) and hence we are rich enough to educate students for their own sakes as well as for the sake of society. This, indeed, may sound like a theory of the "invisible hand" in which private vices become public values. In a way it is. But in more subtle terms what I am suggesting is that individuals live in society and respond to its existential problems. Since society is changing, since it is being changed, by education among other things, we must teach people that education is a lifelong affair, that it is not completed by four years of undergraduate work or even by later years of graduate study. In order to achieve this, I think we need a better understanding of the place of innovation in academic life, more hospitality to experiment, and more tact and subtlety in our encounters with students.

In dealing with students of the sort the better selective colleges and universities are now attracting, the teacher finds, it seems to me, that there is often a very delicate balance between grandiosity and self-distrust. Students have been told that they are bright and capable, and they have often tested their powers in large and competitive high schools. Yet the mass media bring them within range of national and even international models of performance, so that for example, a student who may one day think he is a future Picasso may the next day decide that he is a despicable amateur simply messing around with paint. Many in my own generation of teachers do not perhaps fully appreciate this kind of vulnerability in the talented young; or if they do, they may feel that tough, abrasive criticism is the best remedy for it. In my own view, we really know quite little about how to nurture rather than destroy or dry up talent, at least where that talent does not make itself evident in already approved and readily harnessed ways. No educational experience is likely ever fully to solidify the balance between grandiosity and narcissism on the one side, and self-distrust and fear of failure on the other. But both with individuals and in our larger social life, it seems to me necessary to maintain a certain tension between the real and the ideal of such a sort that individual students are not driven into cynicism either about themselves or about the ideal. Education must always work with an unstable dialectic in which students transform themselves in college and help transform the institutions into which they come. Educational experiments are costly, but they can serve in modest degree to bridge the generational gap between teachers and students, and hence to suggest still further experiments. And, so far as I can see, the backing and support for such experiments is, in the superior institution, more likely to come from the administration than from the faculty. Therefore I believe we cannot dispense with the college president as an educational leader and innovator, however many other tasks he must also accept in the way of mediation and day-to-day management.

7

To

Know

and

To Do

Milton Mayer

The age of confidence that began with the Renaissance seems to have ended at Verdun. It persisted (for another few years) in an America far from the ruins of Europe. It persists no longer. Pessimism (or apathy, which is predigested pessimism) is pervasive now, and the characteristic hope is that things will grow no worse; at best, that some part of the *status quo ante* can be recaptured. We are wistful, in America about the "positive values" of the Great Depression, in Europe about the stability before (and even between) the wars. Human progress is no longer axiomatic.

The modern world is built upon that axiom. It dates from Bacon's dictum that knowledge is power—an idea that would have astounded the fallen Oedipus no less than the fallen Adam. The idea swept mechanics with Newton at the beginning of the eighteenth century and flowered in the history of Gibbon, the economics of Smith, and the politics of Jefferson at the end; proved itself invulnerable in science, philosophy, and rhetoric with Darwin, Mill, and Marx in the nineteenth; reflected all its robust triumphs in the retreat of Victoria and the charge of T. R. at the opening of the twentieth; and in Woodrow Wilson survived until Versailles, where Clemenceau (after two years of Verdum) said serenely that "there is nothing very new to learn about this war or the end it was fought for. . . . Prudence required some measure of lip service to the 'ideals' of foolish Americans. . . ."

The prophet of old said of the great nation of his time, "They are wise to do evil, but to do good they have no knowledge." If the prophet was right, Verdun was a hard lesson that had to be learned some time. And the foolish Americans were not to be foolish much longer: National Socialism and the Second World War (F.D.R. modestly called it "the War for Survival") taught them the lesson that Europe learned at Mort Homme Hill a generation before: Man was not going to be an unmitigated success.

Bacon was none the less right and the Renaissance none the less real: Knowledge *was* power. Man armed with knowledge was, and is, as a god. Freed from demonology and dogma, he poured forth an immediate cornucopia of wonders and transformed "the world" of the medieval (and Mesopotamian) oxcart. He pours them forth still, in an ever-increasing tempo. Bacon's man is doing great—greater every day.

But the mastery of nature is discovered to be an independent compulsion; like the Dybbuk, it needs no command to fetch water faster and faster. The water rises, and the power of knowledge is a consternation: Rare indeed the commencement orator who does not wag his head over the discrepancy between man's moral and intellectual (or social and scientific) progress. He still says "progress," to be sure, implying that the difficulty is morality's pace rather than its nature. And the locale assumes that there is an integral connection between morality and education that we'd better tighten up a little.

What if the orator is deluded on both these points? What if morality is not progressive? What if there is no necessary, or even probable, connection between morality and knowledge? And what if (*horribile dictu!*) the human crisis is first and last a moral crisis and not an intellectual crisis in the least?

When the President of the United States says that "science has no conscience of its own. . . . Whether it becomes a force for good or ill depends on man," he is doing more than quoting Rabelais; he is saying something revolutionary about education and about American education. He is calling upon us to de-emphasize science and emphasize something else.

What? Philosophy? Has philosophy a conscience of its own? Theology? What if none of the sciences—not even the highest—has a
conscience of its own? If the President and Rabelais are right, the inference is cataclysmic: Education is of conditional service to man, and
if the condition is not met, it is of no service at all.

The Know-Nothings, whose tribe increases, McCarthy in, McCarthy
out, are making the right (if insufficient) inference. When men
become desperately, if incoherently, aware that their therapist has no
therapy, they turn against him. "Fascism," said Mussolini's official
philosopher, "is anti-intellectualism." And Hitler's said, "We think
with our blood." Fascism, Nazism, Birchism, "scientific Marxism" are
the moral fruit of moral frustration. They may be bad moralities, but
they are moralities, and men who cannot have a good morality are
driven by frustration to a bad one.

The anti-intellectual exempts the intellectual *arts*—certainly medicine—from his fury. But he has no stomach for egg-headedness in the
moral order (which is also the political). He will have no discussion,
no dialogue, no democracy. He will have a morality uninfected by
reason, which does not deliver him in his hour of need. The university
which produced the atomic bomb had as its motto: *Let Knowledge
Grow from More to More, that Human Life May Be Enriched.* Along-
side that motto, on a tennis court fence where a low structure once
stood, there is a plaque commemorating the achievement of the first
sustained nuclear chain reaction. The plaque's inscription was to have
begun with the words, "For good or for evil . . ." until somebody
suggested that the university's motto would then have to read, *"that
Human Life Be Enriched or Impoverished."*

The disorder lit by the bomb is a moral disorder. When most men
have less than thirty dollars a year and the per capita expenditure on
war in "peacetime" is forty, what is there that intelligence can tell us?
When the most knowledgeable (and therefore the richest) societies,
with the longest history of civilized institutions, lead the world in
suicide, insanity, alcoholism, divorce, crime, delinquency, and the
splendid control of disease (including venereal disease), what critical
need have they—or, for that matter, the least knowledgeable societies—
for knowledge?

What the issues of economic and social justice want is not research,
but the will to do the research. What they want is the determination
to pursue these remote goods above the immediate goods of advantage
provided by nationalism and militarism, by war and by racism and by

tyranny and by the free market. We are wise to do evil; wise enough, for the moment.

The two most literate societies in the world launched the last war, and the two most elaborately schooled threaten to launch the next one. But I do not speak of literacy and schooling here. I speak of education, and I speak of it as an expensively educated man. I do not recall one of the crises of my life—there have been more than six—which I might have met better had I known something more or something else. My need was not to know, but to do; was, at fifteen, and is, at fifty. And now, in my decline, I must try to establish for education (my own profession) a claim to a relevant place in the moral muddle. I think I can—but I'm afraid that it will not be the place it now occupies.

With the spread of Communism to the Orient and the instant-progress movement in Africa and Latin America, faith in education is everywhere established. What for Jefferson was the keystone of the democratic arch is now the keystone of the democratic and anti-democratic arches. But Jefferson is misread. He wanted every citizen of the United States to have had three years of schooling. He could not have settled for much less; even a junior citizen should know how to make change and read the label on the bottle. But this is hardly to say that schooling was to be the national religion. If this is what it has become, it is not for Jeffersonian reasons but because an agnostic society which has no need to employ its young people, and no time to watch them, had to find a well to drown them in; and in a society as sociable as ours, it would naturally be a well of togetherness.

But the character of education is important, and what the rising generation needs most must decide it, whatever necessary or dispensable divagations may invest the procedure. What the young need most is whatever they will need in later life, for they will be old much longer than they are young, and unprotected longer than they are protected. If, then, the lifelong crisis of man is moral, it would seem that education should, in some way, if possible, be trained upon morality. We should not make any such requirement of bingo or tap-dancing or swinging on the old front gate. We may make it of education because education is the great public enterprise.

The schoolhouse is the national ground cover, and schooling the national habit. Jefferson was as fearful as Adams—their correspondence of 1818 is conclusive—of the democratic form of government. In his fearfulness he talked up education (and Madison with him) beyond either its known efficacy or his own proposal for its content and duration. The American devotion to the school is the result: the consuming faith that the more schools there are and the longer they confine their charges (even unto the "lifelong education" of the book sets), the better off we shall all be.

We pedagogues have been willing to exploit the national habit insofar as we can cozen the moneyed—and the taxpayer's name leads all the rest—out of their money. We do not urge them to examine the habit's premise, nor do we examine it ourselves. Our trade secret consists in our being supposed to have a secret when we haven't. What we have, and keep, is a skeleton in the multi-purpose closet. Whatever the taxpayer wants, we deliver if we can and promise to deliver if we can't.

It is public pressure that fills the schools—and the colleges—with junk. The pressure is irresistible because we have nothing to resist it with. In the moral crisis we are unable to argue that we are doing something critically useful—or even that we would if the law allowed. Why shouldn't driver training be compulsory? Driving is a moral problem, without intellectual content beyond the grasp of a high-grade moron; the public wants the moral problem solved and thinks, mistakenly, that it can be solved by teaching; and we are unable to plead that we are preoccupied with much more pressing moral problems and unwilling to confess that this one cannot be solved pedagogically.

A few years ago Professor I. I. Rabi, the Nobel physicist, observed with humanistic satisfaction that "nowadays everyone connected with education, whether in the public schools or in the colleges, is pressing for greater emphasis on the humanities." Immediately thereafter the Soviet Union launched the first Sputnik, and everyone connected with education pressed for greater emphasis on the sciences. On December 20, 1957, the Kiplinger *Washington Letter* predicted that "education will swing heavily to science from this time out," and on December 30, President Eisenhower submitted to a generous Congress "a plan for expanding scientific education at a federal-state cost of about $1,800,000,000 over the next four years."

Out went the humanities (or the superficial survey courses that passed for humanities), in went science (or the superficial surveys of science), and up went the pre-professional preparation of technicians and mechanics. Why not? Had the schools been doing anything so important that the curriculum should not be transformed the instant the

Russians presented a moral problem—the *evil* of Communist success—that the American people wanted solved? The schools stood ready to hand, requiring only the replacement of staff and library by a different staff and laboratory.

What was missing from the schools, at this point, was an understood purpose, aggressively advanced against all comers; a purpose that would justify either their going on doing what they were doing or their doing something else. But purpose applied to people is moral purpose: What did the schools think they were preparing people for? Could they prove it, or even argue it? In the order of human action the end is the first principle; what was missing was that battered old shuttlecock, a philosophy of education.

Ours is the first age since that of Greece and Rome in which schooling is secular—and America's is the only public schooling now or ever that is rigidly secular. (Westerners are amazed to learn that religious instruction is still given by clerics in the schools of the *atheist* Communist countries). In the Christian theocracies, as in the Jewish before and the Islamic after, the asserted objective of education was morality as a means to salvation. It was supposed, right or wrong, that works followed faith and that faith was supported by knowledge. When, therefore, knowledge appeared to challenge faith, there was trouble with the Holy Office. "It is your business," Barberini is said to have told Galileo, "to teach men how the heavens go, ours to teach them how to go to Heaven."

The settled conviction that men might be *taught* how to go to Heaven was maintained—if never demonstrated—long after the age of the priests. In 1701, Yale undertook to transmit not only *Veritas* but *Lux;* more than a century later Oberlin was consecrated by its charter to "the total abolition of all forms of sin"; and the present Haverford catalogue asserts that more important than the skills of learning "is the desire and moral capacity to use these skills for worthwhile ends." The prospective Haverfordian is left to understand that a church-related college will not leave the desire and moral capacity unattended to.

If such an institution thinks that it can attend to such matters, there is no legal impediment to its trying; it is over the wall of separation upon which the safety and security of the secular state rests like Humpty Dumpty. But *public* education, at all levels, is forbidden by the First Amendment to abolish all forms of sin or tamper with the desire and moral capacity. What ever made us think that it could if it tried? What evidence has there ever been that even under the most sacred auspices education could make men good?

Logomachos wants to know if God is corporeal or spiritual when we encounter Him in the Eucharist.

"How should I know?" says Dondindac.

"What! You don't know what a spirit is?"

"Not in the least: Of what use would it be to me? Should I be more just? Should I be a better husband, a better father, a better master, a better citizen?"

The centuries of sacred education may have produced especially good churchmen. Had the churchmen been especially good men, Dante would have had to do without the first two parts of his three-part comedy and Luther without all ninety-five of his Ninety-Five Theses.

The parochial schools are not peripherally religious like Yale or Oberlin or Haverford. They are blatantly so, and their objective is, accordingly, the improvement of the pupil as a soul which will be known by its fruits. They mean to make men good. But where is the evidence that they do or can? Their alumni are all fine fellows, but I do not know that they are finer than the alumni of Yale—or of the City College of New York. And they should be, if morality can be taught.

But the parochial objective was, after all, more than ordinarily clear to Father Adam. He knew his origin better than we know ours. He knew what he was to do and not to do. He knew the penalty and the reward (which he was already enjoying). And he fell. He fell in knowledge. Indeed, we are told that there is no other way to fall; the received doctrine of the salvation of Abraham testifies that ignorance of the Law is an excuse.

Morality, whatever else it is, is action. We know that action and knowledge are wholly separable, *e.g.*, in the case of the mathematician *qua* mathematician. But the separability appears in all the other disciplines—in the logician whose personal life is eccentric, in the gluttonous physician, in the physicist who rounds a sharp curve at 80 m.p.h. One of the greatest living political scientists dismisses civil disobedience as anarchy because law is the indispensable condition of community—and asks a friend to slip a Swiss watch through customs.

If there were any causal, or even correlative, connection between knowledge and action, a weighted analysis should show (at least tendentially) that college graduates are better behaved in later life than non-college graduates and the top of the class better behaved than the bottom. But there is no evidence that this is the case, not even when, as in H. H. Newman's classic study of identical twins, the factors other than education have been rigorously reduced. Avid readers of John Marquand are aware that disgraceful people may leave the academic grove (and return for Alumni Reunion) no less disgraceful than they entered it. We cannot blame the academy. But we cannot demonstrate its counterweight.

Without much hope of a hearing in the new nations—or the old— Arnold Toynbee, in *A Study of History,* wonders where schooling gets us: "The bread of universal education is no sooner cast upon the waters of social life than a shoal of sharks rises from the depths and devours it under the philanthropists' eyes." Observing that the Yellow Press was invented (in England) twenty years after the introduction of compulsory public education—that is, as soon as there was a generation able to read it—he finds that literate peoples "are in danger of falling under an intellectual tyranny of one kind or another, whether it be exercised by private capitalists or by public authorities." Toynbee's remedy is to "raise the level of mass-cultivation." How? By education? And how by education?

We are not asking whether the educationally disadvantaged are good, rather whether the advantaged are better. The Governor of Alabama is a graduate of its university and its law school and may be assumed to have a passing acquaintance with ethnology. The restrictive real-estate covenant in the North is not a product of the unschooled, nor the country club their special province. The late Rabbi Emil G. Hirsch was once asked—in the dining room of a club whose members were all university men—the meaning of the Hebrew which was written on a wall plaque. "It says," he replied, " 'We Don't Take Jews.' "

If the Bachelors ought, as such, to be better men than the rest of us, the Masters ought to be better still. But the evidence that they are (or that their erudition is the reason they are) is wanting, not only in the logician, the physicist, and the political scientist, but in the professoriat as a whole. "We imagined," said the late G. A. Borgese of Fascism, "that the universities would be the last to surrender. They were the first." And Professor Carl Hermann argued that in taking the Nazi loyalty oath he himself was responsible for the evils of the system, "for," he said, "if I had been prepared to say No, it would have meant that men like me were. But we were not."

One of the causes of pluralism was the Renaissance religion of reason. It involved a progressive misunderstanding of the Greeks—the adjective became the noun in Aristotle's celebrated definition of man as the rational animal—and a rejection of the medieval Schoolman's commentary on the Greek analysis of human nature: "Speaking simply, the intellectual virtues, which perfect the reason, are more excellent than the moral virtues, which perfect the appetite. . . . But if we consider virtue in relation to action, then moral virtue, which perfects the appetite, whose function it is to move the other powers to action, is more excellent."

Descartes' *Cogito*—echoed by Locke's *homo rationalis,* Rousseau's faculty of self-improvement, and Hegel's perfectibility—laid the foundation of the new rationalism which battened on science and its application. At one end of the era stands Laplace: "If we were able to make an exact catalogue of all particles and forces in a speck of dust, the laws of the universe would hold no more mysteries for us"; at the other, two centuries later, Justice Holmes, who saw "no reason for attributing to man a significance different in kind from that which belongs to a baboon or a grain of sand." This was the modern man's credo; two thousand years earlier Lucretius explained the universe as atoms in motion.

Lucretius found the life of man "crushed by the weight of religion." Relieved of the weight, man ascended into the dream-world of Kant's "sovereignty in which reason alone shall have sway." A new Serpent would never emerge from the illimitable passion for knowledge— Faust or no Faust. And thus the prophetic horrors of the industrial revolution were ignored (except by Marx) in the achievement of man's emancipation from diabolism.

Religion yielded to philosophy, philosophy to science; and the new hierarchy transformed the university (and then the college) curriculum. The "hard" disciplines were the natural sciences, the "soft" the humanities. Economics and anthropology found that they enjoyed respectability insofar as they could demonstrate their "hardness," and sociology and psychology confected their arcane (and therefore scientific) jargons.

By the middle of the nineteenth century the intellect, and the intellect alone, was avowed the proper object of education. And in this avowal Cardinal Newman and John Stuart Mill—the Christian and the "atheist"—were in vehement agreement. But they were both careful to cover their bets: Mill tells us (in his St. Andrews inaugural) that the ultimate end of study is to make men "more effective combatants in the great fight which never ceases to rage between Good and Evil"; and Newman lets it be known that the Church founds a university "not for talent, genius, or knowledge for their own sake, but for the sake of her children, with a view to their spiritual welfare and their religious influence and usefulness."

If they were hedging, they had reason to. A man simply cannot proclaim the primacy of morality—as Mill did—and dismiss it from education, least of all a university president. For mankind will not support a public institution, including war, that does not have a moral purpose or the color of one. There are no apostles of wickedness; Capone, protesting that "Insull's doing it, everybody's doing it," is appealing his behavior to the accepted moral standard; and worse men have appealed theirs to a still higher one.

Nor is goodness, praised by hypocrites, praised hypocritically. Men want to be good and to live (if in no more elevated an interest than that of security) among good men; and if they have not found it feasible to be good themselves, they want their children to be good. Ask a man—ask a bad man—at the cradle of his son whether he would rather be the father of a clever scoundrel or a decent boor.

The instinct is just as sound publicly as privately. We know that it is good men who are wanted in the community—and only then good doctors and good hod-carriers and good philologists. We know that what was said of old is true, that the state is not made of oak or rock, but of men; and as the men are, so will the state be. We know that goodness—and not law at all—is the bond of men in community and that even a band of thieves is held together by goodness and by goodness alone. Good men will make good laws, and if they make bad laws they will correct them; but bad men will subvert good laws and good societies; we have seen, and see, it happening.

In the international as in the domestic order, the central issue is morality's: pain and pleasure. Where else arises man's mote-and-beam trouble? In his eye? What is it, then, that the Communist, who wants free elections in Mississippi but not in Germany, cannot see; or the

anti-Communist who wants bases ninety yards from Russia but not
ninety miles from Florida? It is the pain-pleasure equation that argues
that "we had to do it to end the war"—the argument of the German
at Rotterdam, the Englishman at Dresden, the American at Nagasaki;
the same equation that sends us to war because of "atrocities against
civilian populations" and that, after Rotterdam, Dresden, and Nagasaki,
arraigns the losers (in the court of the winners) for "crimes against
humanity."

But resistance to pleasure and endurance of pain is the trial of the
psyche, or soul, to which the mind may or may not be impervious.
*Tobacco is a filthy weed/It satisfies no human need/I like it/Yep, I
like it.* The doggerel of our great-grandfathers is still the answer (and
the doctor's answer) to cancer. The crisis is, in a word, a crisis of willing, not wishing (and least of all knowing); and unless we can discover a nexus between knowledge and action, the best education is at
best an amenity and at worst a vanity without which a man may lead
a good life and with which he may or may not.

Our search for the nexus takes us at once to the epistemological
commonplace that one kind of knowledge appears—in the life of the
race—to accumulate and another doesn't. The kind that accumulates
answers the question, *What is?* and ends in knowing. The kind that
doesn't answers the question, *What is to be done?* and ends in doing.

The comprehension of the physical (including the physiological)
universe does not require twentieth-century man to know that the seat
of fever is the blood—or that the world is flat—before he can learn that
it isn't. He starts from the latest break-through. Aristotelian physics
was at last replaced by Newtonian, and Newtonian after a short time
by Einsteinian; except for historical interest, the twentieth-century
physicist may begin with Einstein, and the twentieth-century physician
need never have heard of Galen or Harvey. Our cumulative knowledge
is science—in its very broadest sense—and the arts that apply it.

But there are no break-throughs in normative knowledge. Relativity
is new, but moral relativism is as old as Thrasymachus. Each generation (and each individual in it) begins at the beginning. Child psychology is able to tell us why our children are as good and as bad as
we were; but their and our agonies abide, and the man who says sadly
(and rightly), "I'm a failure as a father," overlooks the consolation he
might take from his father's failure as a son.

"The ancients," says Mark Twain, "stole all our ideas from us."

Everything we can say in the realm of the "ought" is a platitude. The *Odyssey* takes us the long, long way home of the tired businessman who *really* loves his wife; the *Apology* assembles the Un-Athenian Activities Committee; and Sophocles owes his biggest Broadway success to his study of Freud. The ingenious inventor—man—has no ethical ingenuity or political invention (including world government).

Some few—fewer than fifty years ago—will say that we *do* better nowadays even if we don't know better than our ancestors or the modern "primitives." The progressive case for ethics and politics may be made in detail, but not in general; nor is it likely to be attempted in the year 1964. It will, of course, sidestep war and argue, say, slavery; and if it overcomes the point that slavery is inefficient in the machine age, it will still have to overcome the point that the white man's enslavement of the black is not ancient at all, but modern; and so on.

We may have better manners than our ancestors past and present —or manners we like better—but manners aren't morals. The Melanesian cannibal, when Malinowski told him of the casualty rate at Verdun, asked how so many men could be eaten before they spoiled, and when the European smiled and said, "We don't eat men in Europe," the cannibal said, "Then why do you kill them?" Two millennia earlier the barbarian eating his dead father horrified the Greek, and the barbarian asked him what the Greeks did when their fathers died. "We burn them," said the Greek. "But that," said the barbarian, "is blasphemy."

The overriding difficulty is that no man, including modern man, is competent to sit in judgment on his own case. *We* would rather compare Florence Nightingale with Attila than Bull Connor with Epictetus. Belsen and Dachau leave us still saying that it can't happen here, but we can no longer say that it can't happen now; and the progressive case has to be made for modern man, not for a happy variant like the American.

As soon as the carpenter chooses to carpenter—to apply the science upon which the art of carpentry rests—his choice is gone. He may not use a thirty-six-inch yardstick on the doorway and a thirty-seven on the door. His knowledge is binding, "absolute," and compels the course of his action. It does not, however, compel him to act; he may choose not to carpenter. Moral knowledge, too, has a special sense in which its end is not action, but knowledge alone: The *sciences* of ethics and politics may be studied without reference to their application. Like Greek or Latin—or higher mathematics or physics or chemistry—they are good in themselves because they perfect the intellect. But I am a man and a citizen confronted constantly by ethical and political choice. I must use or misuse my knowledge—or, unlike the non-carpentering carpenter, abdicate it at my peril. I must carpenter my life and my community all my life.

But I am free, as the carpenter is not, to use the two yardsticks. *His* house will fall down if he does. Mine may—but it may not. He won't get away with it. But I may. The uniform yardstick is the best (indeed, the only) policy for the carpenter, but honesty has not yet been proved to be the best policy for the man and the citizen.

The moral sanctions of religion are as compelling as those of carpentry, but they are not to be demonstrated or (not being knowledge) taught. Without them, Kant can only plead with me to take my hand from my neighbor's pocket to avoid the inconvenience of every man's hand in every other man's pocket; but my neighbor's pocket is immediate (and the policeman is around the corner) and the inconvenience contingent. Euclid, on the other hand, says, "Thou shalt" and "Thou shalt not," and subdues the carpenter's whimsey at once.

The hard thing is to think straight in moral matters because the hard thing is to get a hearing from appetite. Appetite—which "moves the other powers to action"—will not listen to arguments which threaten its interest. The arguments of science as such do not. The arguments of morality do. And if we need a definition of morality, we have it in those issues in which the subject and the object are one: appetitive man and the things that are dear to his appetite. It is about me—and my family and friends, my race and religion, my country and species —that I can't "think" straight. I am a victim of what elementary psychology calls reflexivity.

What stands in the way of my mastery of the physical universe? External objects and the means to be fashioned for coping with them. Full tilt, then, to the fray; with a will, *but an unperturbed will,* against the common obstacles. Whose passion is so strong that he can not see straight when he sees an X-ray picture? But you say you think I should give up smoking, and you have here some roentgenological evidence to lay before me. Away with it! Why that old geezer on TV said he'd been smoking a couple of packs a day for ninety years. I like it; yep, I like it.

Whoever deals with himself deals unscientifically—including that hero of the endless serial, the Man in White. This practitioner of science is exercised just now to save the elderly from socialism. Would it be bad medicine, and for whom? For them, or for him? We go back to 1932, when the American Medical Association called *private* health insurance "socialism and communism, inciting to revolution"; and to 1937, when it called the same private health insurance "the American way." The question is not a scientific one; it is political—belonging, perhaps, to that branch of politics known as political economy. Beneath the White beats the heart of the Man.

But not when we see him in Surgery. Here he has not himself to work on, but an organism whose function it is his business to maintain. You stay the knife in his hand and ask him if this *man,* this Haman, this Hitler, ought to live or die. He says it is none of his business, and you ask him whose it is. He doesn't know; perhaps another of the applied sciences'; try the psychiatrist down the hall.

The psychiatrist is named Freud. You ask him the question and he takes his *New Introductory Lectures* down from the shelf and reads to you: "The physician who is called in to treat a case of pneumonia has no need to consider whether the patient is a good man, a suicide, or a criminal; whether he deserves to remain alive, or whether it is for his advantage to do so."

"And the psychiatrist is a physician?"

He nods and goes on reading: "It is not the business of the analyst to decide between parties."

"What is the business of the analyst?"

"To send them away"—he is still reading—"as healthy and as efficient as possible."

"Healthy! Efficient! But this is Haman! This is Hitler! Where is the scientist who decides between parties?" The psychiatrist—or as the Greek has it, doctor of the soul—shrugs and says, "Keep going down the hall."

Down the hall is the judge instructing the jury in that which is capable of being instructed—the law. But in that which is not—the good and evil of men which brings them into court—the jury is the judge. And who are the jury? Twelve ordinary men, whose only competence is their relative objectivity to the case at bar. The petit juror, and not the jurist, is the best judge of morals, just as the petit voter, and not the political scientist, is the best judge of politics. What morality judgment seems to want most is the dispassion of the scientist without the scientist's science.

The centuries in which moral knowledge claimed to be able to make men good were the centuries of a universal religious faith in which morality had its roots; the centuries in which government was theocratic. They were the centuries, too, in which education was narrowly confined. The natural law (upon which morality was laid) was delineated in a language the people could not understand. The age was (as far as we know) no more or less moral than ours, certainly no less. But on the nature and content of morality Machiavelli himself agreed with Moses.

Once the sovereign pattern was broken by the impact of pluralism, secularism, and science, philosophical systems of morality sprang up, some of them (like Kant's and Bentham's) intellectually coherent, all of them systematically splendid. But they did not touch the lives of men. They had, progressively, the patina of science, but they were as unproductive of goodness as pre-scientific Platonism or Christian Thomism or post-Christian *How to Win Friends and Influence People*. They did not (until Marx tried in our time) even enter the arena in which a man and his life stand naked.

The proliferation of competing systems ultimately deprived moral knowledge of the unity, and therefore of the authority, with which it was once advanced as an index to action. Nowadays we have surveys of philosophy, with *General Philosophy* as a text. We conduct a peep show. We do not pretend that we are teaching something we know— we leave that to the sciences—but a congerie of doctrines all of which fall before the law of contradiction (which doesn't need to be taught). Like Freud, we do not decide between parties.

The survey saves us from all sorts of difficulties. It eliminates the queasiness that relates philosophy to sentimentality and preaching. It dodges the parental prerogative (no longer claimed by the Church) to tell the child what is right and wrong, and the parental storm that engulfs the occasional teacher who presumes to teach *a* doctrine (or to have one). It thus preserves the "independence" of the schools from the yahoos. The philosophers are safe—which is as good as safe and sound. They don't raise moral, or even intelligible, issues. The child who asks the fourth- (or fourteenth-) grade teacher, "Why should I be honest?" or, "Where do we go when we die?" can be sent down the long, long hall.

Natural science, unlike moral science, never did claim to make men good, or to deal with men at all. (To be sure, it fortifies certain moral virtues such as patience, persistence, initiative, and open-mindedness; but so do burglary and philosophy.) In its humility it teaches what it knows and what it knows can be taught. Its way is the easy one of universal agreement. (The Nazis did not use their Aryan physics to develop their rockets.) Its world is real, its materials sensible and generally manipulable, its methods exact, its conclusions demonstrable. And it works. It delivers the goods.

The goods it delivers are those we need greatly in peace and even more in war. In peace it enables us to live longer and less laboriously, in war to fight longer and more effectively. It doesn't tell us, or try to tell us, what to live for or fight for, or whether labor is bad for us or longevity good for us. These are the "insoluble" problems that have to be taken to the man still farther down the ever-lengthening hall.

The genius of the Nazi V-2 was captured by the Americans and is presently one of the chief ornaments of their military technology; his brother, another genius, was captured by the Russians and is one of the chief ornaments of *theirs*. These men's science did not help them choose in moral matters; I take it that *both* of them cannot have chosen well, and, actually, neither appears to have chosen at all whether he should serve German, Russian, or American purposes. It may be that the Russian form of government can do with men whose learning is so thoroughly nonmoral that they cannot even recognize, much less make, moral choices. Ours cannot.

Such men are men and citizens in a free society. Must they be stripped of their civil and political rights, and instead be given Nobel prizes all, on the ground that their single-minded service to us left them no time to learn how to govern themselves and others?

The atomic bomb was devised by men who had devoted their lives to mathematics, physics, and chemistry. Perhaps the bomb should have been used, as it was, but sixty-five of the leading men who made it pleaded secretly with Mr. Truman that it not be used. Of their colleagues who took the opposite view at the end of July, 1945, many, perhaps most, entrenched themselves behind the scientific attitude of suspended judgment. (Mr. Truman might have envied them their trench; he had a sign on his desk reading, "The buck stops here.") But one of their number (a Nobel laureate) took a strong religious position: "If anybody should feel guilty," he said, "it is God, who put the facts there."

If a knowledge of nuclear physics does not help a man decide whether to use an atomic bomb, what makes me suppose that a knowledge of the internal-combustion engine will help me decide whether to stop my car when I see a man bleeding by the road? The priest and the Levite were graduates of the Harvard Medical School, as the Samaritan was not; the Samaritan misplaced the tourniquet; too bad, but he was the only hope of him who had fallen among thieves.

Physicians and metaphysicians in all probability act as well as the rest of us, and the politics of the local bar are in all probability no more retrogressive (if they are retrogressive at all) than those of the barflies in the same community. But their good behavior cannot be traced to their education. The decision of the nation's lawyers to straddle the civil rights issue—in the summer of 1963—was reported as the only possible compromise between the Northern and Southern delegates to the American Bar Association meeting.

Consider, said Socrates, the effectiveness of the teachers of everything else and the ineffectiveness of those who pretend to teach morality. Consider, too (he went on), the best men of our own and of former times; men who, moreover, could command the best teaching facilities for their sons: They spared no pains to make them good, and they failed. The Socratic conclusion (on that occasion) was that morality cannot be taught. But it *is* acquired somehow (along with immorality), and, like other habits, it is more easily acquired young than old. Can the school, on or about whose premises morality is being acquired, do anything purposive about it and still remain a school?

The nature of the case forces on us an order of subject matters, and of effort devoted to them. Since we cannot teach everybody (or even anybody) everything, we have got to ask ourselves how much—and how much of what—a man needs to know in this life and how much of that is within our capacity and time to teach. The question is hard-rock difficult, and we may do well to back into it by asking what knowledge a man can get along without.

We are told that modern civilization is complicated and that, therefore, we need more knowledge than our forebears to keep out of trouble. But I find in my own case that there is nothing wrong with me that a little incorruptibility wouldn't take care of, anytime, anywhere. I lie as a matter of course, and cheat and steal when I "have to." I oversell my employer's product, and switch jobs and oversell his competitor's. I don't look for trouble or even stay on my own side of the street when I see it coming. I jettison principle when the wind howls, keep my mouth shut when I shouldn't, and open it loudly to say I agree when I don't. I thank God that I am as other men are, and on that basis excuse my derelictions. And what I profess on Sunday morning would ruin me if I practiced it on Monday. On the occasions of unavoidable moral choice I mobilize my good reasons for doing bad things and emerge, at best, as a trimmer whose object all sublime is to get on in the modern world.

Morality aside, I am told that I have to have more technological knowledge than my father in order to keep up with technology. Why isn't just the opposite true? The construction of my automobile is much more intricate than that of the Model T—so much more so that neither I nor the mechanic can take the automatic transmission apart. But the automatic transmission requires less knowledge *of me* than the old stick-shift. What is more, I drive better than the automatic transmission specialist (who's a drunkard).

The community is crawling with specialists, none of whom has time to stay on top of his specialty. It would be folly of me to try to stay on top of *all* of them; I'd be behind the changing times in no time. Then there's my Hi-Fi; am I to be an automatic transmission man *and* an electronist (or electronicist, or electronologist) besides?

When Herbert Hoover (and he an engineer) was asked about Telstar, he said, "I belong to a generation that just doesn't grasp all that." Don't we all? And what difference does it make? So, too, with regard to the other historic disciplines. I would not think of stirring without my lawyer and my lawyer's lawyer. My doctor sends me to a specialist, who sends me to a great specialist, who confesses himself puzzled; shall I drop my electronics now and brush up on modern medicine? No use. My ancestors had to take care of themselves in these matters; they needed to know all kinds of things I don't and, in any case, can't.

I am told, then, that the fortunate form of government under which

I live requires a great deal of knowledge of me as a modern citizen. I take a gander at its problems and I am back where I was with the automatic transmission. Public finance is impossible to comprehend if I mean to comprehend anything else; and the public financiers (who do not mean to comprehend anything else) are at odds with each other. My greatest-grandfather had to decide his political destinies in town meeting, but he did not have to know whether Korea was in the Mediterranean or the Caribbean or have a judicious opinion on Guinea, Guiana, and Ghana. I am producing more history than I can possibly consume. Beyond being a just man and looking for just men to govern, I (like the just man who governs) am helpless without my bureaucracy.

Shame on the man who shirks his political duties in a freedom-loving democracy. But what is it that makes him shirk them? Would my apathetic neighbor have been less apathetic in a less complicated society? I think not. Democracy and freedom belong most truly to the realm of desire and action. For every lover of democracy and freedom bewildered by the multiplicity and flux of events there are ten who haven't the love. Give us men to do or die for democracy and freedom, and a set of technologists to serve us, and we shall see what we can do.

The basic institutions of our polity were just as complex in the simple society of the Mediterranean world as they are in ours. The institutions failed, and not because the facts were multifarious and evanescent. In the still simpler society of Asia Minor it was the Ten Commandments that were too complicated, and the Sermon on the Mount. The conversion of knowledge to precept and precept to action takes prudence, and a man wants some sort of head for it; but as an excuse for inaction, or bad action, complexity is one with the suspended judgment of the physicist who devises the bomb.

If I am to be trained professionally to be an electronologist (or an endocrinologist) or a desk man in the bowels of the State Department, I shall have to begin my training at birth and, in the avalanche of knowledge set before me, prepare myself for nothing else. If, on the other hand, I mean to do something less confining, the time is already upon us when I need only to push the button every time the bell rings—a performance which Pavlov's dog discovered long since—is better learned on the job than from books. We may, then, consider the elimination of both professional and vocational study from the preparation of modern man for the moral crisis.

We are asked if we mean to dispense with natural science. We reply: With as much of it as we have to. It is nice to know that the earth goes around the sun and the blood around the heart, and that the angle of reflection is equal to the angle of incidence, and that man and a candle flame both metabolize. It is nicer to know them than to have to depend upon the navigator, the physiologist, the mathematician, or the biologist who knows them. But the competence we want *and for which we cannot depend upon another* is moral competence and we cannot get it from science.

But the experimental method of science is a peculiar contribution to the intellectual enterprise. Can we find a moral use for it? Perhaps, in its distinction from the nonexperimental method of the humanities and the social sciences, yes. If our student learns both procedures (along with the principles that underlie them), we may hope that he will never confuse the two and try to investigate essentially human materials scientifically (as the Nazi physicians did) or essentially scientific materials humanistically (as the party out of power does). The conditions under which we study men—including ourselves—are not controlled conditions. We may shoot a cabbage full of enzymes and see what happens, but not a man. *Human* life is not an experiment—at least not our experiment.

Shall we consider taking time from science and investing it in esthetics? Music is said to have an inordinate power to soothe the savage breast—which comes closer to the moral crisis than all your metabolism. True, our student may not "take" to music; or he may take to the wrong music and find his breast inflamed. But our case is parlous anyway. The arts at least summon the passions—the same passions that morality regulates—to loveliness and blandishes them from the raw banality of their untutored state. Besides, they vivify the imagination, which transmutes the impossible to the possible and, in doing so, seems to bring unattainable goods (and, to be sure, evils) within our reach.

But we must aim at appreciation, and not at theory: It is not musicology that soothes the savage breast. The practice, too, of the arts (the least as well as the most pretentious of them) may steal up on our objective, however circuitously. Art's worth, like morality's, is not in its utility but in itself; and artistic, like moral, endeavor has the nuance of creation. So, too, are the works of science, but they are much later and rarer to come by, while the child who has painted or grown a flower has had the creative experience to savor while young. He has done something he wasn't sure he could do; and that, too, is common to art and morality.

Like all of the pursuits we contemplate here, artistic creation has its drawback. It is proud, and pride induceth a fall. We want lowliness to restrain it, and lowliness is not the necessary consequence of failure; irritation is likelier. Lowliness comes from our recognition of our place in the order of things. It is hard to teach; hard at least for men to teach, and wanting wholly in texts. But nature tries to teach it. Perhaps our pupil, on his holiday, can be brought to nature and turned loose in it, far from the madding freeway, to let it have a go at instructing him in proper majesty and in proper awe. A flier, of course; but so is everything we can think of, and a 1 per cent chance is 1 per cent better than no chances at all.

The trouble with the arts—music no less than medicine—is that the artist may be both an artist and a swine. And this is true of the liberal artist, too. The liberal arts, of hoariest tradition, are those of formulation: in their Greco-Roman expression the verbal trivium of grammar, rhetoric, and logic; and the numerical quadrivium of arithmetic, geometry, music (harmony), and astronomy. They were enjoying a small but insistent renaissance in America until Sputnik demanded the substitution of productive—once thought of as servile—for nonproductive study.

The argument for them runs that it is better for a man to be intellectually enlightened than intellectually unenlightened. And it is—if by "man" we mean "mind." If it is possible for a man to be a grammatical, rhetorical, and logical swine, why shouldn't we exhaust the possibilities of making him honorable (or at least exhaust ourselves looking for them) before we do him the dubious favor of putting tools, even the finest tools, in his hand? Watch out, with your arts of reasoning, or you will have equipped a monster to rationalize his monstrosities. You will have beefed up a part of a man—the part uniquely proper to men and to angels, and to fallen angels.

"O-ho, so you belong to the 'whole man' school of Dewey?" Of course I do. So do you. Do you not want the man to be—and there-fore to grow—whole? Was it Dewey or your liberal artist in Athens who prayed in the *Phaedrus* that the inner and the outer man be as one? Why, if you do not belong to the "whole man" school, do you festoon the school with nonacademic activities? You say that it is be-cause of popular pressure (which we both deplore), and I say that you are uneasy in your avowal of the intellect as the proper object of your occupation. You are as uneasy as the secular culture behind its wall of separation with *In God We Trust* as its motto. Neither you nor the culture knows where, or how, or exactly why to draw the line that cuts the man into pieces. You draw it—but you are careful to draw it blurred.

Dewey was wrong in his belief that there is a science of pedagogy —as if a man could be taught to be a Dewey—and we are just begin-ning to recover from the "teacher's college," which, like the journalism schools, failed so wonderfully to produce its announced product. But Dewey was righter than he was wrong. He was right to insist, with Carlyle, that the end of man is an action and not a thought; righter still to reject the compartmentalization of man implicit no less in the liberal than it is in the servile arts. The child comes to school —as the man to life—with his sneezes, his lusts, his dreams, and his grandfather's grandfather all in one bundle; and on them his docility, or teachability, depends.

Is there anything clearly teachable (as Dewey's techniques were not) that will serve us less tangentially than the odds and ends we have already salvaged for our curriculum? What of the study of man as a moral—and therefore immoral—being? We have argued against the moral utility of the teachable, and here we have the teachable again. But morality can be taught *about,* and Augustine insists that "we ought to know the causes of good and evil as far as man in this life may know them, in order to avoid the mistakes and troubles of which this life is full." Is there a way or ways in which human action may (*may* is as much as we ask for) be influenced by the knowledge of human action?

That it need not be, we know; we know that the humanists are not necessarily good men or any better than the biologist or the janitor who empties the biologist's wastebasket. And the supposition that social scientists are politically liberal rests upon the susceptibility of their field to controversy, not upon them. There are social—unlike humanistic or scientific—doctrines that the public does not want mentioned unless they are mentioned pejoratively. And there are social scientists, and not a few, who will mention them pejoratively, and not a few more who will mention them not at all. It takes more than science to make a man good.

The sciences that deal with man as man are ethics, politics, metaphysics, psychology, sociology, social anthropology, theology, and the principles of both jurisprudence and economics. They commend themselves to our curriculum in four analytically (if not operationally) distinct ways: (1) They may, by pressing the human dilemma, urge its sensitivity upon the student and intensify such sensitivity as he already has. (2) A studied awareness of good and evil may increase a man's ability (even if he may not be able to be good himself) to distinguish a good man from a bad one. (3) The knowledge of good and evil may somehow, as Socrates suggested, support or "anchor" the good man's goodness. (4) The acquaintance of good and bad men— living and dead—may inspire our imitation of the one and dishearten our resemblance to the other.

Erasmus says that man learns at the school of example and will attend no other. We do not, however, hire living teachers as exemplars, but as instructors of subject matters. I may apply until I am blue in the face, submitting the evidence of my impeccable character. —Do you know Kant?—No, I do not know Kant.—I'm sorry, but we are looking for a moral philosopher; his personal life is his own affair.

Erasmus may have been wrong. The proverbial preacher's son is not an argument for example except in reverse. And of the two greatest exemplars who ever lived, one was the master of such deplorable persons as Alcibiades and Critias, and the other, of unparalleled exemplarity, had twelve followers one of whom betrayed him, one of whom denied him, and all of whom ran away from him in his time of trouble. Still we know that man (like the other primates) has a strong tendency to imitate—a tendency that our critical need may not be above exploiting.

But we cannot plant moral exemplars in the educational system— or expect them to last long if we do. We cannot even get them a job if they exemplify both the very moral and the very unpopular. What we can do is confront the student with the spectacle—however remote in time or place—of men engaged in moral struggle and hope that he will meditate upon it. And on this long chance, and on the still longer that his meditation will be transubstantiated into action, there may be a place in the curriculum for the great tales (in whatever form, including belles-lettres and history) of men and of peoples, along with the sciences that deal with man as man.

The sciences that deal with man as man are, if less moving, more eminently teachable than belles-lettres, and their lesson is more immediately apprehensible than history (above the names-and-dates level). They try to tell us what man is and isn't; as history tries to tell us what he has and hasn't been and done; and as poetry tries to tell us what he might and might not be and do. And these three kinds of knowledge, and they alone, speak directly to the human crisis. Whether our student listens is, of course, outside our present pedagogical power to ensure.

We grant that the apprehension of them involves the liberal arts as the tools of the thinking and talking trades, a kind of graduate literacy. Why shouldn't we turn them to our purpose by following the practice of Plato in the Dialogues and use morality as the *material* of liberal arts instruction? The ancients had too few books available. We have too many. But good books are better than bad books, and Great Books are great even though the two words are capitalized. The test of our texts is the lucidity with which they plumb the passions of men, whenever they were written and in whatever language. (A reading knowledge of two or three of the great languages justifies their inclusion in our curriculum apart from their excellence as intellectual arts.)

An article of faith underlies every argument I have been able to make in behalf of education's use to moral man: the faith that what goes into the head will find its way into the heart. For the heart is the heart of the matter, and the matter, today, yesterday, tomorrow, is to pick up one's cross and carry it in defiance of the Devil and all his works and pomps. If the faith is false, as it may be, I do not know what can be said at all for the systematic transmission of knowledge as an undertaking of either public or private importance.

The ancients took a cyclical view of the human condition. Men (even gods) soared and plummeted in a lifetime, in a single day, and "those cities which were once great are now nothing, while those that are now great were once nothing." With the Renaissance behind us, the invalidity of the cyclical view is still to be demonstrated. We do not have to be worse off than earlier worlds to go the way they did; we need only be no better off than they were. And we could be much worse off than we are. But we can hardly say that we are well off, or that education is responsible for our not being worse. Nor do new methodologies for teaching the things that don't move us move us any further than the construction of more stately mansions for cyclotrons.

We are not visionary these days, no more so (if no less) than our fathers who stoned the prophets. And our children (unless they are black) reject neither the image we present nor our preoccupation with images. There is a reality—the reality of where we are and how we get there; of what we can and cannot do; and of what, if anything, can be done about it. The belief of the more recent fathers that education and research would disclose that reality has been sterile, and its sterility illuminates our situation.

We are vestigial Greeks. We adhere to knowledge, but we have cut ourselves off from the mysticism that threaded Greek rationalism. An Italian in thirteenth-century Paris, Aquinas by name, was the liveliest of all the Greeks: He undertook to prove the existence of God by reason alone. We dying Greeks undertake to prove we-care-not-what by reason alone; and we succeed; and our success in the end undoes us. The thrall of Emerson's Things holds us in *its* meaningless mystique.

It is doubtful that educators can contribute much to the resolution of the moral crisis, whose resolution is the key to every other. They are inside the institution whose utility is in question and whose faith the question threatens. Nor is our consideration of the curriculum central. For the reform that is called for is not a reform of education, but a reform that *calls for* a reform of education. It is not a reform at all, but a revolution. It is the revolution of man, and it wants something more than our bootstraps and our marvelous machines.

We know what goodness is, and we always have. Moses knew, and Machiavelli. But we do not know how to make men good. It is going on two and a half millennia since the first discussion of education opened with the question, "Can you tell me, Socrates, whether virtue is acquired by teaching or by practice . . . or in what other way?" We are not able to answer the question. Perhaps it is not to be answered—in which event we may concentrate on a succession (better yet, a continuum) of gayeties in contended conscience. But perhaps another two and a half millennia of unrelenting inquiry will produce the answer; all the more reason for getting started at once.

8

On the

Future of

Humanistic

Education

John Courtney Murray, S.J.

The issue of the future of humanistic education arises, I suppose, because the future of man himself has become an issue in our day. Is the present moment the portent of a new epoch of history, a new age of humanity, a new sort of humanism, a new type of man? Must there consequently be a new kind of education, for which the tradition offers no model?

No one will deny that the signs of the times are portentous. It seems to be the fact that the crisis of history in which the whole world is presently engaged promises to be perpetual, at least in the sense that its duration and final resolution outdistance all possible foresight. The symbol of its perpetuity is the nuclear stockpile, here and also over there, undestroyed, perhaps indestructible, destined to permanent presence, a hidden threat to the future of civilization. The modalities of the crisis and its manifestations will undoubtedly alter, as time alters all things, but only so as to make its root more plain and its nature more explicit.

There is also the problem of politics, or, more exactly, the problem of scientific technocracy versus liberal politics. We already observe the phenomenon vaguely known as the "new politics," which is beginning to be visible in what is called, with equal vagueness (whether in English, French, German, or Italian), the New Left. One cannot yet speak of a party; the phenomenon is still too amorphous. It chiefly appears as a fact, the uniquitous fact of collegial expertise in collaboration with government, directing the exercise of political power. Do we therefore stand on the threshold of Saint-Simon's "new regime"? "As long as governments exercise patronage over the learned, in theory and practice, we remain in the old regime. But from the moment the learned exercise patronage over government the new regime really begins." Such a regime will, indeed, be new; but what will it be like? In any event, "socialism" will not be the word for it. Its new axiom of control seems likely to transcend all the principles of socialism, in any of its forms. Whatever is theoretically possible from a scientific viewpoint (it may well say) can be translated into political reality. Politics is only administration. The people are to be managed, not governed.

Again, there is the psychological problem that is the still undissipated legacy of Freud. The advance of civilization requires that man should sustain an unrelenting, rigidly controlled effort to master and organize the things of the world, including himself, by the techniques of conscious reason. He must therefore renounce the forces of instinct, deny them gratification, repress them. This, it seems, is not done with impunity. Its consequence is not self-fulfillment and happiness but psychic misery and loss of personal identity. As civilization advances, the Marxist proletariat will, indeed, vanish, only to be succeeded by the new Freudian proletariat, chained in neurotic misery amid material abundance. Auden's phrase, "the Age of Anxiety," will be filled with meaning.

Furthermore, it may be that Ortega y Gasset touched the portentous meaning of the moment when he said that today "man has no nature, he has only his history." Technology promises at least to alter in radical fashion the contours of nature, if not to erase the once-sacred distinction between nature and artifice. Technology also promises to change the whole course of events, and perhaps, if Jacques Ellul is right, to make their course "self-determining in a closed circle." If Derek Price is correct in his projection of the exponential growth-curve of scientific activity since 1662 (the founding of the Royal Society), we shall eventually reach "a state where civilization is saturated with science." Then what? Will Kant have been proven wrong? Will civilization, which is an affair of the sciences, have overwhelmed culture, which is the moral state of man? In any case, we already confront the question that George A. Baker phrased: "Can science make history and make it orderly, provided that human beings are persuaded or coerced to act according to the precepts of order? Is proper technocratic organization, in effect, nothing less than the general will itself and a guarantee against the worst forms of coercion?"

The question might be put in another way if you admit, with Ellul, that a deterministic bent is inherent in technology. Will technology, which is man's own creation, eventually become his creator? Will it make man over into its own image, not free, but captive to the same determinisms to which the creator himself is subject? In the end, will man have lost, by undertaking to win, his perennial conflict with the energies of the material world and with the momentum of historical forces?

Perhaps Bruce Mazlish put the issue most sharply when he said, "Faustian man is everywhere on the stage of the world." His symbol— significantly not plastic, or even a thing of earth—is boundless space. It symbolizes his will to a limitless striving, supported by powers that are believed to be bottomless in their resources. The act to which he immediately aspires, as the evidence of his arrival in history and the announcement of his program, is to put a man on the moon. His motive seems not to be the wish to escape the human condition, as Hannah Arendt suggested, but, as Mazlish more correctly divines, the will to reveal the human condition and to fulfill its potentialities of power for the advancement of civilization.

Finally, there is the issue presently involved in the very notion of the advancement of civilization. It is not the old issue which Francis Bacon raised, which is the "elder" and which the "younger" age of the world? No one will now quarrel with his answer, that "our own times" are the elder, the "more advanced age." The new issue concerns the final meaning of the idea that was the morning star of modernity, the idea of progress. The idea has been newly qualified in conformity with the notion of progress in scientific knowledge and activity. Scientific progress is an unbrokenly continuous process, pursued for its own sake, toward a truth that forever recedes in consequence of the very pursuit of it. The process is not animated by any vision of fixed and final goals in the form of eternal and unchanging truths; for science there are no such truths. As with the progress of science, so with the progress of culture. Culture is indeed the moral state of man; but its structure and substance, like the structure and substance of the state of material well-being which science provides, cannot be foreseen or determined in advance. Only in the pursuit of his goals does man discover what his goals are. He finds out what he wants to do, and must do, by finding out what he can do, and by doing it. The chase itself produces the quarry. And in the end man's only goal is—progress. The cultural concept of progress, like the technological concept, is open-ended. Progress is endless and it is its own end. This perhaps is what Ortega y Gasset meant. Man has no nature, that is, no form, and therefore no finality. He is only history, process, action—what the existentialists call an "ex-sistence" without an essence.

I do not know to what extent this Faustian ideology is explicit in the American mind. To some extent, however, it seems to be implicit in the general action of American civilization. It may be undergoing a pragmatic, not theoretical, evolution. To the same extent, there is evidence for the view of those who hold that an indigenous brand of Marxism is developing among us, with the consequence that American and Communist civilization are set on converging courses. (I am not speaking of forms of government, among which ours is still hardly more than an historical upstart, not yet tested in stern encounter with the newly emergent forces of history.) If this be the case, the end may be foreseen. There is no need or room in the world for two Doctor Faustuses.

These issues, and others of the sort, are brought up when there is talk of the New Age of Humanity. How one conceives them and wrestles with them in one's own mind depends, I suppose, on whether or not one is inclined to the tragic vision. More concretely, what matters is whether one is convinced that man is intelligent and free in the classical Christian sense, or not so convinced. More profoundly, what matters is whether or not one believes in God, Creator of the universe, Master of history, the End of man, who is only in the image of the Pantocrator, not the Pantocrator himself.

The concern here, however, is with the bearing of the current prognosis of the New Man on the public institution of humanistic education. One's thought on this issue will be guided, I expect, by one's judgment on a prior issue. One can accept as a half-truth, because it is half true, Dr. Conant's weary definition of education as "what goes on in schools and colleges." The question then is, to what extent should education involve itself in all the cultural problems of the present moment, and with what function in mind, and to what end. Whether we need to be rescued from the New Man or rescued by him, to what extent may we look to education for rescue?

I take it that the day is long past when a Francis W. Parker could require of the citizen, as he did in 1894, that he "should say in his heart: 'I await the regeneration of the world from the teaching of the common schools [add: the universities] of America.'" I further take it that none of us will address to American education the plea that it banish the Faustian man from the face of our fair country and halt the advance of his New Humanism. We might be content quietly to plead that education should not plunge into the business of producing the Faustian man and of fostering his dream. We might in consequence ask that the Deweyan premise of education be finally abandoned: "Since in reality there is nothing to which growth is relative save more growth, there is nothing to which education is subordinate save more education." In its own small way this is Faustianism. In reality human growth is relative to the ends of growth, which are inscribed in man's nature. Education is subordinate to the ends of education, which have been defined by the tradition of humanism.

For my part, I see nothing in the prognosis of a new age of humanity that would require us to abandon or radically to alter the fourfold structure of aims in terms of which the tradition of humanistic education has stated its ideal. The ideal has been to put the student in the way of developing a power of diction, a view of reality, a set of values, and a sense of style.

By diction I mean, for the moment, all that traditional humanism, in dependence on Quintilian (A.D. 35–c. 100), has meant by a finished power of utterance (*perfecta eloquentia*). In his *Institutio oratoria* (*The Training of an Orator*), Quintilian defined the majestic verb "eloqui" simply as the power "to utter, and to convey to the listener, what you have in mind." Diction in this sense means command of words, the ability to find in language the exact equivalent of the thought in mind, and the further quality of fluency. Diction, however, also includes the capacity to order discourse with a sense of logic and thus endow it with force, and to compose discourse with the care that issues in elegance, which is a thing of restraint, propriety, polish, grace. This art of utterance stands highest in the order of the skills which education seeks to develop. The mark of the humanist is the manner in which he uses his tongue, in the several senses of that word. Today we might speak of a power of communication, except that Quintilian would wince at the shallowness of meaning that the word has taken on. His orator was trained to fulfill Cato's definition, "a good man skilled in speaking," a man who had the public in mind, and who also had in mind something that needed utterance, because it was true, and therefore would serve the public good.

What the humanist is supposed to have in mind, needing utterance, is, in the end, a view of reality in Newman's sense of the word "view." In *The Idea of a University,* he contrasts the "genuine philosophical habit of mind," which is at once the possession and the quest for a view, with "that spurious philosophism which shows itself in what, for want of a word, I may call 'viewiness.' " The contrast is between a grasp of things in their ordered intelligibility and what is pejoratively called "knowledgeability," which is a thing of bits and pieces, the property of the famous gentleman who "knew everything—and nothing else." This aspect of the ideal of humanistic education serves more often as the measure of its failure than of its success. In 1953-54 a survey of twenty-one colleges and universities, made for the Fund for the Advancement of Education, discovered that the "pervasive problem" was the problem of "coherence." The discovery was not new. Long before, Woodrow Wilson had spoken of "the feudal system of learning," in which "there is no common mastery, but everywhere separate baronies of knowledge, where a few strong men rule and many ignorant men are held vassals." My concern, however, is not with the factual state of education but with its ideal. The survey itself acknowledged the ideal in multiple references to the need for synthesis, integration, coherence, a unifying purpose and idea, a design, a synoptic view.

To achieve a view requires a certain comprehensiveness and versatility of intellect, a command over the mind's full range of powers, the faculty of entering with comparative ease into any subject of thought, the active power of insight that prompts one to ask the right questions, a flexibility of intelligence that enables one to assume a variety of viewpoints, the capacity to grasp the relations between things and to throw them into system. The effort to build a view begins with the profound sense that intelligence is, as Aristotle said it was, *capax fieri omnia,* a universally responsive capacity for spiritual identification with, and therefore knowledge of, all that is real. To put it more simply, the quest for a view begins with the awakening of the spirit of wonder that is the root of the desire for understanding.

The spirit of wonder is man's native endowment. What is not an endowment but a most painful acquisition is an understanding of what Wilson called the "constitution of learning." Little success will attend any effort to order one's knowledge, unless one understands what the order of knowledge is and why it is an order. Therefore one must come to understand what understanding is, and what the ways of understanding are, and why there are several, not just one. From another point of view, one must come to understand the virtualities of man's intellectual consciousness—how they are multiple, not single. In a metaphor, one must understand that truth is not a ranch-style structure, all on one level, with a single door of entry, but a many-storied edifice through which one ascends by those different modes of access which are the variant methodologies of inquiry. To say all this is, of course, to raise a whole spectrum of philosophical issues. They are precisely the issues that must be raised in the course of a humanistic education, because its aim is to put the student in the way of building a view of reality. The essential humanist refusal is to diminish the range of man's intelligence and thus contract the dimensions of reality.

I am implying, of acourse, that the subject matter of a humanistic education is the whole of reality, or, if you will, all truth, in its unity and in all the inner differentiations within its unity. Out of this implication a multitude of educational problems arise which cannot be touched here. I must, however, note that within the tradition of humanistic education the canon for the inclusion or exclusion of this or that subject matter or field of study was never considered to be relevance. The canon is too vague to serve as a heuristic principle. Relevance to whom? Why? When? Under what circumstances? How? And what precisely does relevance mean? The issue of relevance is best left to be solved *ambulando*. One must wait to discover by experience the uses of what one knows and the consequences of ignorance. The humanist is not greatly disposed to argue the issue of relevance. Not being a pedant, he is prepared to agree with Whitehead that all education is and ought to be useful, in the sense that all understanding is useful.

The tradition of humanistic education has never regarded the student as a naked intelligence inhabiting a world of concepts and propositions, in which the only issues are truth and error, certitude and probability, adequacy or inadequacy of formulation, logic or fallacy in argument. The student's attention was directed to the real world as it is, a world of good and evil, beauty and ugliness, order and disorder, in which man is called upon not only to think but also to act—to do things and make things. The aim, therefore, was to cultivate a power of moral judgment and the esthetic sense that is called taste. Newman has the phrase for this aim: "the instinctive just estimate of things as they pass before us." The estimate, whether moral or esthetic, is instinctive, but only because the sense of right and wrong, of the beautiful and the ugly, has been subjected to rigorous discipline and refined by the further necessary tutelage of experience. The estimate is just, because it is not merely visceral; valid reasons can be adduced for it, if need be. The right word here might be "appreciation," the capacity to set a just value on what presents itself, not only in the intellectual order of thought but in the practical orders of doing and making. The power of evaluation supposes the possession of a set of values, anchored in the order of reality and ordered in proper hierarchy. Humanistic education, therefore, has looked to the development of a set of values, moral and esthetic.

Finally, the tradition has considered that humanistic education should somehow instill what Whitehead called "the most austere of all mental qualities," the sense for style. In the well-known passage in his Presidential Address to the Mathematical Association of England in 1916, he spoke of the sense for style as "the ultimate morality of mind" and also the final utility of education. "It is," he said, "an aesthetic sense, based on admiration for the direct attainment of a foreseen end, simply and without waste." In all the affairs of men, certainly in all the affairs of intelligence, blindness or lack of focus with regard to the end in view, round-aboutness and muddle and wastage of effort in pursuit of the end assume somewhat the character of *hamartia, sin.* Where they are found, something essential is "missing" (the root meaning of *hamartia*), and the privation is a manner of evil. "Style," Whitehead concludes, "is the last acquirement of the educated mind; it is also the most useful. It pervades the whole being." Style is not, indeed, wisdom, which remains the highest of the intellectual virtues. Style is, however, a quality of wisdom as of the four other intellectual virtues —knowledge and understanding, art and prudence.

The foregoing may do as a highly condensed and generalized summary of the four traditional aims of humanistic education—diction, a view, values, and style. I maintain that this ideal, in its fourfold structure, will be as valid in the future as it has been in the past. The only objection to the ideal is that it may be impossible of attainment in the course of "what goes on in schools and colleges." The objection is irrelevant. The ideal always lay beyond reach; but one became an educated man in the process of reaching for it.

The whole issue, however, is not thus easily disposed of. There is some substance to the talk about the new epoch of history and the new man. Moreover, I happen to be a conservative who believes in innovation, as true conservatives must, lest in the end they find themselves with nothing worth conserving. Therefore, I further maintain that the educational tradition, in order to be true to itself, must undergo that organic process of change which is known as "growth." It only remains to know what the dynamism of growth is, what directions the progress in the tradition should take, and what new forms the development should show forth.

In the realm of doctrine or theory the dynamism of development is readily identified. It is the change of perspective that is brought about by the asking of either a new question, or of an old question in a new mode of statement or with a new note of urgency. The classic theological instance is Nicaea. The new question asked by Arius altered the perspective in which the writings of the New Testament had viewed the Logos-Son. The New Testament question was asked in intersubjective categories, I and Thou, and formally raised the issue of presence and function: Art thou the Christ—the Lord-with-us, the Savior-of-us? The Arian question was asked in ontological categories and formally raised the issue of being and nature: Is the Son God or creature? The Nicene answer, given in the famous *homoousion,* affirmed the scriptural doctrine but in the new perspective. Thus it was a development, a growth in understanding. Another theological instance confronts us today, as the polemical question (Who has the one true faith—Catholic, Protestant, Orthodox?) gives place to the ecumenical question (How shall Catholic, Protestant, and Orthodox move together toward unity in the true faith?). A change of perspective has occurred which affects almost every single theological issue and will surely result in an enrichment of the Christian tradition.

The same dynamism of development has operated in the field of political theory. There has been in the West a political tradition, a tradition of growth in the understanding and practice of politics. Its growth has been occasioned by changes of perspective; these in turn occurred as new questions arose, or, more exactly, as one or other essential political question took precedence over others; and this in turn happened in consequence of the changing experiences of particular cultures in different periods of history. For classical antiquity the political question was justice; for medieval times it was the political relationship, its origin and limits—that is, the question of authority; for modern times it was the freedom of the individual citizen. In our own times, as Hans Morgenthau tirelessly points out, the political question is power and the struggle for power. The experience of totalitarianism has raised the question—that is, given primacy to it. And its primacy creates a new perspective within which the Western political tradition is given an opportunity for new growth in the understanding of itself.

The same complex of factors—new experience, new question, new perspective on an old problem—could furnish the dynamism for organic developments in the tradition of humanistic education. The new experience is easily identified; it prompts all the talk about the new age and the new man. It is the scientific experience, using the term in its broadest meaning. The new educational question, however, has not yet been formulated with clarity. A confused argument is, indeed, going on, but it seems to be hardly more than a reverberating echo of the seventeenth-century quarrel between the "ancients" and the "moderns," which was satirized by Jonathan Swift in *The Battle of the Books*. In Swift's version, which has the truth of caricature, the quarrel concerned occupancy of the higher and larger of the two tops of the Parnassus. Traditionally, it had belonged to the ancients; the Moderns coveted it. Hence they sent the demand, "either that the ancients would remove themselves and their effects down to the lower summit, which the moderns would graciously surrender to them, and advance in their place; or else the said ancients will give leave to the moderns to come with shovels and mattocks, and level the said hill as low as they shall think it convenient."

The same issue seems to appear in today's battle of the books, when the state of the question is conceived to be science *versus* the humanities. This conception of the issue releases only a sectarian quarrel, not a useful argument. The state of the question is altered when the positivist philosophers of science join the fray, as they enthusiastically do. (For the most part, scientists themselves are above the battle, or possibly beneath it; generally they want to get on with their work in the laboratory or at the desk, and not be bothered about education.) The positivist or pragmatist takes up the position that there are not two tops to Parnassus—the hill of true and certain knowledge—but only one, and now it is securely occupied by science. The humanities can make no valid cognitive claims for themselves; all such claims must be submitted to the test of scientific verification. In its extreme form, the position seems to assert that there is no Parnassus at all, but only a way of climbing it—that is, there is no definitive and universal truth, but only a method for its endless pursuit.

There are, moreover, those who attempt to reconcile the contending parties by saying that science deals with "facts," whereas the humanities deal with "values," and therefore there should be no quarrel. This position, of course, stultifies the humanist and makes the scientist quite rightly mad. His rejoinder is that science today is not value-free, that it is itself a value, and that it creates values for society as for the individual. The contention is true enough, but, so far from advancing the argument, it disguises or further confuses the real issue. And the confusion is worse confounded when the humanities are reduced to literature and the fine arts, under exclusion of philosophy, on the ground, as Douglas Bush has pointed out, that "modern philosophy seems to be suspended somewhere between linguistics and mathematics," both of which, incidentally, are now considered to be scientific disciplines. Thus the old battle of the books, which was at least serious and even sprightly in its day, runs drearily down to the level of the trivial and nugatory, the partisan and the passionate.

The result is lamentable, because an issue of the highest importance lies somewhere buried beneath all the misstatements, confusions, and sectarianisms. If the issue could be unearthed and defined, we might come close to understanding the schism in the soul of our civilization which began to open sometime in the *quattrocento* and has been widening ever since—in more recent times, in consequence of the scientific experience. The issue, I suspect, is multifaceted; and it is by no means easy to define it in any of its facets. In so far as it is philosophical, it clearly involves a theory of knowledge and knowing. What is at stake is a metaphysic of cognition—the question of the dynamic structure of intelligence itself and of the processes whereby intellectual consciousness moves from the moment of wonder to the moment of the attainment of truth. Consequently at stake is an ontology—the question of the structure of the real and its isomorphism with the structure of intelligence. Finally at stake is an epistomology—the question of the criterion whereby to test the validity of insight and the certainty of affirmation.

If one could arrive at a view on these related questions, one would understand the meaning of the verb "to know" and of the correlative verb "to be," when there is question of Aquinas, Aristotle, Locke, Spinoza, Newton, Einstein, Bohr, Gödel, Spengler, Shakespeare, Picasso, Mother Hubbard, and the man in the street, to cite random symbols of the modes of knowing: theological, philosophical, scientific, mathematical, historical, artistic, common-sensical. Here, I suggest, is the broad area in which the true lines of the philosophical battle of the books are to be drawn.

I do not think that this battle, which is only an engagement in a larger war, can be fought to a conclusion in the course of "what goes on in schools and colleges." (I really should not use the military image. The issue is a schism in the soul of civilization. And in a case of spiritual schism an image from the world of medicine, "healing," or from the higher world of religion, "conversion," would be more apt.) What, then, can education undertake to do, in response to today's dominant experience? What might be the directions and the forms of progress? Some few suggestions can be offered with regard to ways in which the four traditional aims of education may be enlarged and also brought to new focus.

A new issue of diction has arisen. If the Faustian man has arrived on the scene, it is important that the humanist should be able to talk to him. This means that his language must be learned. I do not mean his jargon, but his nonverbal language, which is mathematics, and his logic, which is the special logic of the scientific method of inquiry. As Ernest Nagel said, "To accept the conclusions of science without a thorough familiarity with its method of warranting them is to remain ignorant of the critical spirit that is the life of science." No educated man today can afford this ignorance. There is, moreover, the need to obviate the danger to which Margaret Mead has called attention, the danger of developing, as other civilizations before us have developed, "special esoteric groups," whose members can communicate only with one another. This development she says, is "schismogenic," self-perpetuating and self-aggravating. Again, if it be true that these esoteric groups, in combination, are fashioning a new age of man, the humanist cannot afford to be left out of their conversation. Its subject matter is his own—man and the world of man. Moreover, the scientific conversation is political in some Greek sense, as the scientific enterprise is a public enterprise. Scientists frequently vaunt the latter fact (though some of them make the disastrous mistake of supposing that humanism, like religion, is a purely private matter). The conversation ought, therefore, to be somehow open to the public. Furthermore, since the scientists are talking, not just about themselves and about what they are doing, but about the future of man, their conversation is of universal import. We the People should know what they are saying and what they are up to. There is, therefore, the problem of translation downward, so to speak, from the world of expertise to the world in which the rest of us live. The humanist, the man of diction, who is in command of all the forms of literary art, from the learned essay to the light theater-piece, and who is also the "good man speaking skilfully," should somehow let us know what is in store for us—in some more responsible ways than by scary stories of unsafe fail-safe systems.

Finally, there is the problem of diction as it touches the scientist himself. Privately, he may, indeed, be dealing with the ineffable, with what can be communicated only in nonverbal symbols. The ineffable is, however, useless to political man, who lives in a world whose motive power is chiefly the power of speech. If, therefore, science is relevant to political man, as science says it is, the scientist must somehow learn intelligibly to use his tongue. Above all, he is not permitted to ascend to the arrogance of saying, as he sometimes does, "You would not understand." The rest of us would be tempted to the quick retort: "The trouble is that you do not understand what understanding is." We know today the scientific fact, verified in experiment, that a child of ten can be brought to understand almost anything if the teacher understands not only his subject but also the nature and processes of understanding in any subject. Incidentally, the arrogant statement and the just retort embody an implicit statement of an aspect of our current cultural schism. Part of the trouble does seem to be that Science understands science, but it does not understand understanding.

In what concerns the second aim of education—the quest of a view of reality—the new perspective derivative from the scientific experiences makes possible a development. The central reality of which traditional humanism sought to fashion a view was man, taking "man" to mean "I-with-the-others-in-the-world," that is, the person, society, and the human environment in both its cosmic and in its humanly created aspects. In an older humanism man was simply the subject who undertook the inquiry. He was Ulysses, setting out "to gain experience of the world and of the vices and worth of men," pressing onward even into the "unpeopled world to be discovered by following the sun," and still further daring to pursue his quest into the transcendent world where God dwells in inaccessible light. Moreover, he had at his disposal, as his tool of research, only his own intelligence, tutored in the logic of philosophical inquiry, stored with knowledge of what men had thought and said, made and done. Finally, what aroused his wonder was simply the world of common human experience; this was the world of which he had to render an account, in all the aspects of it that progressively aroused his curiosity. In our day, however, man is no longer simply the inquiring subjects; he is also the object of inquiry. The inquiry is objective, skeptical, professionally neutral. And man has at his disposal, as tools of research, whole batteries of scientific instruments, new kinds of mathematics, new techniques of statistical estimate and so on. Finally, these new artificial hands, so to speak, have made accessible to man a whole new world of experience, the special experience, unknown to the old humanist, which is called "scientific."

The instant question is: What has science found out about man? The detailed and unfolding answer to this question needs to be made the common property of all educated men and women today. Therefore, as part of its aim to put the student in the way of acquiring a view of reality, humanistic education needs to develop what Robert J. Henle, S.J., calls a "program of cultural assimilation of science." It is not simply that the student must be exposed to the scientific experience by serious study of the scientific disciplines, to some depth at least in one or other of them. It is a matter of conveying to the student—to adapt Henle's terms—the scientific "story" of the cosmos and the scientific "picture" of man in the cosmos, in so far as the story and the picture can presently be constructed out of the certified findings of all the sciences, from genetics to geopolitics. We know today how important the body-image is to the individual, how panic ensues when it is lost —in the course, for instance, of controlled experiments in the limited environment, so called. This body-image is largely an affair of the unconscious. For his own spiritual security man also needs a conscious image of himself and his world—the kind of image that every age has needed to construct for itself, if only by recourse to myth and fantasy. Science can now construct this image with a relative measure of factual accuracy. And the rest of us ought to know what it is; it belongs, as it were, to us, as a man's body-image is a part of himself.

If the scientific view of man and his world were to become the common intellectual possession of scientist and humanist, expert and non-expert, some small step would have been taken toward the integration of science and humanism in our culture. There is, however, a more compelling reason why this effort at the cultural assimilation of science is imperative in education. Unless the student comes to know the scientific story of the world and the scientific picture of man (together, as I said, with a firm grasp of the method whereby the story was put together and the picture drawn, and thus of the level of explanation on which the picture and the story have their validity), he cannot intelligently get on toward his higher aim, which is the building of a view of *all* reality. That is to say, he cannot grapple with the question of whether the scientific perspective is the only perspective within which the truth about man comes into view; whether the scientific view is therefore the total view; or whether it is open to completion by inclusion within a wider framework of systematic understanding whose architecture is designed by philosophy and theology.

This question pertains to the pervasive issue with which humanistic education must continually concern itself—the spiritual and intellectual schism in our culture. I state the issue in the first instance as that of openness, in a reciprocal sense. Is the scientific story and picture of man open to, or closed against, the story and the picture which, in different ways, philosophy and theology have to tell or draw, and does this openness also reveal itself from the standpoint of philosophy and theology? Christian theology begins in biblical "recital-theology," so called, a telling of the story of the world and man—the story of creation and redemption—and a foretelling of the way in which the story will come out. Christian theology goes on to systematize the content and meaning of the story in the form of doctrine, which, in synthesis with such propositions about man and the world as philosophy may certify, presents a picture of man-in-his-world. There are, therefore, two stories and two pictures. How are they related? Does one cancel the other or complete the other? Is man to acquiesce in an irreducibly dualistic view of himself? Or is he to reduce the dualism to some sort of monism? Or can he account for the difference of views, render intelligible the diversity of perspectives, and compose the views into one, under respect for the respective character of the explanatory value of each? Here, I suggest, is a stimulating new focus for the second traditional aim of education. (I am supposing, of course, that theology will gradually find place in the higher education of the future.)

The third aim is the cultivation of the capacity to make valid judgments both of worth and of utility. Here the new focus would concern such judgments as they bear on science and technology, in themselves, and in their relation to other areas of intellectual achievement and moral aspiration. The sciences today present themselves for judgment in a variety of ways. They are systems of true statements, in the scientific sense of truth, which are conclusions of controlled investigation; these systems are part of the public knowledge. The sciences are disciplines that employ a distinctive logic of inquiry, by whose canons and criteria they evaluate claims to knowledge. They are disciplines whose pursuit forms the mind and imparts to it a special quality and a characteristic bent. They are sets of techniques whose import is pragmatic, in that they make it possible to manipulate, regulate, impart chosen directions to the energies of the cosmos and of man himself, and also to manage the course of events. They are collectively a massive enterprise within the liberal society, which profoundly affects its ethos and the whole moral as well as material condition of man. In their ensemble they constitute a revelation of the spirit of man, a manifestation of his power over his own history and nature. In all these aspects science presents itself for value-judgment with regard to both its worth and its utility. Therefore, it becomes an aim of humanistic education to see that the student is equipped to pass this multiple judgment with discriminating nicety, in the light of both fact and rational standards.

The educated man is not permitted to be contemptuous of science, as if it were all an affair of "atoms and the void." Conversely, he will not permit himself to be seduced by science, as if it were the contemporary golden bull, symbol of divinity. In particular, he will stand against the temptation inherent in the contemporary climate, which is to be intimidated by science, as if it were Doctor Faustus.

Nothing need be added, I think, about the sense for style. Whitehead may or may not have been wholly right when he said, "Civilization advances by extending the number of important operations which we can perform without thinking about them." In any case, style is what you don't think about when in action, on penalty of awkwardness. Similarly, style is what you don't talk about when discoursing on education, on penalty of superfluity. In a true sense, style is not really an aim of education but a result. Aims need to be defined; but one must simply wait for results.

Acknowledgments

The suggestion for the preparation of *Humanistic Education and Western Civilization* was made by Mr. W. H. Ferry of the Center for the Study of Democratic Institutions. Without his enthusiasm and energy it is doubtful that the distinguished contributors to this volume could have been persuaded to set aside their already crowded schedules in order to accommodate the editor's desire for original essays on humanistic education and Western civilization. Particular thanks and appreciation are due, therefore, to Mr. Ferry and to the co-operativeness of the contributors who succeeded, on relatively short notice, in making possible this volume in honor of Robert M. Hutchins' sixty-fifth birthday on January 17, 1964. Lastly, as a personal note, the task of organizing this book and of writing the only essay in it which treats specifically of Mr. Hutchins' career has been a particular delight. When I was a student at the University of Chicago, Mr. Hutchins was a phantom *daimon*—he was always present and rarely seen, except on those occasions when, elevated before us in the lectern of Rockefeller Chapel, he seemed to us undergraduates rather too awesome to be quite human. Only later, when I worked with him as publisher and editor of his book, *Freedom, Education and the Fund* did I discover that, in addition to being both educator and moralist, he was one of the most thoroughly gracious and generous human beings I have ever had the good fortune to meet.

September 22, 1963   ARTHUR A. COHEN

Notes on Contributors

Mortimer J. Adler is Director of the Institute for Philosophical Research, Chicago, and Associate Editor of Great Books of the Western World. His books include (with Louis Kelso) *The Capitalist Manifesto* and (with Milton Mayer) *The Revolution in Education*.

Elisabeth Mann Borgese, daughter of Thomas Mann, is the author of the recently published *Ascent of Woman* and also of *To Whom It May Concern*.

Scott Buchanan, philosopher and Consultant to the Center for the Study of Democratic Institutions, is former Dean of St. John's College, Annapolis, Maryland. He has written, among other books, *Essay in Politics* and *Poetry and Mathematics*, which was recently reissued as a paperback.

Arthur A. Cohen is Director of the Religion Department of Holt, Rinehart and Winston. Mr. Cohen was a member of the project, "Religion and the Free Society," sponsored by the Fund for the Republic. He is the author, among other works, of *Martin Buber, The Natural and the Supernatural Jew: An Historical and Theological Introduction,* and the forthcoming *The Myth of the Judeo-Christian Tradition.*

Bertrand de Jouvenel, French economist and political scientist, President of SEDEIS (Société d'Études et de Documentation Économique, Industrielles et Sociales). His *Du Pouvoir* and *De La Souvraineté* have been translated into English, Italian, Spanish, Arabic, and Japanese.

William O. Douglas has been Associate Justice of the United States Supreme

Court since 1939. Author of many books, he is also Co-Chairman of the Board of Directors of the Fund for the Republic.

Phillip C. Jessup is a judge of the International Court of Justice. He was previously Professor of International Law and Diplomacy at Columbia University. His writings include *The Use of International Law* and (with H. J. Taubenfeld) *Controls for Outer Space.*

Humayun Kabir, Minister of Scientific Research and Cultural Affairs of the Indian Government, is a Consultant to the Fund for Advancement of Education and author of *Science, Democracy and Islam, Education in New India,* and others.

Richard P. McKeon, Distinguished Service Professor of Greek and Philosophy at the University of Chicago, is Vice-President of the International Federation of Philosophical Societies, author of *The Freedom to Read* (with R. K. Merton and W. Gellhorn) and *Thought, Action and Passion* and Editor of *Selections from Medieval Philosophers* and Aristotle's "Basic Works."

Milton Mayer, journalist and lecturer, contributes to many periodicals. He has been Visiting Professor at the Comenius Theological Faculty in Prague, and is co-author of *The Revolution in Education.*

John Courtney Murray, S.J., is Professor of Theology at Woodstock College, Maryland, and Editor of *Theological Studies.* He has written *We Hold These Truths.* He is also Consultant to the Center for the Study of Democratic Institutions.

David Riesman is Professor of Social Science at Harvard University. He has written *The Lonely Crowd* (with Reuel Denney), *Individualism Reconsidered* and *Constraint and Variety in American Education.*

Rexford G. Tugwell, educator, author, and government administrator, is associated with the University of Puerto Rico and with Columbia University. Mr. Tugwell was a member of the "brain trust" that was instrumental in drafting plans for the New Deal, and served as Undersecretary of Agriculture. His later posts included Chief Planner for New York City and Governor of Puerto Rico. He is the author of many books, the latest being *The Light of Other Days.*

F. Champion Ward, former Professor of Philosophy and Dean of The College, University of Chicago, is now Director of the Near East and Africa Program of the Ford Foundation.

O. Meredith Wilson is President of the University of Minnesota and former President of the University of Oregon. He is a member of the Educational Committee of the Aspen Institute of Humanistic Studies, Director of the Center for Advanced Study in the Behavioral Sciences, and a member of the Business Ethics Advisory Council of the U.S. Department of Commerce.